Awakening Democracy Through Public Work

AWAKENING DEMOCRACY
Through Public Work

Pedagogies of Empowerment

Harry C. Boyte

*with Marie-Louise Ström, Isak Tranvik, Tami L. Moore,
Susan O'Connor, and Donna R. Patterson*

VANDERBILT UNIVERSITY PRESS
NASHVILLE

© 2018 by Vanderbilt University Press
Nashville, Tennessee 37235
All rights reserved
First printing 2018

Cover art: *Dreams Escape My Lips*, linocut, 2012, Phillip Mabote

Library of Congress Cataloging-in-Publication Data on file
LC control number 2018006255
LC classification number LC220.5.B69 2018
Dewey classification number 361.3/7—dc23
LC record available at *lccn.loc.gov/2018006255*

ISBN 978-0-8265-2217-7 (hardcover)
ISBN 978-0-8265-2218-4 (paperback)
ISBN 978-0-8265-2219-1 (ebook)

To Dennis Donovan, a master coach

CONTENTS

ACKNOWLEDGMENTS

Awakening Democracy through Public Work is a venture in public work. It draws from a remarkable network of co-creators.

The book project began with the suggestion of David Mathews, president of the Kettering Foundation, that I do a book on Public Achievement (PA). It evolved into the larger story of public work, including many examples in other settings, from colleges to African villages to American communities. Our network of public work practitioners, organizers, and scholars has long worked with David, John Dedrick, Derek Barker, Melinda Gilmore, and other colleagues at the Kettering Foundation on themes of public work. I greatly appreciate the learning partnerships we have created with them. And I appreciate the way the Kettering Foundation has been at the center of a learning community of great diversity, exploring themes such as the role of technocratic power almost invisible in conventional scholarly treatments of democracy.

The networks, participants, coaches, teachers, organizers, and leaders in Public Achievement are central voices and co-creators of this book project. There are many to thank, including Jim Scheibel, Nan Skelton, and our working group in the earliest days. In the fall of 2016 PA leaders and organizers came together at Kettering to review the history of a quarter century, as well as to brainstorm and develop a list of people to interview. The group included Dennis Donovan, Elaine Eschenbacher, Nan Skelton, James Farr, Melissa Bass, Roudy Hildreth, John (J.) Theis, Shelley Robertson, Juan Jackson, Jamie Minor, D'Ann Urbaniak Lesch, Jeff Maurer, Susan O'Connor, and Isak Tranvik. John Dedrick and Derek Barker from Kettering participated. Isak had discovered public work and Public Achievement as a graduate student in political science at Duke. He spent the summer of 2016 doing detailed archival research, and his research was an immense resource for the conversation. Isak also coauthored Chapter 2, "Education as a Civic Question," drawing on his own experience in Teach for America.

Public Achievement incubated at the Humphrey Institute (now Humphrey School), and there are many colleagues there to whom I owe debts of appreciation. Let me thank especially several deans including the late Harlan Cleveland, the late Ed Schuh, and the late John Brandl, as well as John Adams and Brian Atwood for their strong support. I also want to thank Robert Kudrle, Barbara Crosby, John Bryson, Ken Keller, and Samuel Myers for creating an intellectual community around Public Achievement and public work.

As the book took shape, Scott Peters, Dennis Donovan, Elaine Eschenbacher, and Tami Moore gave ongoing feedback, discussion, and direction setting for the manuscript. Tami coauthored Chapter 5, "Public Work Abroad," and did extremely helpful interviews of Public Achievement leaders, teachers, and participants who experimented with Public Achievement in the former Soviet-bloc countries. Susan O'Connor and Donna Patterson, who were our partners in bringing Public Achievement into special education work, coauthored Chapter 7, "Tackling the Empowerment Gap." They contributed extensive knowledge of the field of disabilities studies and interviewed young special education teachers who had coached in Public Achievement. Their commitment to developing "citizen teachers" and their vision of transforming special education from a field of remediation to one where young people are empowered to take leadership in their own education is a model for professional education broadly, at Augsburg and beyond.

Higher education is an "upstream" culture-shaping force in knowledge societies like the United States. It plays invisible but formative roles in shaping democracy's possibilities. Against the grain of an institutional landscape which has become highly meritocratic, colleagues and partners in higher education who seek to revitalize the democratic and public purposes of colleges and universities have formed a key community contributing to our work this work and also preparing large numbers of their graduates to take leadership in turning jobs into public work. Chapter 8, on civic organizing to strengthen higher education's public and democratic identity, draws heavily on this community. I especially want to thank the group, convened by the Kettering Foundation, of college and university presidents interested in reclaiming roles as "public philosophers," with whom I work. Adam Weinberg of Denison University and Paul Pribbenow of Augsburg University, co-initiators of this group, are a continuing source of wisdom and insight. Maria Avila, Scott Peters, David

Hoffman, Laurel Kennedy, Erik Farley have contributed to Chapter 8. I also thank colleagues in Imagining America, ADP, and ACP, including Julie Ellison, Tim Eatman, Scott Peters, George Mehaffy, Cecilia Orphan, Jen Domagal-Goldman, Jon Carson, Nancy Kantor, and Nancy Cantor.

The citizen professional is a new frontier of democracy, speaking to the aspirations of a young generation. Chapter 9 draws on insights and practices of longtime colleagues Bill Doherty, founder of the Citizen Professional Center at the University of Minnesota, Tai Mendenhall, Bobby Milstein of Rethink Health, and Albert Dzur, an outstanding theorist of democratic professionalism. Our colleagues Katie Clark, Cheryl Leuning, Joyce Miller, and Katherine Baumgartner, with other faculty, have developed the concept of "citizen nurse" as agent of change in health systems. Mike Huggins, the city manager in Eau Claire whom we have worked with for more than twenty years—pioneering citizen profession models in government—helped us to craft the case study of Clear Vision Eau Claire. Augsburg University, where we settled in 2009 after many years at the University of Minnesota, has been a fertile environment for concepts and practices of civic agency and citizen professionalism. I thank Paul Pribbenow, Garry Hesser, Michael Lansing, Peg Finders, Joaquin Munoz, Joe Underhill, Mike Grewe, Joe Underhill, Rachel Lloyd, and Jacqui deVries for their welcome.

Several people provided critical feedback and help. Mike Ames, director of Vanderbilt University Press and a partner over years in publishing books about public work, insisted from the beginning for clarity of focus and presentation, and I most certainly owe him a considerable debt of gratitude. Jeremy Rehwaldt, copy editor, did an outstanding job. Two outside reviewers, Peter Levine and Meira Levinson, made wise commentary, and Levinson gave a final, trenchant review of the book draft that was extremely helpful. Two leaders of the Citizen Student Movement, Ali Oosterhuis and Steven Vogel, both independent students of mine through the Humphrey School, gave detailed feedback on several chapters. Isak Tranvik was an insightful and incisive commentator throughout.

Finally, I want to express my deepest appreciation to Marie-Louise Ström, my life partner. Our collaboration was enriched by the fact that most of her work took place in African countries, as described in Chapter 6. Idasa (the Institute for Democracy in South Africa), where she directed democracy education was an invaluable touchstone. Partnerships with Idasa helped in developing the concept of public work in comparative and cross-cultural ways, and I am appreciative of Idasa leaders Paul Graham, Ivor Jenkins, and Marietjie

Oelofsen, as well as other South African colleagues, especially Kim Berman, Xolela Mangcu, and Peter Vale.

Marie is also my important collaborator in developing the concept, pedagogies, and practices of public work. We are building a new educational initiative, the Public Work Academy, to consolidate and advance the lessons of *Awakening Democracy through Public Work.*

INTRODUCTION

A Movement for Civic Repair

Harry C. Boyte

I work with many young people through the youth civic education and empowerment initiative called Public Achievement (PA). They describe looming disasters and escalating conflicts they hear about in the news and learn about from teachers in their schools. They also talk poignantly about public problems they experience in their lives, problems that echo those of so many others.

Young people may feel discouraged, but they hunger for stories of hope. Finding such a story began for me in the African American freedom movement as a young man working for the Southern Christian Leadership Conference (SCLC), the organization headed by Martin Luther King. Like many "southern whites" in the movement, black political, civic, and cultural self-assertion moved me to reclaim my own cultural heritage, Scottish American and Scotch Irish. The movement also taught me about agency, the power of people to shape their environments. I had grown up in the European American community of Atlanta in the 1950s as a son of outspoken critics of segregation. Few in this community who were against segregation ever voiced their views publicly for fear of reprisal. They also thought segregation would last for generations, if not forever. In the movement I learned hope.

The freedom movement's story of agency is mostly unknown to young people today—education is better at describing problems, injustices, and disasters than conveying what young people and other ordinary citizens might do about them. But I find intense interest among young people of all cultural and partisan backgrounds when the freedom movement story is presented as an account of how people like themselves made change.

This story is now told at the National Museum of African American History and Culture, located in the Mall of America. The vastness of the museum's collection can be overwhelming, but it serves a purpose, telling the story of the struggle for freedom and empowerment against enormous obstacles in the midst of suffering and injustice. For black Americans, agency involved creating a multitude of empowering institutions, developing political and civic capacities, refining practices for making change, generating a profound nonviolent philosophy, and forming complex, contradictory, but also productive partnerships with government bodies at every level. These experiences transformed victimhood into agency for millions. The transformation is expressed in the movement's self-description as a "freedom movement."

The museum does not sugarcoat the horrors of slavery and segregation. But it pairs these with stories of resistance, empowerment, civic repair, and the struggle for freedom. It tells stories of solidarity in the belly of slave ships and describes those who chose to die by jumping into the ocean rather than lose their freedom. It depicts rebellions in the colonies, in some cases involving poor and working-class European Americans, coalitions that moved the planter elites to create the concept of "whiteness" itself as a way to divide those of European background from those of African descent and from Native Americans.

The museum also describes civic construction: churches and mosques, beauty parlors and other black businesses, women's organizations like the Council of Negro Women, fraternal and sororal organizations. "To shield their families from the unfairness of segregation, African Americans created communities that served their social, political, and religious needs," reads one display. "The activities and organizations they created—from fraternal groups to literary clubs—provided them the opportunity to interact with one another and hold positions denied to them otherwise. Building communities together, they also developed the skills in oratory, organization, and leadership that ultimately served them so well in demanding their rights as citizens." Civic institutions and relationships created a base for partnering—in often frustrating but crucial ways—with government agencies and policy makers to dismantle Jim Crow.

All these elements fed citizenship schools across the South. "Between 1957 and 1970 civil rights activists established nearly 900 Citizenship Schools in rural areas throughout the South," reads a description in the museum. "The immediate goal of this grassroots educational campaign was to help African Americans pass the literacy tests required for voter registration. However, the schools also trained people to become activists themselves and work for change in their own communities."[1]

I was schooled by these citizenship schools and their vision. They prepared people to fight for "first-class citizenship." People knew government was a necessary if often reluctant ally, but the schools also taught people to be self-reliant, using their skills to solve local problems and to improve local communities, not looking to outsiders to fix things. The movement combined the struggle for racial justice with the work of civic construction. It also generated what can be called "citizen professionals" on an enormous scale—professionals who saw their work in terms of public contributions to the freedom struggle, community building, and the advance of democracy, broader than their specific disciplines.

In the process, people debated the meaning of citizenship. A rough consensus emerged: citizenship is not simply legal status nor is it defined merely by relationships with government. The citizen is someone who solves problems, takes responsibility for building communities, and believes in democracy. Put differently, the citizen is a "co-creator" of communities. We didn't use the term co-creator until it became part of PA in the early 1990s, but the idea that democracy is a work in progress ran throughout the movement. The goal, according to Septima Clark, architect of the citizenship schools (Martin Luther King called her the "mother of the movement"), was "broadening the scope of democracy to include everyone and deepening the concept to include every relationship."[2] In recent years, Dorothy Cotton, director of the SCLC Citizenship Education Program, communicated the message with a song written in the late civil rights movement. "We Are the Ones We've Been Waiting For."[3]

Cotton and Clark were part of a group that also included Ella Baker, Myles Horton, and many local leaders such as Oliver Harvey, a janitor at Duke University where I went to college. Harvey was my mentor for several years as we built support among students for an organizing effort by Duke maids and janitors. Such grassroots-oriented leaders shared what historian Charles Payne calls "an expansive sense of the possibilities of democracy." They "espoused a non-bureaucratic style of work, focused on local problems sensitive to the social structure of local communities, appreciative of the culture of those communities." Moreover, "they stressed a developmental style of politics . . . in which the most important thing was the development of efficacy in those most affected by a problem."[4] I felt strong identification with this group. I also learned deep appreciation for the visionary, philosophical, and political skills of leaders like Martin Luther King, Andy Young, and Bayard Rustin.

Beginning in 1987, a network of partners, including community organizers, educators, academics, and politicians, built on this legacy, developing a different kind of politics and over time elaborating concepts and practices of public work as a way to rebuild civic life and to awaken democracy. We translated themes from the freedom movement and community organizing into other settings, calling our approach citizen politics—politics centered on everyday citizens, not politicians—that teaches skills of negotiating different backgrounds and interests to make change and create a common life.[5]

One early partner was ARC, a group of African American parents who had children with autism. They were finding it difficult to negotiate school bureaucracies and wanted to learn practical political skills. The work took shape against the background of rising anger all over the country during the election of 1992. "If you haven't noticed, Americans are angry this year," said Connie Chung, CBS anchor. "Some are turning anger into action." The journalist Scott Pelley aired a man on talk radio yelling about the "bloodsuckers in government." He interviewed people in ten counties who were trying to secede from Kansas. Then he described the women learning citizen politics in Minneapolis. "We can't just voice complaints," said one. Annette Comb, a single mother with a disabled child, met with the school board. "I used to be quiet," she said. "Now I'm ready to take action." CBS presented their citizen politics as a hopeful alternative to fear and rancor. In a bitter season, Pelley defined it simply: "Some have decided politics can't be left to the politicians."[6]

Twenty-five years later, "politics" has become nastier, with conflict spreading from elections to family meals. Against the grain, a growing number of people have also practiced citizen politics of civic repair as an alternative. Our network has learned many lessons about how to teach it.

Ali Oosterhuis, a University of Minnesota student of Dutch descent, is one of these practitioners and educators. She helped to organize a group calling itself the "Citizen Student Movement." It aims to spread citizen politics to young people. "The mission and purpose of the Citizen Student Movement challenge the norm in a tense and divisive society characterized by hate and isolation instead of public love and acceptance," says Ali.

> In a campus climate in which student groups graffiti hate speech on each other's promotional panels during "Paint the Bridge Day" and trash the front lawns of houses that display "Make America Great Again" banners in their front windows, almost everyone, from undocumented immigrants to Black Lives Matter protesters, to white, male students who feel that their voices are being silenced, feels scared, powerless, and hopeless for the future. People from all walks of life either retreat into the comfort of their "private lives" or they seize the power of protest with newfound animosity toward their enemies. . . . Both contribute to the crumbling of civic life.[7]

Steven Vogel, another organizer of the movement, drafted the statement on their website. "We believe in a new type of politics," he wrote. "In the increasingly ineffective political atmosphere we live in, we want to take back our rightful power as citizens." He reflected on their early organizing experiences. "We [as students] know how to complain and vote, but beyond that, our advocacy often stops." But he finds interest among many students in a different kind of politics. "Despite all of the difficulties, young people's capacity for hope is phenomenal. We come to these meetings every week because we truly believe in our vision of change. In a world of so many looming problems— climate change, rising incarceration, exponentially increasing health care and education costs, and more—[it] gives us hope." Steven worked with a Public Achievement team of fourth and fifth graders at Maxfield, a low-income school in St. Paul. "They organized a field day with the police and UMN student athletes to act as an informal relationship-building activity between the community and the police. It is incredibly motivating." Steven was inspired by their work. "I feel like I truly can do something about the challenges in our community, albeit one step at a time." He is working on one of the Citizen Student Movement's teams doing "public work," working to overcome political polarization on campus.[8]

Citizen politics is relational, empowering, down-to-earth, and oriented to problem-solving, not partisan conflict. It is also elevating, reviving the idea of citizenship in which the point is to live and work nonviolently in a pluralistic civic world, where the marketplace and government are resources but not the center of the action. In one sense it is intensely local, stressing grassroots democratic action. It also reframes strategies for change by emphasizing that the most important task in a troubled world is developing people's civic muscle, a task involving visionary and conceptual work and large-scale political alliance building as well as grassroots civic organizing.

The idea of public work emerged as we sought to translate citizen politics into institutional change and civic repair. A group of institutions—the College of St. Catherine, Minnesota Cooperative Extension, Augustana Nursing Home, the Metropolitan Regional Council, and several others—wanted to revitalize the civic *identities* of their institutions, not simply to undertake civic engagement *activities*. We soon realized that for institutional civic identity to develop requires "making work more public."

Public work, sustained, uncoerced effort by a mix of people who create things of lasting civic or public significance, makes work more public in several different ways. Work is done in more open and "public" fashion. It is undertaken by a mix of diverse people: "a public." It is filled with public purpose. Public work is an approach to citizenship in which *citizens are co-creators, builders of the common world, not simply voters and volunteers who fit into that*

*world or protesters who oppose it. Democracy itself is a way of life, not simply elec-
tions, and it is built through civic labors in a myriad of settings.*

This concept of public work has proved to be a powerful resource in many
settings, including colleges, universities, and professions. Public work emphasizes the importance of sustained relationship-building, which goes against the
grain of professional and other cultures based on information and activities
and programs. Maria Avila, a Mexican American community organizer who
pioneered in bringing relational organizing practices into higher education,
explained that it involves "building something based on people who [are]
clear about their interests and passions, the things that matter to them deeply
and enough to sustain their involvement over time," different from the "pre-
dominate culture of wanting quick, concrete, predictable results and . . . [that]
undervalues process and relationality."[9]

Making work more public helps institutions look *outward*, stressing the
civic possibilities of work and workplaces, including colleges, congregations,
schools, businesses, unions, nonprofits, and government agencies. Public work
requires and develops *citizen professionals* who build and sustain such settings.
It involves free spaces where citizens learn to work across differences. It creates
community wealth, including schools, public spaces, and libraries, as well as
music and healthy civic norms and values—a commonwealth of public useful-
ness and beauty. Citizen politics and public work are antidotes to hopelessness.
They counter the culture of irresponsibility that arises when citizens are seen
and see themselves simply as consumers.

Awakening Democracy through Public Work tells the story of public work
and how it is taught, learned, and practiced and how it develops civic muscle
in communities. The book also gives examples of how public work has taken
shape in Public Achievement and in other pedagogies under other banners. It
explores its spread beyond the United States to other societies. Today, public
work and its pedagogies have taken root in communities across the United
States and in many other countries—in Poland, Azerbaijan, and the Gaza Strip
as well as Japan, South Africa, and Ghana. Public work has been translated
into professions, colleges, and government as well as K-12 schools. In Africa,
public work has generated a vision of "democratic society," not simply "democratic state." In Burundi, public work led to a nationwide initiative to bridge
divisions between police and villagers.

Public work revives the idea of a world we create together and of the politics of a common life.

New Resources for Civic Repair

Today, millions of Americans are disgusted with what they understand as polarized politics. Citizenship itself—not legal status but action for the general welfare, which can include the action of undocumented citizens and refugees who develop capacities and undertake work to build their communities—can seem like an echo from the distant past. This dismal view of politics is widespread around the globe.

Contributing to political polarization, social fragmentation has also been growing. "There really is less of a safety net of close friends and confidants," said Lynn Smith-Lovin, a Duke sociologist who studies social erosion. "We're not saying people are completely isolated. They may have 600 friends on Facebook.com and email 25 people a day. But they are not discussing matters that are personally important."[10] Over the last decade this erosion has worsened. Dhruv Khullar, a resident physician at Massachusetts General Hospital and a faculty member of Harvard Medical School, reported that since the 1980s the number of adults who report loneliness has skyrocketed. Social relationship and social networks have shrunk.[11] One study finds that young people under 35, the most prolific social media networkers, are also those who feel most alone.[12]

Despite decades of civic and social unraveling, new resources for repairing the social fabric and civic life are appearing. The late Elinor Ostrom won the Nobel Prize in economics in 2009 for her work on citizen-centered governance of common resources such as forests, irrigation systems, and fisheries. She was also a cofounder of the new field of civic studies, which identifies and disseminates resources for civic life and citizen action. Public work and its citizen politics are a philosophical pillar of civic studies.

In the spirit of civic studies are signs of a reorientation across the political spectrum to move beyond partisan warfare to focus on the repair of the civic fabric and the development of civic muscle, communities' capacities to act across differences on common challenges. Former president Barack Obama's new foundation has this emphasis. "The moment we're in right now, [partisan] politics is the tail and not the dog," Obama said at the launch of the foundation in Chicago on October 30, 2017. "What's wrong with our politics is a reflection of something that's wrong with the civic culture, not just in the United States but around the world."[13] The website of the foundation describes its efforts as an "experiment in citizenship" and its mission "to inspire and empower people to change their world."[14] Conservative thinkers such as Yuval Levin, Russ Douthat, and David Brooks similarly draw attention to repair of civic ties.

Some have long championed civic life as an arena different from markets and states. Elizabeth Kautz, the mayor of Burnsville, Minnesota, has focused on this theme since 1994, calling on citizens of the city to do public work across partisan divisions, with government as a partner. The city's successes in addressing a range of challenges led the National Conference of Mayors to elect her as president, the first suburban mayor—and the first woman—to be chosen for the position.

The Kettering Foundation calls civic life "the wetlands of democracy," a phrase coined by David Mathews. For decades Kettering has promoted deliberation among different viewpoints, one of the methods which the citizen students find extremely useful. Kettering focuses on addressing problems *of* democracy such as polarization and declining trust in institutions. The foundation distinguishes these from problems *in* democracy—that is, the issues that dominate in public debates, from gun control to immigration. Another group, the Center for Public Justice, working from a Christian perspective, promotes an inclusive commonwealth with limits on government's work "to promoting policies and practices that uphold the ability of other institutions and associations to make their full contributions to human flourishing."[15]

A movement for civic repair draws upon the nation's founding ideals as expressed especially in the Declaration of Independence. In her book *Our Declaration*, Danielle Allen, an African American political philosopher now at Harvard, describes how she became aware of the power of this story, what she calls America's egalitarian ideal, as she taught working-class students taking a night class in Chicago. "As my night students metabolized the philosophical argument and rhetorical art of the Declaration, many of them, and I along with them experienced a personal metamorphosis," she recalled. Despite her extensive education, Allen realized for the first time in her life that the Declaration of Independence "makes a cogent philosophical case for political equality . . . that democratic citizens desperately need to understand." Such equality involves empowering citizens to protect themselves from domination, and more. "Political equality is not . . . merely freedom from domination. The best way to avoid being dominated is to help build the world . . . to help, like an architect, determine its pattern and structure. The point of political equality is not merely to secure spaces free from domination but also to engage all members of a community equally in the work of creating and constantly recreating that community."[16]

The ideals of equality, citizen agency, and civic construction are not unique to America.[17] But the Declaration of Independence expressed them with unique force. Americans sometimes put them into practice, and this was noticed by visitors. Reflecting on his travels across the country in the 1830s, the French observer Alexis de Tocqueville compared European nations in which the citizenry relied on government or great leaders with the self-organizing efforts of citizens in America. "In democratic peoples, associations must take the place of the powerful particular persons," he wrote in his classic text, *Democracy in America*. "In democratic countries the science of association is the mother science; the progress of all the others depends on the progress of that one."[18] Tocqueville located the "science of association" in a citizen politics different from partisan politics, through which citizens learn civic skills, habits, and values as they argue, negotiate, and create a shared way of life.[19]

Langston Hughes, poet of the Harlem Renaissance and titan of America's democratic imagination, expressed the spirit which animates democracy in his poem "Let America Be America Again," written in the depth of the Great Depression in 1935. Hughes confronts "the world as it is," including America's injustices, with brutal honesty: "I am the poor white, fooled and pushed apart . . . the Negro bearing slavery's scars . . . the red man driven from the land . . . the immigrant clutching the hope I seek and finding only the same old stupid plan of dog eat dog, of mighty crush the weak . . . of grab the gold! . . . of work the man! . . . of owning everything for one's own greed!" In co-creative politics, unflinching engagement with "the world as it is" is the start of serious work to make change. But to act, one needs also to hold "the world as it is" in tension with hope for "the world as it should be." Hughes accomplishes this task brilliantly, with the language of possibility based on faith in American democratic ideals. "Let America be the dream the dreamers dreamed . . . that great strong land of love where never kings connive nor tyrants scheme that any . . . be crushed by one above . . . a land where Liberty is crowned with no false patriot wreathe, but opportunity is real, and life is free, equality is in the air we breathe." Put simply, Hughes puts recognition of painful reality together with commitment to act on ideals. "I say it plain, America never was America to me, and yet I swear this oath—America will be!"[20]

This combination encapsulates public work at its best. The rest of the book explains why and how. In the spirit of Hughes, it also describes mistakes and setbacks as well as successes.

Outline of the Book

Chapter 1 describes the "reinvention of citizen politics," detailing an early, iconic effort in PA as well as my own background in the freedom movement, community organizing, and research into citizen action and the commonwealth tradition that expresses civic construction. It shows how public work, a politics of civic repair and civic empowerment, contrasts with citizen activism today which uses an "us against them," good-versus-evil framework.

Chapter 2, coauthored with Isak Tranvik, describes how much educators crave a rich purpose in education beyond testing, are eager to see teaching as a highly respected craft, and are worried about the replacement of human beings with smart machines. Public Achievement provides one hopeful and practical way to make change in K-12 schools. Chapter 3 tells how Public Achievement found a home in Saint Bernard's Grade School in the North End neighborhood of Saint Paul, Minnesota. It was here that the PA pedagogy came into its own.

Chapter 4 describes how Public Achievement spread across the country in a jazz-like fashion. It also describes the role of Public Achievement in the emPowerU initiative of the Heartland Foundation in rural Missouri, which has involved twenty thousand young people and increased young people's intentions to stay in the region. Chapter 5, coauthored with Tami Lee Moore and Marie-Louise Ström, tells the story of public work "going abroad," using case studies from sixteen former Soviet societies and from its adaptation in Southern and East Africa. It points to "democratic internationalism," akin to what I experienced in the freedom movement, which sees the work of democratizing change in a time of enormous challenge as a global process, creating possibilities for new alliances and learning across the world.

Chapter 6, again coauthored with Marie Ström, tells how approaches to teaching public work are rooted in four democratic pedagogies. Chapter 7, coauthored with Susan O'Connor and Donna R. Patterson, details the ways special educators at Augsburg University and in partnering schools in the Twin Cities are using public work to transform special education, putting into practice themes from the field of disability studies. Chapter 8, "Artisans of a Common Life," uses Pope Francis's vivid phrase to describe educators who teach the skills and habits of a civic culture, giving an account of examples of public work in higher education. These include the Citizen Student Movement Ali and Steven are helping to organize, the patient relational organizing Maria Avila pioneers, and the creation of a civic architecture that sustains civic learning. Chapter 9, "Awakening Democracy," includes innovations in professions and professional training called "citizen professionalism" and the field of civic studies, including its closely allied the philosophy of science called "civic science." It tells story of citizen professionals in family therapy, nursing, and other scientific fields. Finally, it details an experiment in Eau Claire, Wisconsin, in which the city manager, Mike Huggins, reframed government as a catalyst for public work by citizens across the community and its institutions. The result,

Clear Visions Eau Claire, points to new frontiers of local democracy centered on citizens, not government. Clear Vision has begun to reorient professionals in business, education, and elsewhere to seeing their work in more public and community-building terms. Mike Huggins and Elizabeth Kautz, like other leaders profiled in this book, recall the biblical story of Nehemiah in which the leader summoned the Hebrews to rebuild the walls of Jerusalem, rather than do the work on their behalf.

What does public work look like? The question leads to the tale of two playgrounds.

1

Reinventing Citizen Politics

Harry C. Boyte

Public Achievement and Dr. King are alike because we
both made a difference in the world peacefully.
We both look at the problems and solve them
instead of blaming people.
—Matt Anderson, fourth-grade student at Saint Bernard's[1]

A Tale of Two Playgrounds
A Playground Built

The iconic story of Public Achievement is the tale of how teams of children at Saint Bernard's Grade School in Saint Paul worked for five years to build a playground, turning around neighborhood sentiment about the project and gathering support from city officials. The playground story contrasts with the frustrated aspirations of teenagers who wanted to build a playground in Brooklyn, New York. The differences illustrate how citizen politics contrasts with most citizen activism.

In the late fall of 1998, just as snow began to fall, the lot donated by Saint Bernard's Catholic Parish to children to build a playground filled early one morning. Children, teachers, and neighbors joined with college students and a few faculty from the University of Minnesota to assemble a playground. Some adults helped children put together swing sets. Others dug sand pits. Church women served refreshments. At the end of the day, all dedicated the playground with a plaque etched with drawings of cat feet: "PAWS: Public Achievement Works."

The incoming governor, Jesse Ventura, visited the new playground on February 26 and in his State of the State address the next week recognized five team members with the Governor's Award for a Better Minnesota for "reforming Minnesota every day through their good works." Joe Lynch, an eighth grader at Saint Bernard's who accepted the award for the group, was portrayed in Ventura's flamboyant style as a "citizen hero prevailing against all odds."[2]

In Public Achievement, teams of young people—generally ranging from elementary through high school students, sometimes in recent years including college students—work over the school year on issues they choose. Their issues must be legal, tackled nonviolently, and make a public contribution. Saint Bernard's set the pattern often used for choosing issues. They began at the start of the school year with an "issues convention." Students discussed problems in the school, the neighborhood, and the larger world, then voted to determine their priorities and arrive at a workable number of groups. Coaches came from Jim Farr's political science class, "Citizen Education," at the University of Minnesota. Earlier teams at Saint Bernard's had chosen issues such as reviving a parish carnival called Springfest, developing a curriculum to address and prevent sexual harassment, changing school uniform policy, and responding to the problem of gangs and violence in the neighborhood.[3] In 1993 one team chose to work on the playground issue.

Children and adults alike had long been concerned about the lack of a playground. Students at Saint Bernard's spent recesses in a parking lot. "I saw a lot of kids get hurt," Lynch explained to a reporter for the *St. Paul Pioneer Press*. "I saw a girl get a concussion. It was pretty boring too. We played kick ball but usually the ball went into the neighbor's yard."[4]

Parents had tried to build a playground a couple of years earlier but backed down when neighbors voiced opposition, fearing it would be a magnet for vandalism and gangs. The children took on the work themselves. "By the second year I knew it would happen," Lynch remembered.[5]

How it happened is the most important part of the story, about empowering civic skills and habits learned through practice. Years later, Joey's younger sister Alaina, who also worked on the playground, remembered the overall lesson. "It was a 'no-brainer' to have a playground for kids instead of an old lot, but that didn't mean that making it happen was straightforward," Alaina explained. She learned about city politics. "Public Achievement opened my eyes to the processes of government—petitions, connecting with the city council, commenting, obtaining permits. [These were] not things I would have thought about as a ten- or eleven-year-old otherwise." She also learned about neighborhood politics. "I learned there are multiple sides to every idea. Even something that seemed straightforward to me could have negative ramifications from another point of view." For her, the gang issue was "not a huge concern. The neighborhood gangs would hang out in the empty lot." But others saw it differently. "We had to demonstrate that we had a plan for mitigating any risk—a fence, with the playground closed after certain hours." She learned about different perspectives and also "about compromise."[6]

The teams got the parish council on their side. They negotiated zoning changes with city officials. They raised more than $60,000 from local businesses in the North End Business Association and other groups. To accomplish these tasks, the children learned how to interview people, write letters, give speeches, and call people they didn't know on the phone. They worked to understand the views of adults they originally thought were opponents. They mapped power, did research, and negotiated. Throughout, they had a sense that their efforts were public work, suggested in the name young people chose for the park: Public Achievement Works. They also learned political concepts—power, interests, and politics itself. "For most of my life, I've wanted to get involved with politics," said Jeremy Carr, a pioneer of Public Achievement. "When [Public Achievement] came around and I found I could do the stuff I wanted to change—and got adults to treat me seriously—I got excited." This also was the opportunity the principal, Dennis Donovan, was looking for. "We wanted kids doing citizenship-type things," he said. "More than just reading to other little kids."[7]

The framework in Public Achievement stresses a different kind of politics, co-creative politics that revolves around diverse citizens' needs, interests, and capacities, and that teaches the skills and habits of working with people who differ from one another. Issues chosen in Public Achievement sometimes have to do with injustices, such as landmines, child labor, or the rights of LGBT young people. Sometimes they address concrete problems such as broken toilet stalls in bathrooms. Many issues concern changing school and community culture, such as bullying and cyberbullying, disrespect for people with disabilities, sexual harassment, vandalism, racial prejudice, or the image of young people in the mass media. Sometimes young people create public goods and artifacts such as a song, a play, a school curriculum—or a playground. In Public Achievement, young people are conceived as co-creators, citizens today, not simply citizens-in-waiting. They help to build democracy in their schools, neighborhoods, and society.

A number of evaluations have found that young people, college coaches, and sometimes teachers and community members develop political skills and civic identity in Public Achievement: chairing meetings, interviewing, deliberating, negotiating interests, speaking publicly, writing, holding each other accountable, doing research on issues, and evaluating their own efforts, to mention a few. Jim Farr, the political scientist who began bringing his UMN class to Saint Bernard's to coach each week, saw significant learning opportunities for his own college students. "The only way to really think about citizen education is to practice it," he explained. "If you have a civic and pedagogical mission at the University, as I do, you want to get your students out of the classroom into the broader classroom of public life, to let them engage in public work, and to help educate younger citizens [in] identifying and solving their own problems."[8] He could see his own students learning civic and political skills and habits as they served as coaches.[9]

In 1999, Angela Matthews, a young adult leader of Public Achievement from Northern Ireland, spoke to a Twin Cities Public Achievement conference that included young people from third grade through college. She asked, "How many of you like politics?" Most raised their hands. Then she made her point: "It's because we're doing politics; it's not simply something politicians do."[10]

Students in Public Achievement also learn that citizenship is active. "Citizenship means taking action, not sitting back and watching," said Chou Vang, a six grader.[11] They learn it is about power, not dominating "power over" but "power to," what we call agency, the capacity to act intentionally to shape the world around oneself. "Civic" agency adds a cooperative, collective dimension. "I got a lot of empowerment from Public Achievement," said Tamisha Anderson twenty years later. Tamisha, an African American student at Saint Bernard's, worked on the playground and on a team trying to change clothing rules in the school. "We didn't get white shoes, but we got the uniforms changed. It was empowering to know that your voice matters regardless of what color or size or age you are." The lessons stayed with her. "I use [the example of] 'the little train that could' to this day with kids I talk to. I push them to stay involved even though they get knocked down."[12]

Zach Baumann, who is of German American background, worked for several years on the playground. "We had neighborhood meetings. We worked with the city to get the zoning changed and interacted with local business leaders to try to get some money. We met with the county commissioners." Zach said he learned to be accountable, which he saw as "a huge deal for people that age. You were letting down your team if you dropped the ball. We knew we had to rely on each other to get things done." He also learned to work across differences. "Civic involvement has a stereotypically liberal quality in a lot of the media, but it's about conservative values, taking responsibility for what's going on, contributing how you can to improve your world, not about asking somebody to do something for you." He worked with both liberal and conservative kids. "I didn't care what someone else's thoughts on immigration were. We were trying to get the playground. That's one of the biggest things Public

Achievement can bring, the ability to put aside your differences for a common goal. In fact, you don't have to like the person to work with them. Standing up and walking out of the room isn't going to accomplish anything."[13]

Both Tamisha and Zach recall how Public Achievement filled the school with energy. "It was so great to see all these kids want to learn something, want to change something, want to add something, want to remove something," Tamisha remembered. "We would race to Public Achievement and get down to business." Zach said, "We felt we were doing something important that had a lot of support." The importance of the work animated their lives. "It led to a lot more engagement with the school because we felt we could say if we thought something was wrong or should be different. I don't think there is any section of my life it didn't reach one way or another."[14]

Speaking today as an adult, Zach believes that what he learned in Public Achievement is crucial for the country. "The principles of Public Achievement, the abilities that it teaches and the agency that it gives, are the last vestige of the foundation of America. So much of our political environment is so divisive. People have lost a sense that they have a voice, that what they say matters."[15]

Alaina Lynch brought the skills and habits she learned in Public Achievement to her work on the staff of Congresswoman Betty McCollum from Saint Paul. "I saw the lessons repeated over and over again—doing your homework, building your case, connecting with like-minded people, considering others' perspectives, and making compromises, from local projects to national legislation. The people who get things done, whose ideas move forward, are the ones willing to put in the time and effort to collaborate with people at all levels, rather than considering them to be an obstacle." She, like Zach, feels such knowledge and skills are largely absent today. "These are very basic concepts, but I was surprised as a Congressional staffer how many people hurt their own causes by not checking these simple boxes—not having local support, or data to back up an idea, not considering multiple perspectives, not being willing to compromise. I was lucky to have exposure to these concepts at a young age through Public Achievement."[16]

The loss of political skills, habits, and civic concepts is a problem not only for individuals but also for society. It has been exacerbated by the loss of institutional and community settings where people develop such capacities and learn to respect others who are different from themselves. This loss of civic muscle has been accompanied by the narrowing of government's role to government "for the people," delivering services and benefits, not "of the people, by the people." Government is rarely seen as civic partner.

A Playground Lost

Young people's typical experiences with citizen activism differ markedly from the story of Saint Bernard's. A second playground story illustrates this.[17]

Daniel May worked for the New York affiliate of ACORN, a nationwide activist citizen organization, after graduating from college. Growing up in Minneapolis, the son of friends of mine, and committed to Jewish ideals of social justice, he heard many of my stories about the Saint Bernard's youth organizing. When a group of teens in the Brooklyn neighborhood where he was working told him they wanted to get a playground, it was natural that he propose the project to the regional director of ACORN. She was skeptical. "What does a playground have to do with power?" she asked. She believed energy should go into mobilizing citizens for progressive causes and raising consciousness about corporate and right-wing enemies. Her conclusion was that Daniel could work with the teenagers on the issue only under certain conditions. He had to be able to "cut" the issue in a progressive way, which is organizing language for identifying a clear enemy. He had to figure out how it could be used to organize a protest.

This approach did not make much sense to Daniel. It wasn't likely to get a playground, even if they could figure out who the enemy was. Through the summer ACORN became active in the mayor's election. The playground issue was dropped. Daniel felt relief as "organizing" came to mean voter mobilization. "Our organizing clay suddenly makes sense when poured into this mold," he said. "Some camaraderie is really beginning to creep into walls that seemed to house folks who talked about quitting over cigarettes nearly every day. Campaigning is all about numbers, mobilizing the base and turning out the regulars. We don't even pretend to develop leaders or build anything sustainable."[18]

This episode is a case study of young people's common experiences with what is called "politics." Over the last generation, many activist citizen groups have emerged that purport to be educating citizens generally and young people specifically for political life, increasing citizen participation and empowerment, and creating responsive government. But their approach is like ACORN's. They often use the language of organizing. But what they mean is "mobilizing."

Today's mobilizing developed in stages and has accelerated with the digital revolution. In 1974 Citizens for a Better Environment invented the modern canvass powered by a formula. The canvass involves paid staff going door-to-door on an issue, raising money and collecting signatures. The formula that makes it work identifies the enemy and defines the issue in radically reductionist, good-versus-evil terms, a Manichean politics. Manichean approaches make mass activation *efficient* because hatred and its close cousin anger are relatively uncomplicated emotions to manipulate. "We've discovered how to sell progressive politics door-to-door, like selling encyclopedias," was the boast of the canvass creators. Canvassers are generally barred from having discussions with those at the door that might complicate the issue at hand.

For years I defended the canvass, coauthoring *Citizen Action and the New American Populism* with Steve Max and Heather Booth, founder of the Midwest Academy training center that was the hub for spreading the method. I remember well the urgency we felt in the 1970s faced with massive mobilization by large corporate interests to roll back environmental, consumer, affirmative action, progressive tax, and other legislation from the 1960s. We saw ourselves as political realists in contrast to what we saw as the romanticism and hyperbolic rhetoric of the student movements of the late 1960s. My first book, *The Backyard Revolution: Understanding the New Citizen Movement*, began as a description of the corporate mobilization and what could be done about it. We saw the canvass as a way to fight back through large-scale citizen activation. The canvass produced successes on environmental, consumer, and other issues even during the Reagan presidency. We estimated that the canvass reached twelve million households a year in the mid-1980s.[19]

Over the past four decades many canvass operations have developed, including environmental and consumer organizations and the Public Interest Research Group (PIRG) network on college campuses. ACORN was one of the earliest and largest examples. But at the Humphrey Institute I discovered that most of my students had canvassed. Almost all felt burnout and disillusionment with its scripted qualities. Dana Fisher's study of the effects of the canvass, *Activism, Inc.*, expands this account based on many interviews.[20]

I also began to realize another problem: the Manichean formula escaped the canvass and spread like the southern creeper kudzu. It polarizes civic life, objectifies and abstracts "the enemy," erodes citizenship, communicates that politics is warfare, and narrows government to a "target" for gaining resources, not a partner in problem-solving. New technologies dramatically augment its reach, now employed in robo-calls, Internet mobilizations, talk radio, and Michael Moore's documentaries. An *NBC News* report by Chuck Todd and Carrie Dann, "How Big Data Broke American Politics," details the increasingly polarized campaigns and politics over the last two decades. "Polarization isn't new, but it's definitely worse than it was 20 years ago," they write. "And thanks to technology and the manipulation of demographic data, those charged with the setting and resetting of American politics . . . have set the stage and conditioned the country for a more permanent polarized atmosphere."[21]

These patterns took many forms across the country. Linda Honold, former chair of the Wisconsin Democratic Party, led implementation of a strategy developed by 125 progressive leaders from labor unions, environmental groups, women's organizations, and others. As a young single mother on welfare, she had used welfare and jobs programs as well as public universities to get out of poverty. After spending time in business and getting a doctorate in organizational theory, she joined the activist world out of a desire to champion such programs. But her tenure as state chair of the Democratic Party was frustrating. "It used a 50 percent plus one approach that didn't engage people." Many groups in the progressive coalition use the good versus evil formula. Even groups that don't use the canvass use a mobilizing approach, getting people out to rallies, town meetings, press conferences, and other events. Her research showed that it feeds people's anger at government.[22]

When I was invited to begin a democracy project from the Humphrey Institute in 1987, what became the Center for Democracy and Citizenship in 1994, I was motivated to launch Public Achievement as an explicit alternative for young people to such good versus evil politics.[23] To understand the elements that went into the project, some of my "public narrative"—my experiences in the freedom movement, community organizing, and writing and research—may be useful.

A Public Narrative

In the freedom movement, I learned the distinction between "mobilizing" and "organizing." Mobilizing—demonstrations, protests, sit-ins, and the like—was more visible. Organizing was slower and developed public talents. Both were shaped by a nonviolent philosophy that taught not to demonize opponents and to look for possibilities even in enemies. These qualities generated the movement's public appeal and political savvy.

Charles Payne describes how movement leaders distinguished between mobilizing and organizing. Though mobilizing is better known, grassroots organizing took place in communities across the South on a large scale under the radar. Citizenship schools and related efforts created seedbeds for what Payne called "developmental politics."[24] "Whether a community achieved this or that tactical objective was likely to matter less than whether the people in it came to see themselves as having the right and the capacity to have some say-so in their own lives."[25] The roots of Public Achievement begin in this developmental politics.

This cross-partisan, developmental politics flourished in the self-organizing efforts of people as they created associations and built communities, often in partnership with government. Through the twentieth century such politics weakened as civic centers such as local schools and colleges, congregations, libraries, ethnic groups, and locally rooted unions and businesses turned into service centers where trained experts treat people as clients and customers. In the 1930s popular politics revived in the movements of the Great Depression that sought to enlist broad support, across partisan divisions, for the struggles against fascism. I believe that the great work *In Defense of Politics*, by the British philosopher Bernard Crick, drew on this popular politics. Crick called politics "a great and civilizing activity," built on negotiation and compromise among diverse interests. An emphasis on ideological *unity*, he said, destroyed the defining quality of politics, namely *plurality*. Crick defended politics against forces that he saw as obliterating plurality, including nationalism, technology, and mass democracy, as well as conservative, liberal, and socialist ideologies.[26]

Organizers of the freedom movement such as Ella Baker, Septima Clark, Myles Horton, and Bayard Rustin also participated in the popular movements of the 1930s, and their politics resembled Crick's. So did Oliver Harvey's politics. Harvey was a janitor at Duke University who led a successful effort over years to organize the nonacademic employees. He told me about earlier movements like the struggle against the poll tax, used to keep both poor whites and blacks from voting, and interracial union organizing efforts in textile and tobacco factories in Durham. He also contrasted the effort among maids and janitors with the penchant of students and faculty for protests. In his view, righteous protests against the institution damaged the efforts of nonacademic employees, who were framing their efforts as a way to contribute to Duke's educational mission.

In addition to grassroots, cross-partisan politics, the freedom movement was infused with nonviolent philosophy, which differs from pacifism—that is, the refusal of violence in any circumstance—and is also different from current views that define nonviolence as tactical.[27] Nonviolence in the freedom movement tradition involves spiritual, moral, and psychological disciplines that refuse to demonize opponents or see them in reductionist terms. In *Stride toward Freedom*, Martin Luther King develops a profound account. Nonviolence is struggle, not inaction. It seeks to understand opponents, not defeat or humiliate them. It distinguishes between evil actions and those who commit them. It starts with change in oneself. "Hate . . . corrodes the personality and eats away at its vital unity," King wrote. "The nonviolent approach . . . first does something to the hearts and souls of those committed to it. It gives them new self-respect. It calls up resources of strength and courage they did not know they had." Finally, King proposes a kind of love: not personal love, but goodwill toward one's enemies as well as one's friends. King called this *agape*, from the Greek, meaning disinterested love. I believe a better term is *public love*, a horizon of respect for the potential of one's adversaries to contribute to a common life.[28] This philosophy and its expression in the enormous dignity and public presence of ordinary people who animated the movement had a large impact on me, an angry young southerner of Scottish descent who tended to be sharply critical of peers and family who supported segregation.

Citizenship schools, infused with nonviolence and grassroots politics, taught people to see themselves not as victims but as change agents. Dorothy Cotton, my boss in the citizenship schools, listened to people's stories of suffering for the first two days of the five-day training session held at the Dorchester Center in Georgia, where people came from across the South to learn how to create local citizenship schools in their communities. The third day she would issue a challenge: "You're never going to be a first-class citizen if you are a victim," she said.

My views of grassroots politics and nonviolence were further developed by King's suggestion that I do community organizing among poor whites.[29] I organized in Edgemont, a white mill community in Durham, North Carolina, experimenting with the politics I had learned in the citizenship schools with people who reminded me of my southern working-class, Scottish American relatives. A few in Edgemont were members of the Ku Klux Klan. Others, such as Basie and Doug Hicks, had battled racial prejudice all their lives. The Klan influence subsided noticeably as the neighborhood gained a little power. After our first victory, getting the city to oil dirt streets so dust wouldn't blow into people's houses, neighborhood women reached out to black women across the railroad tracks. I learned in Edgemont that there are resources in every community for building democracy.

The citizenship ethos of the movement was evident on the vast public stage of the March on Washington, held on August 28, 1963. The march drew on a deep relational process taking place in communities before the event itself. As Zeynep Tufekci, a scholar of marches, put it in the *New York Times* when comparing the March on Washington in 1963 with the Women's March after Trump's inauguration in 2017, "The [1963] march drew a quarter of a million people but it represented much more effort, commitment, and preparation than would a protest of similar size today," in the world of social media such as Facebook and Twitter, cell phones, and email. She emphasized the patient process of building relationships and discussing the meaning of the march in advance, which is different from what takes place in today's mobilizing campaigns.[30]

The program notes of the 1963 march urged participants to act with dignity and discipline even if provoked by those who sought to disrupt the march. "In a neighborhood dispute there may be stunts, rough words and hot insults, but when a whole people speaks to its government the quality of the action and the dialogue needs to reflect the worth of that people and the responsibility of that government." The marchers embodied citizenship in their dignified demeanor, marching as a "whole people" speaking to government, taking responsibility for "the quality of [their] action and the dialogue," showing their "worth."[31] Bayard Rustin, march organizer, stressed that the goal was to "win over the middle" of American society, not to rally the already convinced.[32] These lessons are woven into Public Achievement.

In the 1970s I started writing about different currents of citizen action and was especially impressed with the ways citizen politics was gaining maturity in what is called broad-based community organizing. Such organizing, particularly the network called the Industrial Areas Foundation, with its own 1930s roots, generated several discrete practices such as one-on-ones, power mapping, an ongoing process of reflection, and a sustained focus on developing public skills and habits.[33]

I brought these concepts and experiences to civic engagement work through the Humphrey Institute. I also brought interest in the "commonwealth" tradition in American political culture. Over several years of PA and other citizen politics efforts, the concept of public work emerged.

The Commonwealth

In American history, "commonwealth" was the idiom of choice for American radicals, organizers, small farmers, and business owners battling concentrated economic power, for suffragists and feminists, and for those who struggled against racial oppression. The "cooperative commonwealth," the "maternal commonwealth," and the "commonwealth of freedom"—or simply "the commonwealth"—created a distinctive American vocabulary of change that balanced pursuit of private wealth with concern for creating and sustaining a common world. "The great problem to be solved by the American people is this: whether or not there is strength enough in democracy, virtue enough in our civilization, and power enough in our religion to have mercy and deal justly with four millions of people lately translated from the old oligarchy of slavery to the new commonwealth of freedom," said the African American poet Frances Harper in 1875.[34]

If "commonwealth" was the lingua franca of democratizing movements, it also had cross-partisan appeal. The term was used by conservative intellectuals; business, civic, and political leaders; and more generally by people of diverse partisan views to express the constructive work of building civic life, sometimes in partnership with government, other times independently. "The last duty of the commonwealth is that of erecting and maintaining those public institutions and those public works which, though they may be of the highest degree advantageous to a great society, are, however, of such a nature that the profit could never repay the expense of any individual or small number," wrote Adam Smith, architect of modern market economics.[35]

The commonwealth had two interrelated roots. It drew from traditions of popular government such as the British "commonwealth" that for a time replaced the monarchy. It also drew from "the commons," grazing and pasture lands, streams, and forests of general benefit for which whole communities had responsibilities and in which they had rights of use. In *Common Wealth: A Return to Citizen Politics*, a book that helped to launch the civic engagement work through the Humphrey Institute, I connected citizen politics with the commonwealth tradition through a focus on power dynamics, arguing that citizen politics represents a tradition different from the politics of left or right. In the American commonwealth tradition, "civic autonomy" replaces a distributive view of politics through the state, the centerpiece of left-wing theory and practice. The commonwealth that people helped manage, often in partnership with government, also replaces the right wing's focus on markets. These themes intimated Elinor Ostrom's much more elaborated theory of citizen-centered governance of common pool resources, which she and her colleagues were developing independently.

When Jim Farr suggested the theme "public work," a term used by some in cooperative extension in the early twentieth century, we organized a conference on the idea in 1992. I saw parallels between the "public work" young people were doing in Public Achievement and the commonwealth tradition. We tied together public work and the commonwealth in which citizens are at the center.

In the American case, public goods such as schools, libraries, community centers, wells, roads, and bridges were created by citizens, not by aristocrats or monarchs or handed down from antiquity. As David Mathews observed, "Nineteenth-century self-rule . . . was a sweaty, hands-on, problem-solving politics . . . rooted in collective decision making and acting—especially acting." He continues, "Settlers on the frontier had to be producers, not just consumers. They had to join forces to build forts, roads, and libraries. . . . They also established the first public schools. Their efforts were examples of 'public work,' meaning work done by not just for the public."[36] Historians Oscar Handlin and Mary Handlin said that the concept of commonwealth conveyed collective effort itself: "For the farmers and seamen, for the fishermen, artisans and new merchants, commonwealth repeated the lessons they knew from the organization of churches and towns . . . the value of common action."[37]

Minnesota usage illustrates both republican government and commons created by citizens. Commonwealth came to expression in popular movements and in civic contributions by business and other civic leaders alike. "The Cooperative Commonwealth Program" of the Farmer-Labor Party, leading to Floyd Olson's election as governor and considerable party gains in the Minnesota legislature, is a landmark in progressive vision, growing out of populist farmer, labor, and cooperative movements. In Minnesota, commonwealth was a term used by elites as well as by common people. The *St. Paul Pioneer Press*, on the seventh-fifth anniversary of the state, profiled Charles M. Loring, president of the Minneapolis park board from 1883 to 1890 and architect of the city's park system, as a contributor to the commonwealth of the state. "He published articles, gave illustrated lectures, and in various other ways made clear to the people of the state the advantages of parks and civic improvement."[38] Lotus Coffman, the University of Minnesota's president from 1920 to 1938, entitled his inaugural address "The University and the Commonwealth."

The novelist Marilynne Robinson was implying these ideas in her conversation with President Obama in the fall of 2015, reprinted in the *New York Review of Books*. "Democracy," she said, "was something people collectively made." Making democracy created a culture of mutual respect.[39]

Civic construction of the commonwealth was not only a feature of nineteenth-century rural America. In the Great Depression government played a key role as partner in citizen construction. The Civilian Conservation Corps (CCC), for example, involved more than three million young men in public works projects. They acted out of practical self-interest, not high ideals. They needed jobs. The CCC camps, run by the army, were scarcely models of democratic decision making. But their work also had democratic dimensions. As people made a commonwealth of goods, they became a commonwealth of citizens.

The CCC brought people together across differences. As Al Hammer told Nan Kari, in an interview for our coauthored *Building America: The Democratic Promise of Public Work*, "The CCC got people like me out into the public. It gave me a chance to meet and work with people different than me from all over the country—farm boys, city boys, mountain boys, all worked together."[40]

Public work was educative in other ways. C. H. Blanchard observed that "the CCC enrollees feel a part-ownership as citizens in the forest that they have seen improve through the labor of their hands." Participants often developed a strong sense of public purpose. Scott Leavitt of the U.S. Forest Service explained that "there has come to the boys of the Corps a dawning understanding of the inspiring and satisfying fact that they are taking an integral and indispensable part in a great program vitally essential to the welfare, possibly even to the ultimate existence, of this country."[41]

Over the last several decades the culture of democratic respect has eroded in concert with the decline of public work. Susan Faludi's *Stiffed: The Betrayal of the American Man* explores the changing identities of men, from African American shipyard workers to football players and television executives. Men by the beginning of the twenty-first century were "in an unfamiliar world where male worth is measured only by participation in a celebrity-driven consumer culture." With productive measures of success—supporting a family, contributing to the community, helping to build the nation—in shards, men resembled Betty Friedan's "trapped housewives" of the 1960s, without words to name their discontent in a culture "drained of context, saturated with a competitive individualism that has been robbed of craft or utility and ruled by commercial values that revolve around who has the most, the best, the biggest, the fastest."[42]

We came to see public work as reviving not only traditions of the commonwealth but also people's identities as civic producers, not simply consumers. Both aspirations and obstacles to public work can be found across society. And education is a useful case in point to explore.

2

Education as a Civic Question

Harry C. Boyte with Isak Tranvik

Educational reform in the United States has often been driven by a combination of blame and punishment. "We tend to frame our indictments in terms of decline," wrote Mike Rose, a keen observer of education, in *Lives on the Boundary*. "[It is] a harsh, laced-with-doom assault stripped of the historical realities of American education—of its struggle to broaden rather than narrow access, of the increasing social as well as cognitive demands made on it." Rose invokes the image of the ancient goddess of grammar, Grammatica, to invoke the tone: severe, holding pincer and scalpel, right hand grasping a bird by its neck, its mouth ready to squawk. "How fitting the choices of emblem were—the living thing being strangled . . . the scalpel, the pincers reminders to the teacher to be vigilant for error," he writes.[1]

Today, "data" has become the new goddess of grammar. And the authority of the algorithm extends far beyond the reach of the teacher-goddess Rose describes; students, teachers, and even entire schools can be caught between this new Grammatica's pincer and scalpel. Decisions about instruction, curriculum, and assessments, not to mention hiring, firing, and "consolidation," are heavily informed by quantitative evidence of student growth, or lack thereof, usually measured by results on standardized tests. A few years of subpar performance on annual assessments can have dire consequences for teachers and whole schools and communities. When students fail to show growth on these exams, the teacher is held responsible; when teachers fail to move their students along, schools are warned; and when a school doesn't meet mandated academic targets, it can be closed. The narrative of blame and punishment, then, is flourishing decades after Rose wrote.[2]

To be sure, technological transformation and the ready availability of data bring many benefits in education. In the classroom, students everywhere have access to information that only a few decades ago was housed at a select few elite institutions. Teachers can monitor student learning in real-time. Technology enables creative lesson planning and even flipped classrooms. Perhaps most importantly, teachers, parents, and administrators are now able to identify common misunderstandings or gaps in student learning; students are less likely to be lost in the shuffle when their learning is tracked and monitored. When we act on the view of data and technology as educational tools, not ends in themselves, the digital revolution can be a powerful resource.

The problem is that digital technology is now often employed in the service of what historian Robert Kanigel calls "the credo of efficiency," focused on getting "there" faster and faster with little discussion of whether "there" is the best place to go. This dynamic appears across society. In politics it accelerates trends toward mobilizing as Manichean politics, described in Chapter 1, seeing opponents as enemies whose vast complexity is entirely lost. In education, it erodes the relationships and larger sense of purpose at the heart of teaching and learning.

"The datafication of everything . . . leaves behind whatever can't be quantified," writes Sue Halpern in the *New York Review of Books*.[3] Datafication relies on proxies used to represent vastly more complex realities, with the biases of the programmers written in. Today, algorithms are used to predict who will commit a crime, to influence sentencing, to determine hiring, and to determine one's credit rating. They also increasingly are present in education. Cathy O'Neil begins *Weapons of Math Destruction* with the story of Sarah Wysocki, an elementary school teacher in Washington. Though she received excellent reviews from her principal and from parents, Wysocki received a termination notice because her score in the system for evaluation of teachers, generated by an algorithm, outweighed positive evaluations from humans. The algorithm, developed by Mathematica Policy Research, may well have compared the test results of her students to their scores the year before, when others taught them. Such an analysis could be wrong on many grounds. Did earlier teachers doctor the test numbers upward to protect themselves? Did several of her students have a bad day when they took the test (the small numbers would radically skew her score)? No one knows; such algorithms are kept secret. "Verdicts . . . land like dictates from the algorithmic gods," writes O'Neil.[4]

By the beginning of the twenty-first century, pressure to address the educational needs of low-income, minority and other disadvantaged students joined with accelerating technological change to produce "No Child Left Behind" (NCLB), the 2002 act that passed with support from both Democrats and Republicans in Congress. NCLB doubled down on the carrot-and-stick approach Rose described, strengthening the federal role—and weakening local power. It made every school accountable for student outcomes, defined largely in terms of test scores. States were required to test students in reading and math from grades 3 through 8 and again in high school. Scores, especially for particular subgroups including students in special education, racial minorities, children from low-income backgrounds, and English language learners, were reported to officials. Growth was monitored by "Adequate Yearly Progress" reports with schools facing a series of escalating sanctions for not reaching predetermined targets. When schools fail to meet their targets, they run the risk of being designated "turnaround schools." Teachers at these schools are rarely part of the "turnaround." When a school receives this designation, all teachers are fired and state-appointed administrators can rehire no more than half the old staff. During the Obama administration it became clear that no state would ever hit the 95 percent "proficiency" goal—that 95 percent of students would score proficient on English and mathematics exams—established when the law was passed in 2002. Many states were granted waivers to spare them the harshest punishments.[5] In return, states had to commit to evaluating teachers in light of students' performance on standardized tests.[6]

Some originally enthusiastic NCLB champions began to raise questions. Diane Ravitch, appointed to be assistant secretary of education under George W. H. Bush and later to the National Assessment Government Board, which assesses educational progress, originally supported NCLB. But she had a change of heart. The NCLB model, she writes, "assumes that students be constantly tested and that the results of these tests are the most important measures and outcomes of education."[7] More troublingly, she says, "The scores can be used not only to grade the quality of every school, but to punish or reward students, teachers, principals, and schools." One critical problem with this approach is that "a teacher may look highly effective one year but ineffective the next, depending on which students end up in his or her classroom. Research has demonstrated that those who teach students with disabilities, students who are just learning English, and other students with high needs are less likely to get big test score gains and more likely to be rated as 'bad' teachers. By imposing such indiscriminate standards, some excellent teachers will be fired, and others of less distinction will get bonuses." As a result, teachers are often left feeling undervalued and under attack.

Ravitch's concerns are heightened by advances in education technology. Increased computing power and smart-learning machines make it easier than ever to monitor and analyze student performance on assessments. Unsurprisingly, then, the tech industry has begun pouring money into education, both philanthropically and for profit. DreamBox, a math program funded by Netflix founder Reed Hastings, uses an algorithm that processes up to fifty thousand data points per student per hour to create personalized lessons. Mark Zuckerberg has helped develop and promote technology that helps students teach themselves.[8] One for-profit Silicon Valley startup operating in Africa, Bridge International Academies, has all but removed trained teachers from the classroom. Bridge "teachers," usually without any professional training, read scripts developed by former Boston-area charter school teachers to their African students.[9] While the technology varies from place to place and entrepreneur to entrepreneur, the ultimate goal is often quantifiable growth on standardized assessments.

Such developments left Paul Barnwell, a veteran high school educator, wondering whether he would soon be obsolete. While sympathetic to using technology to identify and target student needs, he worries about its misuse: "[Personalized learning] initiatives often become software or technology-based, with digital 'instruction' adjusting based on competency levels or skills of its student users. It's not about student passion or authentic projects—it's all about remediating and measuring specific academic skills." Technology, then, is employed in service of a predetermined and unquestioned end: quantifiable growth. "Instead of a teacher striving to know a student on multiple levels—from understanding the nuances of his or her academic skills, to building positive relationships and crafting learning experiences based on more than numerical reading scores—educators are sidelined when a machine takes over. Personalized learning often becomes inherently impersonal; it's a sterile approach to messy, complex classroom processes."[10]

Isak Tranvik, one of this chapter's coauthors, vividly recalls how overwhelming the emphasis on "skill acquisition" can be for young teachers. The importance of test scores, especially at lower-performing schools, leaves little space for discussion about students' future flourishing, much less conversations about education and democracy. The exam and the skills students need to succeed on it can evolve into much more than a proximate goal for the larger vision that most teachers have for their students. It subtly becomes the "end" itself. Every day brings more skills to master, more benchmarks to meet, more practice tests to take. Every minute of every class is planned, every student knows the task that needs to be completed, and every last assessment is carefully evaluated. Arne Duncan, the former secretary of education during the Obama administration and longtime defender of using testing data to evaluate school performance, acknowledges that standardized testing can have unintended consequences. In a 2014 policy memo he says that he "believes testing issues today are sucking the oxygen out of the room in a lot of schools."[11]

While Duncan does not reject standardized tests outright, he notes that "too much testing can rob school buildings of joy, and cause unnecessary stress." One might add that strict testing regimes have the tendency to diminish or neglect teachers' power or sense of agency. Teachers can feel as though they are cogs in a machine. To use Duncan's metaphor, a singular emphasis on efficiency leaves schools lifeless.

Even in terms of testing it is more productive to focus on supporting, valuing, and developing teaching as a respected craft than to see technology as the answer. In Finland, for instance, the alternative strategy is to reward and support, not punish. Finnish schools encourage teacher collaboration including local development of tests. The country pays teachers well and holds the profession of teaching in high regard. "Finnish teachers are driven by a sense of intrinsic motivation, not by the hope of a bonus or fear of being fired. Intrinsic motivation is also what they seek to instill in their students," says Ravitch. Standardized tests don't exist in Finland. In their absence "teachers must develop, appeal to, and rely on their students' interest in learning." Interestingly, in international benchmark tests Finnish students score the highest in the world.[12]

Students as well as teachers chafe at the current patterns in schools. David Hoffman, on the student affairs staff at the University of Maryland, Baltimore County (UMBC), has worked with a group of students and staff for several years to translate the citizen politics approach in Public Achievement into the student government and other aspects of campus life at the university. He wrote his dissertation, "Becoming Real," based on iterative interviews with a group of students about their previous experiences in K-12 education; the students gave feedback throughout and the questions emerged from a common discussion.

Looking back at their experiences before coming to college, students at UMBC whom Hoffman interviewed saw their earlier experiences as highly scripted—designed for them by adults—and observed that their peers seemed often to be role-playing. "I grew up in a society that everything I did wasn't real," said Yasmin, an Iranian immigrant who had grown up in the United States. "It always seemed like I was preparing myself for something." Another student, Kati, recalled that school felt a good deal like her authoritarian parent. "Sit down in your seat and raise your hand and don't speak unless you're spoken to . . . don't complain, and don't challenge authority." They reminded Hoffman of his own experiences, "the games of masking genuine emotions to please or placate adults, and jumping through hoops to accumulate credentials." The two dominant obstacles to participants' sense of themselves as active agents in the world—externally determined roles and inauthentic peer interactions—continued in college.[13]

Others make similar observations when they seek to understand what schools "look like" from a student perspective. In a widely shared blog post, a veteran educator describes her experience shadowing two students for two full school days. She recalls asking her host student, Cindy, "if [she] felt like she made important contributions to class or if, when she was absent, the class missed out on the benefit of her knowledge or contributions, and she laughed and said no. . . . I was struck by this . . . because it made me realize how little autonomy students have, how little of their learning they are directing or choosing."[14] As the educator notes, even conscientious students must struggle mightily to stay engaged: "Teachers work hard, but I now think that conscientious students work harder."

A former "conscientious student" agrees: "I have seen my friends and family from the reservation [the Pascua Yaqui Tribe in Arizona] not complete school, while I did" wrote Joaquin Muñoz, a Native American college professor in his dissertation on Waldolf schools. "Yet even in this successful completion I was challenged by a sense of having an education far from complete, missing essential components." Muñoz became a member of Teach for America in Philadelphia in 2005 after graduating from college, working with Latino students from Puerto Rico, Cuba, and the Dominican Republic, more than 50 percent of whom were English language learners. As a teacher, Muñoz writes, "The goals and perspectives privileged in high stakes testing were never questioned." He had some disagreement "but at the time lacked the language to speak to it."[15]

The focus on technology and testing leaves little room for either teachers and students to pursue other goals. Though this may not be the intent of reformers, this focus pushes out other purposes. Indeed, questions about the purpose of school itself are rarely asked, and older ideas of "democratic excellence," much richer than "testocracy," have been largely forgotten. When the Center for Democracy and Citizenship joined with the National Issues Forums, the Kettering Foundation, and other groups to organize discussions on the purposes of higher education, people were surprised at the question of itself. Dave Senjem, the Republican minority leader of the Minnesota Senate, said, "'What's the purpose of higher education?' is a profound question that we've never discussed in all my years in the legislature."[16]

It's worth remembering that citizen politics was once central to American education, embodied in the very term "common school," schools available to the general citizenry. As Lawrence Cremin described in *Transformation of the School*, "The politics of education . . . exhibited unique tendencies over the past century" by bringing together a wide assortment of people with radically different interests and views. "In almost every state citizens organized to do battle in the cause of public schools. The political coalitions they formed frequently drew together the oddest collections of otherwise disparate interests." The movement for schools, with mechanisms for popular power such as local school boards and parent-teacher associations, left an indelible mark of popular ownership and agency. "By the artful device of lay control the public was entrusted with the continuing definition of the public philosophy taught its children," writes Cremin. "In this political process by which the public defines the commitments of the schools . . . one finds the decisive forces in American educational history."[17]

Today's school policy debates embody the efficiency imperative, centralizing power and eroding schools as civic meeting grounds in order to cut costs and develop quicker and more efficient ways to deliver information. Voucher champions such as Education Secretary Betsy DeVos argue that they "empower parents" through school choice, but this means seeing the market as the best mechanism for allocating resources. As the educator Deborah Meier observes, "The notion that we can leave it to the whims of individual parent choice in marketplace fashion is problematic. Good parents are inclined to put their own children's immediate interests first."[18] "Empowerment," in these terms, means consumer choice, not collective civic concern for each other and for communities.[19]

Policy makers on the side of public schools tout democratic values like diversity and inclusion but often focus on designing efficient means like high-stakes testing with little or no input from lay citizens. Luke Bretherton describes citizen-led school reform efforts. "What comes across time and again is the hostility 'non-experts' provoke," he says. Bretherton argues that increasing public support for schools will require a shift from a technocratic, top-down mindset to approaches that involve the diverse citizenry in school change and school life.[20] Such alternatives are beginning to appear.

Education as a Civic Question

On July 15, 2007, early in the presidential election race, Barack Obama spoke at the Sayre School in Philadelphia "At this time in our society, we desperately need beacons of hope that appeal to our better angels, that inspire us to work together to realize the democratic promise of America for *all* Americans." In Obama's view, community schools like Sayre's serve as a hub, "open to everyone, during the day, evening and on weekends." Such community hubs "create and sustain partnerships for change, involving faith-based institutions, universities, community-based organizations, health and human service agencies, unions, businesses and government agencies." They are based on the "powerful but simple idea: strong communities require strong schools and strong schools require strong communities." By embodying the efficiency principle, school policy debates erode the idea of schools as civic meeting grounds.[21] The Obama administration reached out to educators in higher education and K-12 schools in a short-lived effort to revitalize education's public and civic purposes called the American Commonwealth Partnership and through the Department of Education's commissioning of *A Crucible Moment*, a study organized by the Association of American Colleges and Universities calling for civic learning to become "pervasive" in education. These also led to a Department of Education report on policy changes to strengthen civic education.[22]

Outside policy debates, there are growing foundations for the civic purposes of education. For instance, the Coalition for Community Schools works with hundreds of schools across the country and dozens of partners, including the National School Board Association and the National Parent Teachers Association. The coalition has identified more than five thousand community-oriented schools that see education as occurring not only during school hours but after school and in the summer. These community-oriented schools "offer essential health and social supports and services." They "engage families and communities as assets in the lives of their children and youth." The coalition has a formal commitment to "college, career, and citizenship," based on the concept that "21st century skills will not only guide [students] through their post-secondary and professional career, but that they will make them better . . . citizens in a democratic society." Moreover, the university-assisted Community School Network, organized by the coalition and the Netter Center for Community Partnerships at the University of Pennsylvania, includes seventy colleges and universities. "There is a new energy and growth," said Ira Harkavy, a pioneer in partnerships between K-12 schools and institutions of higher education; he also founded the Netter Center and helped to create the coalition. Since its official launch in 1997, the coalition has used a "large tent" approach, including public, charter, parochial, and private schools.[23] What might a community school look like if it were to focus on civic purposes and develop an identity as a school for democracy?

In his speech at Sayre, Obama drew on a famous speech by the philosopher John Dewey to the National Education Association in 1902, "The School as Social Center." Education was central to the democratic way of life in Dewey's view. Democracy "has to be enacted anew in every generation, in every day and year, in the living relations of person to person in all social forms and institutions." For Dewey, education was at the center of democratic society; democracy was the spirit of education.[24] Dewey advanced the idea of schools as social centers to equip citizens with resources for democratic citizenship in an impersonal and chaotic world. His four core elements follow. They remain relevant to community schools that aspire to become democracy schools.

Throughout his 1902 lecture, Dewey's model was Jane Addams's Hull House. He saw the settlement as a space for sustained, face-to-face mingling of diverse populations in cities like Chicago, and he contrasted such space with the forced and destructive "Americanization" he believed was occurring when different races and cultures encountered each other in impersonal and antagonistic settings. For Dewey, when children were instructed with rote learning in factory-like schools and have little chance to interact, they "are frequently left floating and unstable between the two [their immigrant cultures and the dominant culture]. They even learn to despise the dress, bearing, habits, language and beliefs of their parents." In contrast, at Hull House "the new labor museum . . . show[s] the younger generation something of the skill and art and historic meaning of the older generations. . . . Many a child has awakened to an appreciation of admirable qualities hitherto unknown." According to Dewey, the first element of schools as social centers involved creating a "means for bringing people and their ideas and beliefs together, in such ways as will lessen friction and instability and introduce deeper sympathy and wider understanding."[25]

In today's context where the "relational" approach in education is being replaced with obsessively "informational" approaches, educational sites as places for mingling, developing understanding, and building human relationships across differences have renewed importance. The concept of the school as such a site can make explicit and intentional the animating spirit of community schools as a counter to technocratic patterns. The school as social center also provided, in Dewey's view, an antidote to the loss of "the old agencies" like family and religious group. Dewey the modernist saw many faults in such old agencies, but he acknowledged that they had also kept young people "living decent, respectable, and orderly lives." Schools embedded in communities must supply young people with "compensation for the loss of reverence and the influence of authority." Dewey suggested school activities such as "the social club, the gymnasium, the amateur theatrical presentation, the concert," and others to generate ethical behavior and values.[26]

Such a project of ethical civic repair is more relevant than ever in our age of eroding public standards, and it requires places where widely diverse interests and views on morality can interact over time. A public work perspective goes beyond Dewey's modernist bias. In a public work framework, schools embedded in community life *strengthen* mediating institutions such as families and congregations and fortify civic life beyond schools. They do not substitute schools for such institutions.

In addition, Dewey proposed that educational sites should be open to people of all ages, not simply children. He observed that "life is getting so specialized, the divisions of labor are carried so far, that nothing explains or interprets itself. . . . Hence we must rely upon instruction, upon interpretation come to us through conscious channels" to gain some sense of the larger workings of institutions and society as a whole.[27] If the early twentieth century seemed complicated, today's world represents a quantum leap in complexity. As Hull House equipped new immigrants with knowledge of the whole, schools embedded in the life of communities hold potential to be centers for adult learning in the twenty-first century.

Finally, for Dewey, schools as social centers needed to equip people to deal with a changing world of work. Using examples like the lawyer and the doctor who "must go on studying all his [or her] life," Dewey argued that "what is true of the lawyer and the doctor . . . is true . . . of all sorts and degrees of people. Social, economic, and intellectual conditions are changing at a rate undreamed of in past history. Now, unless the agencies of instruction are kept running more or less parallel with these changes, a considerable body of [people] is bound to find itself . . . left stranded and become a burden for the community to carry."[28] In the age of robots and smart machines, the dangers Dewey saw in the changing world of work more than a century ago are multiplying. Educational sites in the life of communities that attend to these challenges can offer opportunities to help keep people up to date with new skills and hold the potential to push back against today's economic logic of efficiency in which the focus is doing things ever faster and cheaper regardless of human displacement.

A fight in Georgia in 2016 suggested the public appeal of revitalizing schools as civic centers, governed by citizens. The popular Republican governor Nathan Deal put on the ballot a constitutional amendment to allow the governor to take charge of "chronically failing" schools and the tax revenue that supports them. Under his plan, "failed" schools would either be run directly by a new state agency or be converted to charter schools under management contracts, which would also be open to profit-making businesses. Deal claimed that Amendment One would "empower parents" and end "an inexcusable crisis" that left kids trapped in cycles of poverty and crime. The amendment was expected to pass easily, following a charter school initiative in Georgia in 2012 that Deal had supported.

The campaign against Amendment One began defensively, but as the campaign progressed and citizen organizers and local civic leaders became involved, the framework shifted. It stressed the positive theme of local power. The opposition named their group the Committee to Keep Georgia Schools Local. They described the amendment as a power grab and pointed out that the amendment proposed a false solution, with no constructive ideas for changing troubled schools such as better teaching methods, teacher training, or more community tutoring. The local school coalition attracted a diverse group, including not only the union but also black clergy and inner-city leaders, the Georgia Parent Teacher Association, rural school boards—more than forty passed resolutions opposing the amendment—and Republican strongholds. The amendment was defeated with more than 60 percent voting in opposition.

Gerald Taylor, a veteran community organizer, former director of the Industrial Areas Foundation's Southeastern region, and a pioneer in IAF's relational organizing approach, served as a consultant to the local school coalition. He observed that the campaign shows how far there is to go. After the election, conflicts broke out between some parent-teacher groups and others. But the campaign also showed the potential of a highly diverse coalition to bridge what many have seen as intractable racial and urban-rural divides, using the theme of local power in education. It demonstrated that "good politics" can be "smart politics." In Taylor's view, the key to the coalition's success was the shift from a typical mobilizing approach to an approach that encouraged local creativity. For instance, there was a fight about whether to allow yard signs, first opposed by campaign consultants but won by local communities. The campaign engaged local cultures and local leadership. It stressed contextualizing technology, metrics, and communication with what Taylor calls "social knowledge," stressing a larger vision of schools. "We argued that schools are much more than buildings or even places to teach kids," he said. "They are rallying centers in rural communities and inner cities. They are economic engines. They are community assets where people have ownership."[29]

Such stories suggest the potential of organizing around education as a *civic question*, grounding civic learning in local communities, not as a matter of market choice or state provision. To accomplish this, organizing will require citizen politics and the spread of public work approaches that reinvent "citizen teachers." The first signs of these appeared in Saint Paul, Minnesota, in the 1990s, at Saint Bernard's, the Catholic school where students organized to get a playground.

3

Public Work in Context

Harry C. Boyte

As Genesis recounts, after the word "cultivate,"
another word immediately follows: "care."
Each explains the other. They go hand in
hand. Those who do not cultivate do not care;
those who do not care do not cultivate.
—Pope Francis, 2015[1]

The Politics of Culture

Our first effort to launch Public Achievement in a school took place in Highland Park High School in Saint Paul. It came after years of careful preparation. It was a failure. Despite our intention to create experiences of citizen politics for young people different from the Manichean model of polarized politics, Public Achievement's first large public action was an angry protest. Students went on strike against a "no hat" rule in the school. The strike collapsed, and the rule continued. Students concluded that they were more powerless than they had thought.

Our working group realized a key lesson: the Highland Park High School experiment involved no learning or teaching about the cultural context. The teens were focused on their issue. They didn't pay attention to the messy complications of the place and the people in the place. We began to realize that Public Achievement, if it is to flourish as a pedagogy through which young people develop the confidence and skills to be serious agents of change and contributors to their communities, needs to teach everyone involved to be more attentive to local cultures and their politics.

Simply becoming *aware* of the culture of a place requires intentionality. Being in a school culture is akin to breathing air—that is, it is usually taken for granted. If the school culture is thought about, its norms, practices, and power relationships are assumed to be fixed, carrying the weight of the past. They can be changed, if at all, only by higher-ups. European American myopia about cultures of place (especially among those of English descent, since "WASP" identities are often taken as the norm) is fed by the individualist notion that "getting ahead" requires ignoring cultural roots. This was expressed in advice to immigrants in the 1890s. "Forget your past, your customs, and your ideals," the advice manual read. "Run, work, do, keep your own good in mind. That's the way to get ahead in America."[2] Finally, myopia about cultures in and around schools is fed by an efficiency mindset, where cultures are hidden by the focus on tests and technical skill mastery.

In contrast, the key to student empowerment is learning that the culture of a school or a place is constantly changing. Young people can help shape the change if they learn to negotiate the politics of cultural context. Citizen politics of this kind requires an approach different from the moralistic perspective typical of today's ideologically charged politics, which sees one side (or one group) as "right" and the other as "wrong."[3] Meira Levinson, a professor at the Harvard Graduate School of Education, developed a culturally contextual approach after teaching in inner-city African American schools and seeing firsthand the alienation of black students whose relational identities, growing from networks of families and communities, clashed with competitive and individualist norms in school cultures. The assumption was that students should adopt dominant norms as their own, which carried with it the message, implicit or explicit, that their values were "wrong." In *No Citizen Left Behind*, Levinson proposes a pragmatic alternative to the "good versus evil" cultural frame. She argues for seeing "power [as] relational and contextual" and "empowerment [as] a collective condition, not just an individual possession or state."[4] What she calls strategic code-switching involves students becoming politically savvy about the cultural language of a school, learning "that in every community there is a language and culture of power." Students can "represent and express themselves in ways that members of the majority group . . . will naturally understand and respect . . . instead of teaching [minority] kids that they do things wrong."[5]

Cultural power, like other kinds of relational power, highlights power's generative qualities. It involves the power to *create* identities and cultures. Such a view is also in the tradition of Jane Addams and others in the Hull House settlement described in Chapter 6, where people from diverse backgrounds learned how to negotiate a culturally pluralist space.[6] "Addams's own initial sense of superiority [over poor immigrants] had been grounded partly in her rarified cultural accomplishments," writes Louise Knight in her biography of

Addams. "Perhaps nothing so dramatically marked the significant transformation of her ideas . . . as her eventual abandonment of that attitude." Addams wrote, "The uncultivated person is bounded by a narrow outlook, unable to overcome differences in dress and habit, and his interests are slowly contracting within a circumscribed area." In contrast, she saw a cultivated person as having a "growing understanding of all kinds of people and their varying experiences." Knight adds, "She was describing herself . . . but also many of the working people" around Hull House.[7]

Public Achievement draws on this tradition. It begins with "the world as it is"—including the culture of a place—not from where students or coaches or teachers might want it to be. Participants develop knowledge, skills, and the habids of mind to engage with the actually existing culture of a school and neighborhood to make change. This politics and pedagogy provide a path beyond acquiescence or protests.

Before the Hat Strike

Extensive conversations, relationship-building, and organizing work before our entrance into Highland Park High School created a foundation to recoup from the failed experiment. The background was a partnership with the Minnesota Department of Education and the Mayor's Office of Saint Paul, both of which illustrated the idea of government as civic partner.

After coming to the Humphrey Institute in 1987, I began working with Nan Skelton, assistant commissioner of the Minnesota Department of Education. We sought to add a civic education dimension to youth service. Skelton at the time was organizing a statewide initiative called the Youth Service Model, based on a youth development approach to children. She wanted education policy to focus on young people's talents and capacities, not what was wrong with them. She also wanted communities to broaden their view of where education and learning take place to include many locations beyond classrooms. She invited twelve communities across the state to work with the department in developing community-wide strategies to address the "whole child," not simply academic learning. "Each community devised a plan to make their community work for and with kids. We involved businesses, churches, the schools, the parents, the bars, everybody."[8] We added an explicit citizenship dimension, "vital civic education . . . to produce action plans for youth involvement in community affairs."[9] Several years later, in 1993, Public Achievement was up and running, I was working with the White House Domestic Policy Council, and Nan Skelton had become a program officer for the Lilly

Endowment. We organized a symposium with leaders in the national service movement and the Clinton administration. AmeriCorps added a citizenship curriculum that our center helped design. Meanwhile, we organized a working group to plan our own youth civic education initiative.[10]

We developed a pivotal partnership with Jim Scheibel, who had been elected mayor of Saint Paul in 1989 on a platform that included youth empowerment. Jim, from a white ethnic, working-class background, and I had worked together in the early 1980s in a short-lived effort, the Citizen Heritage Center, seeking to bring awareness of America's rich democratic heritage to citizen action networks. Jim saw himself as a "citizen politician." In high school he was inspired by Catholic activists such as Dorothy Day, the founder of the Catholic Worker movement, and Daniel Berrigan, the antiwar activist who visited his school. After college, Jim became a youth worker in a public housing project, McDonough, and later a community organizer in the West Side neighborhood. "I realized neighborhoods were changed through organizing," he says. "And organizing changes lives." Jim remembers a key moment after the West Side Neighborhood Organization succeeded in getting the city council to create a park. Celebrating with a group of neighborhood leaders, one woman saw herself on the local television news. She said, "This is the first time I was not only reading about history but I was making history." Jim realized the power of seeing oneself as a co-creator. While serving as mayor, Jim championed neighborhoods. "For me that always meant sharing credit. What I accomplished was because I worked with community organizations."[11] In 1990 the city signed a contract with the Humphrey Institute to launch Public Achievement:

> Whereas the City desires to support efforts to teach the City's youth of many backgrounds about their potential for leadership . . . through well-designed community problem solving projects . . . the Mayor's Task Force on Youth has agreed to test a model program called "Public Achievement." The contractor [Project Public Life, Humphrey Institute of Public Affairs, University of Minnesota] shall develop a model program entitled "Public Achievement."[12]

The agreement, officially signed July 27, felt like a momentous beginning.

We created a listening process for teenagers to express their ideas, in partnership with the city and the Humphrey Institute. Carol McGee Johnson, from a leading family of black educators, and I coordinated the work, helped by three young adults—Kate Hogg, Rebecca Breuer, and Denise Beal. The latter two were leaders in a college student–organized service movement called COOL. We held twenty-one discussions with more than three hundred teenagers around Saint Paul, going to their own turf. These ranged from a theater class in Como High School to 4-H, from suburbs to public housing and Totem Town, a halfway house. The goal was to gauge interest in a "youth civic empowerment initiative" with parallels to the freedom movement's citizenship schools. I described how young people played critical roles in the movement, a fact largely unknown to the teenagers.

I asked if there were any problems they were worried about. Every group had a long list. These varied by context. Inner-city teens named problems such as drive-by shootings, crime, gangs, and schools that didn't relate to their lives. Suburban youth surfaced overscheduled families, suicides, drugs, and a hyper-competitive achievement culture. Across the board, young people expressed concern about problems in their immediate environment and the larger world. All were puzzled by the next question, "Do you think you could do anything, yourselves, to address these problems?" They said they had never been asked the question before. Most said they had never learned how to make change, but almost all were interested in learning. It was clear that Public Achievement would have to involve a retrieval process about what democracy means.

The teens helped us design the pedagogical approach. For instance, they proposed the idea of "coaches," adults (they especially liked the idea of college students) who would not do the work on their behalf, "on the field," but would challenge, mentor, and support their own efforts. They agreed strongly with the idea that young people should work as teams on issues they chose themselves. It was not hard to generate interest in politics when we described Public Achievement as "a different kind of politics" in which everyday citizens, not parties or office holders, were at the center and politics teaches the skills of how to make change.

In addition to the discussions, we organized two conferences on young people and politics at the Martin Luther King Center in Saint Paul. The first, "Youth and Democracy: If We Made the Rules," brought together 150 junior and senior high school students from across the state on April 14 and 15, 1989, at the Humphrey Institute. Young people made rules for the event, expressing youthful savvy: "Listen to others," "respect," "compromise," "cooperate, "be excellent to each other," "control your guilt," "control your anger," and "keep an open mind," among others. A song written by participants with help from the folk singer Larry Long, another longtime colleague, conveyed their sense of urgency: "On the streets of broken houses, kids grow old before their time

/ The sirens are screaming / between your house and mine," it began. The
chorus, repeated after each verse, went like this:

It's our thoughts
It's our future
Our voices and our lives
We are young but we're not children
We are fighting for our lives.[13]

The second conference, held on May 17, 1990, officially launched Public Achievement. In the fall, in partnership with several groups, pilot teams
formed to experiment with youth citizen politics. Among the partners were
the West Side Citizen Organization, Saint Anthony United Church of Christ,
Edgecumbe Presbyterian Church, the Inter-Urban Catholic Coalition, Aitkin
County 4-H, and the Lexington/Hamline Neighborhood Connection. Teams
chose issues such as adult-student communication, racism, day care for children of teen mothers, and decision making in schools.[14]

After such preparation we began Public Achievement in Highland Park
High School. The principal agreed to experiment with the civic pedagogy. I
signed up college student coaches from classes at the University of Minnesota.
We went every week to Highland. The college student coaches began working
with students to identify issues. We held weekly coach debriefings. But our
staff working with the coaches and students failed to learn about the cultural
norms and practices of the school or the neighborhood. What was the history
of the school? What was its mission? What did seasoned teachers believe was
important? What were the principal's interests and vision? Why did the staff
and teachers agree to experiment with Public Achievement? What were the
parents and community's relationships with the school? Such questions did
not occur to us.

That spring, when the principal announced a new rule against students
wearing hats, students were outraged. The concept of "empowerment" took
on urgency. Issues quickly narrowed to one: demanding that the hat rule be
rescinded. When the principal refused, hundreds of students walked out on
strike. Undaunted, the principal called a press conference to announce that the
rule would remain in place. Caps of different colors were used to signal different gangs. "I'm not going to allow gangs to advertise in my school," she said.
Facing public outcry about the strike and the seeming defense of gang advertising, the strike collapsed quickly. I asked strike leaders what they had learned.
"It's even worse than we thought," said one. "We can't change anything."

Growing Roots

In response to the strike collapse, I thought a lot about organizing practices that students could learn in order to understand and negotiate their school cultures with any possibility of success, especially around controversial issues. Our team also discussed educational roots of such empowerment in Minnesota that might nourish Public Achievement. Jane Addams was an important source since her Hull House settlement approach had once been a strong presence in the Twin Cities. Addams argued the importance of schools (whether formal or not) as civic centers in the life of communities.

Minnesota has a vibrant history of settlements drawing on the Hull House experience. In the 1920s and 1930s, eleven settlement houses in the Twin Cities helped immigrants integrate their talents and cultures into American society. UMN students often lived upstairs in settlements, getting free room and board in return for sharing with neighborhood children what they were learning. Settlements shaped Richard Green, the first black superintendent of Minneapolis Public Schools, growing up in the 1940s and 1950s. The Phyllis Wheatley Settlement House on the north side of the city was the heart of the African American community, he remembered. Green described Wheatley as a community "commons," a civic center full of public activities and relationships with churches, families, and area businesses that formed a model for what public schools should and could be. The vision inspired educators and families in Minneapolis, where he served as school superintendent in the 1980s. The Wheatley settlement taught hard work, self-discipline, accountability, achievement, and giving back. "Even though we were not a community of wealth, it certainly was a community of cooperation and helping the young people grow up in a healthy manner," he said.[15] We began to think more about Public Achievement as a way for schools to become part of the civic life of communities. Saint Bernard's Grade School, in the North Rice neighborhood of Saint Paul, proved to be fertile ground.

A Home at Saint Bernard's

Dennis Donovan, the principal at Saint Bernard's Grade School when Public Achievement was launched, has an infectious laugh and a wonderful exuberance about the possibilities he sees in almost everyone. I've never met anyone more skilled in building public relationships. His talents draw from extended family ties in both the Italian and Irish neighborhoods of Saint Paul, full of rituals, celebrations, and expectations of reciprocity. Dennis leads a band, the Midas Touch, which has played rock-and-roll music for decades at Mancini's night club. Mancini's is an anchor of ethnic cultures in the West Seventh area of Saint Paul. He knows hundreds of people from the musical world. He knows many hundreds more from decades of teaching, serving as a Catholic school principal, and working as lead organizer for Public Achievement.

Dennis is also passionate about education reform, which he believes should be like Jane Addams understood it, in the old sense of the world, meaning "to draw out," a way to liberate the talents and powers of students for public contribution. At Saint Bernard's he wanted to prepare the students in the working-class and low-income parish to act on values from Catholic social teachings. He also wanted them to have hope. He had had experiences in community organizing, which made his hopes for change more concrete. Dennis had become a leader in a church-based organizing group called the Saint Paul Ecumenical Alliance (SPEAC), part of the Gamaliel Network of broad-based community organizations that shaped Barack Obama as a young organizer in Chicago. "I know what organizing did for me," he explained at our first meeting, a "one-on-one" in organizing language. In a one-on-one, the person initiating the meeting wants to find out "what makes the other person tick," their motivating life story, their passion. The point of the one-on-one is not only to get to know a person on a deeper level but also to find out if there are interests in common. In this case the person "one-on-one'd" was me.

I told Dennis about my experiences in the freedom movement and how I had seen young people transformed as they developed a sense of their "public selves," what they could do in the world and why it mattered. We agreed about how rarely young people have this opportunity. I told him about my appreciation for Catholic social thought.[16]

Dennis was enthusiastic. "The kids in my school feel hopeless," he said. "When they're asked what they want to do when they grow up, they sometimes say they don't think they'll make it. I want students to have hope. I believe they need the same type of opportunities that I've had in SPEAC."

Dennis had become chair of the educational committee of the church-based community organization, bringing together both public and parochial schools to impact school policy in the city. Equally important, from Dennis's perspective, were the changes he and others experienced in the "culture of accountability," built around developing people's public talents. He recalled being "challenged all the time to develop your gifts in a public way. That's what I want for my students." "I used to be scared to talk in front of people and write everything out," he explained. When he was going to give a major speech at a SPEAC event on education he practiced it in front of thirty people. "They gave an honest critique. 'You suck.' 'Where's the passion?' They sent me to talk with Reverend Battle [a eloquent local preacher in the organization]. I realized if I wanted to do something about education change I better get this thing down, so I studied Reverend Battle and watched how he preached. I began to take some risks."[17]

In the fall of 1990 Dennis had organized sixteen Catholic schools to create Martin Luther King Day celebrations for the following year, using an approach similar to that of Public Achievement in which students took the lead in planning what to do. After the hat strike in 1991, he and I began to think about how Public Achievement might work in Saint Bernard's. I realized that Saint Bernard's was a center of community life. At this school, Public Achievement might be both a pedagogy of youth empowerment and a way to build on and strengthen existing community connections.

Saint Bernard's church and its school had opened in 1891. By the early 1900s the students "were packed like sardines in a tin can, in fourteen small rooms." The school and parish played major roles in the North End community. "On Sunday morning, with St. Bernard's bells echoing over the roof . . . the sounds create the shape of the neighborhood," wrote a local architectural writer. "Just like Cockneys of London and the Bow Bells of St. Mary-le-Bow: If you're born within the sound of the bells of St. Bernard's you're a North Ender."[18] Wave after wave of immigrants came to the neighborhood, creating small businesses along Rice Avenue, one of the commercial corridors in the Twin Cities. Central and Eastern Europeans from Germany, Austria, Hungary, and Romania were followed by Poles and Italians and then African Americans, Latinos, and Hmong. Every immigrant community had some Catholic members. There were also conflicts. Older groups often saw new arrivals as competition.

Saint Bernard's Grade School was thus inescapably a site of cultural mingling—Catholic culture, immigrant cultures, neighborhood cultures. It was a meeting ground for children of different backgrounds and also a site of ethnic conflict. Dennis saw Public Achievement as a potential way to empower young people and to improve the school as a civic space where people from different backgrounds learned how to engage each other constructively.

Three teams formed the first year. One was a group of seventh-grade girls who wanted to work on "sexual harassment." Melissa Bass, one of my students at the Humphrey Institute, wanted to try coaching, so she began working with the group. Several conservative Catholic teachers objected to the issue as inappropriate for a Catholic educational institution.

I realized that Melissa, with a background of feminist activism, could well have reacted with anger at the cautiousness of the Catholic teachers, but she had a strong interest in the girls gaining political experience. Dennis worked with Melissa to design a strategy of one-on-one meetings for the girls to undertake with boys, girls, teachers, staff, and others in the school community, aimed at getting different views on the relationships between girls and boys. Virtually everyone agreed that there was tension in these relationships. The team reframed the issue from sexual harassment to "lack of respect." Reframing has since turned out to be a common tactic in Public Achievement, as teams get more input from different vantage points and interests.

With the issue reframed in this way, the skeptical teachers agreed to the project. Over the school year the team developed a multipronged approach, creating a play for younger grades on respect, giving talks in the school and across the city, developing a curriculum on the topic. In the process, Rachel, a young girl from a chaotic family background who had instigated the group, showed striking improvement in her grades and became a fine public leader. I had often seen such change in troubled kids in the freedom movement as they gained a sense of their value and the importance of their work in the world. I didn't know if it would be possible absent such a movement. The first year at Saint Bernard's showed me that it is possible.

Jeff Maurer, the assistant principal whom Dennis describes, variously, as his "right-hand man" and "the logistics guy" for Public Achievement, noted the changes in Rachel. "She had been feisty but didn't have a direction, and came to us with a history of tardiness and difficulties in her studies. Over the course of the year she kept her feistiness and drive but became focused. She got other kids to do things I didn't think they would ever do." Jeff was "hooked," as he said, seeing "how a student could be changed by being involved in the process of identifying an issue and taking action."[19]

The early years at Saint Bernard's established many of the core practices and rituals of the Public Achievement pedagogy. In addition to one-on-one relational meetings, all the teams practiced what we called "power mapping." Power mapping involves putting the issue (whether respect, recycling, bullying, school lunches, land mines, or anything else) in the center of a sheet of paper or on the board and then brainstorming, "Who has an interest in this issue?" Teams are encouraged to go beyond generic categories (such as other students, parents, teachers, janitors) to name specific people they might talk with. Power mapping is a take-off point for relational meetings. Teams revisit the "map" as they gather more information. Like one-on-ones, power mapping is a relational practice. It also radically changes young people's perception of "power." Rather than seeing power only as an abstract category ("others have power; we are powerless"), participants discover many kinds of power, many different interests around any question, and many potential ways to go about tackling a problem.

The third key practice is called "public evaluation" or simply "debriefing." It involves a few minutes at the end of each team meeting during which people reflect on what happened, how they did, and whether people are keeping up the commitments they made. As Zach Baumann described, this proves a powerful way of learning mutual accountability from peers. It also creates a learning culture that reduces the fear of failure. In good Public Achievement teamwork, young people learn that failures are inevitable and can be valuable sources of learning. Team debriefing is complemented by longer coach debriefing with the person who organizes and supports the coaches, the "coach coordinator." At Saint Bernard's, as noted in Chapter 1, Jim Farr from the political science department of the University of Minnesota became a pioneer for this function.

Public Achievement also developed rituals that are common across the network. Teams usually begin their work by setting their own rules, which greatly facilitates holding each other accountable. They give their teams names, such as "Bathroom Busters" for a team that cleaned up a bathroom. They develop mission statements. They designate and rotate roles—moderator, timekeeper, notetaker, evaluation leader, and others. This fluidity gives team members experience with many different kinds of public activity. They role play, practice speaking, work together to write letters, and give each other feedback, in addition to other activities.

Jeff Maurer remembers challenges and triumphs as Public Achievement grew at Saint Bernard's, eventually creating opportunities for students from third grade to eighth grade to participate as more coaches became available. In Public Achievement a strong principle is that participation should be voluntary, with another option, like a study period, for those who don't want to be involved. At Saint Bernard's, as in most sites, the great majority of students chose to be in Public Achievement.

Students are strongly motivated by their projects. I've heard again and again, in many sites, children and teens say, "Public Achievement gives us a chance to do something we love." Skillful teachers can use this motivation to connect to academic subjects. Jeff returns to the example of Rachel. "Her writing and speaking skills vastly improved because the project was something she wanted to accomplish." This was common, he said. "I saw many connections to the basic skills we are wanting to teach, because they are learning them in a real situation [and] using them for a real purpose."

Jeff also enumerates obstacles. "It sounds great, but it's messy," he explains. "It shakes up boundaries. Sometimes [Public Achievement] is seen as a new add-on. Public Achievement can be extra work." There are also logistical difficulties. Jeff constantly balanced conflicting demands on time, resources, and teaching. Finally, there are dynamics of visibility and power. "In Public Achievement teachers are not in the spotlight, the kids are. And kids start questioning some things they had taken for granted." Adding to all these issues, high-stakes testing later, in the twenty-first century, added a large challenge.

At Saint Bernard's, students sometimes strategized to overcome teacher skepticism. "One teacher was dead set against Public Achievement," Jeff recalls. Students decided to enlist her as an ally. "The kids went to her and asked her to edit their writings and look at their pictures and posters [for the issue work they were doing]. She got engaged. In my later years when we moved Public Achievement into the high school, she became a spokesperson for Public Achievement in faculty meetings."[20]

Over several years students took on many campaigns in addition to the playground described in Chapter 1. One group of third graders organized a "peace march" of several hundred children and adults through the neighborhood to visit sites where young people had been shot in drive-by shootings. They involved their parents, another church, and police. By the middle 1990s many visitors were coming to Saint Bernard's from across the country. Students welcomed them, showed them the school, and organized roundtables of PA participants who described their work. Once a group of leading child development scholars visited. They heard the children talk about the peace march and didn't believe it. "All the research says children this age can't do that kind of work," said one. She reminded me of eighteenth-century doctors, whose theory held that blood didn't flow and so they simply could not "see" blood running out of the body.

Children also took on global issues like land mines, connecting with groups across the country who were concerned with the devastation caused by land mines years after wars have ended. Some projects had a humorous side. Charles Schulz, the famous cartoonist and creator of the comic strip *Peanuts*, had grown up in Saint Paul. He was a local hero. One of his friends started a campaign, supported by local businesses, to populate the city with figures from *Peanuts*, including the dog Snoopy, who was installed on Rice Street. One night a vandal removed Snoopy's head. The neighborhood was outraged. Children at Saint Bernard's quickly formed an ad hoc Public Achievement team to bring back Snoopy's head. Soon after they began, the head was discovered in a backyard. Rather than giving up the project, they revised their plan and had a welcome-back party for Snoopy in the neighborhood. "That involved meeting with all sorts of people around animals," Jeff remembers.

"We had a celebration in the gym with the raptors group [concerned about birds]. The police dogs performed. The mayor and other city officials showed up. People could have their picture taken with Snoopy." The result was widely felt throughout the neighborhood. "There was first community anger and then community pride when Snoopy came back home. For a while, until Snoopy found a permanent place in the library, Snoopy stayed at the entrance to Saint Bernard's, where he could be protected by the students who loved him."

Dennis Donovan asked Jeff about a dynamic that Tamisha Anderson noted when she had been interviewed by Donovan. Kids who were seen as "nerds" often flourished in Public Achievement, she said. Jeff added more. "Not only the nerds," says Jeff. "Kids who were seen as troublemakers in the classroom, who didn't go with the flow of the classroom team, became leaders by being part of Public Achievement. Part of it is that they've never had the opportunity to have people listen to them. They're used to being told what to do. This time they have power. There's pride and recognition."

Public Achievement had many ripple effects. "It changed who I was as a teacher," Jeff says. "I engaged students to be part of their education so they would feel they had ownership. In my classroom there was much more discussion on where we were going and why. We brought them into decision making." He also saw changes throughout the school. "Public Achievement became more and more part of the school. It allowed students to have input. We even changed our staff meetings in a Public Achievement way, adding evaluation at the end of the meetings, like in Public Achievement. In classrooms teachers began to evaluate how the lesson went, where we were going. It indicated that students can be contributors. The students learned how to work with adults to make things happen."

By 1997, Saint Bernard's students began to strategize about how they could help spread Public Achievement. They wanted to bring Public Achievement to young people everywhere.

A Larger Stage

Public Achievement in Saint Bernard's had growing momentum. The prestigious National Commission on Civic Renewal, chaired by Democratic senator Sam Nunn from Georgia and William Bennett, Republican secretary of education under Ronald Reagan, and including a cross-partisan group of civic, religious, business, and union leaders, had come out of the Reinventing Citizenship project our Center for Democracy and Citizenship had organized with the Clinton White House. The commission was charged with analyzing the roots of civic decline in America and proposing remedies. To address this task, it heard testimony from a variety of academics and civic groups. Public Achievement was one of the groups chosen to present their experiences, and Tamisha Anderson and Becky Wichlacz went to Washington to do so. Among the community development groups, youth service organizations, civic journalists, and civic education projects, the two girls stood out, as Carmen Sirianni and Lew Friedland describe in their book, *Civic Innovation in America*: "It was two girls from Public Achievement from St. Bernard's School in inner-city Saint Paul, thirteen-year-old Becky Wichlacz and eleven-year-old Tamisha Anderson who gave the most profound and riveting testimony of all the sessions. . . . They engaged the commission directly in a pointed but thoroughly composed and dignified series of exchanges on the efficacy of public work in their own lives, despite coming from fatherless families that a few on the commission might have blamed for most of our civic problems."[21]

In the spring of 1997, Becky helped organize a team of students whose Public Achievement project was to advocate for Public Achievement by engaging leaders in the nation's capital, among them Minnesota congressman Bruce Vento, Senator Paul Wellstone, the National Council of Bishops, and others. "They came to me and said they wanted to spread the word about Public Achievement," remembers Dennis Donovan. "In their minds Washington was the hub of the world. They wanted all kids in the world to do it." With Dennis's help, they found a bus company that would take them to Washington and drive them around the city. They raised $15,000 for the trip. They did research, figured out chaperoning, and took off along with Dennis and two teachers, one of whom was Jeff.

"Students learn lesson in ways of Washington," wrote Bill Salisbury, Washington reporter for the *St. Paul Pioneer Press*. "They got hearings from some movers and shakers. They received words of encouragement. And they got stiffed by a senatorial aide."[22] When they went to see Senator Paul Wellstone, widely acclaimed as a champion of the disadvantaged, two members of his staff gave them a curt dismissal. "You can't visit him. He's busy. He's on the floor of the Senate." The team was angry when they went to supper with Dennis. There they strategized and evaluated. The team decided to write a letter explaining their perspective and to return the next day.

Meanwhile, Salisbury's story about the encounter with Wellstone's aide had an effect. When they arrived at Wellstone's office the next day, the response was far different. The staff got Wellstone off the Senate floor. Wellstone apologized for their treatment, listened to their story, and invited them to speak to a national conference on youth service going on in the city. "They were fantastic," Dennis remembers. Dennis saw something of his own transformation in the way young people from Saint Bernard's had learned public confidence. "Because of Public Achievement they knew how to operate in Washington with powerful people."[23]

Visits to see Public Achievement were a regular occurrence by this time at Saint Bernard's. One included Jerry Kitzi, vice president of the Kauffman Foundation. Joe Lynch, then in sixth grade, explained how the students used mathematics to figure out the dimensions of the playground and what kind of equipment might fit. "Kitzi asked questions," remembers Dennis. "Joey gave him answers when he knew them. He said 'I don't know' on questions he didn't have an answer for." After the roundtable, Kitzi came up and told Dennis that he wanted his kid to experience Public Achievement. Then Kitzi added what Dennis calls "magic words I'll never forget": "You find somebody in Kansas City to do this and I'll fund it."

Soon after, Dennis told Nan Skelton, by then with the Center for Democracy and Citizenship, and me that he wanted to work on Public Achievement full time. We hired him as the organizer and took a group of staff, partners, and Public Achievement students to Kansas City. We found people who were interested. Public Achievement began to grow beyond Minnesota.

4

Building Worlds, Transforming Lives, Making History

Harry C. Boyte

> When men know they are working on what
> belongs to them, they work with far greater
> eagerness and diligence. They learn to love
> the land cultivated by their own hands.
> —Pope Leo XIII, *Rerum Novarum*, 1891

> [The goal] is to plant some seeds in these young
> minds about being a good citizen, caring about
> one's neighborhood and community. Community
> pride, responsibility. That's how we improve
> the quality of life in this community.
> —Mishkat Az-Zubair, Neighborhood Corps
> Director, Kansas City, Missouri[1]

With support from the Kauffman Foundation, the Bradley Foundation, the Kellogg Foundation, and others, we went in search of schools like Saint Bernard's, described in Chapter 3. In many public schools, parochial schools, and community settings, we met teachers, principals, civic partners, and thousands of young people eager to experiment with public work and its citizen politics. As Public Achievement grew, the Center for Democracy and Citizenship became a network coordinator and training resource. We emphasized the idea that young people and educators alike were doing work with public purpose, in public, with diverse publics—what we called public work.

Public Achievement is not expensive to implement. For instance, coaches usually volunteer or do coaching as part of a college course, though Heartland Foundation's adaptation, emPowerU (described later), provides stipends for "facilitators." Educators integrate the pedagogy into their ongoing work. But there are some running costs. It takes organizing and modest financial resources to create connections between schools and colleges, the usual source of coaches; to conduct trainings; to put on conferences and network meetings; to work with teachers and staff in schools; and to publicize the work.

Over the next few years, from 1998 to 2005, the Center for Democracy and Citizenship developed partnerships with funders that enabled us to work with schools in Minnesota, Missouri, Kansas, and Wisconsin. Other schools, finding their own sources of support, joined the network in Colorado, Florida, New Hampshire, and California. In a project directed by Melissa Bass, the coach for Saint Bernard's sexual harassment team described in Chapter 3, 4-H developed a curriculum based on public work. After 2008, as the center began to work in a sustained way with colleges and universities through the American Democracy Project—a consortium of public state colleges and universities that is part of the American Association of State Colleges and Universities—educators experimented with Public Achievement via this network in Kentucky, Arizona, Texas, Georgia, Connecticut, Michigan, and New York. Organizers and educators also adapted public work approaches using other names.

Public Achievement is not a standardized "program," though it has programmatic elements (teams, coaches, young people choosing issues) and practices such as research, power mapping, and relational meetings. It is down-to-earth, practical, and solution-oriented. Three values animate the philosophy: the egalitarianism of the Declaration of Independence, the cultural pluralism described in Chapter 3, and commitment to developing people's potential to build flourishing communities and a democratic society. It involves explicit discussion of core concepts such as public work, citizen politics, citizens as co-creators, free spaces, civic agency, and relational power. But it is not implemented in a standardized way, nor does not have a predetermined goal like teaching an ideology or success in academic test scores.

We often say that Public Achievement is more like jazz than a set piece of music. Its co-creative public work is best understood as an interplay and negotiation of diverse interests and points of view—sometimes contentious, other times blended and harmonious—not a straight line to a predetermined objective. Like jazz, it takes shape in a particular place and culture. It was this sense of politics that I believe led Wynton Marsalis to liken democracy to jazz on the Ken Burns's PBS series: "In American life, you have all these different agendas. You have conflict. And we're attempting to achieve harmony through conflict. It's like an argument with the intent to work something out . . . that's what jazz music is. It's exactly like democracy." Marsalis elaborated the contrast with a set piece of music. "The real power of jazz is that a group of people can come together and improvise . . . negotiate their agendas with each other," he said. "Bach improvised, but he wasn't going to look at the second viola. Whereas in jazz I could go to Milwaukee and there would be three musicians in the bar at 2: 30 in the morning and you never know what they're going to do. The four of us are going to have a conversation in the language of music."[2] Shelly Robertson, a Heartland organizer who helped to birth a citizenship movement in rural Missouri, Nebraska, Iowa, and Kansas, uses the analogy of Doctors without Borders. "Citizen politics is politics without borders," Shelly says. "It doesn't put people in boxes."[3]

What we call "free spaces" are necessary for participants to make choices and to improvise. Free spaces are face-to-face settings where people have room to self-organize, to discuss ideas and develop intellectual imaginations and ideas, and to learn relational skills. They create the unpredictable, open-ended quality of Public Achievement and its adaptations. Sara Evans and I developed the concept of free spaces to name our experiences in the 1960s freedom movement, where we found vibrant intellectual life and learned civic and political skills in places like the Methodist Student Center at Duke. The larger movement was full of free spaces, from black churches and schools to beauty parlors and other businesses and the Brotherhood of Sleeping Car Porters. What generated their freedom was relative autonomy from the norms and power relations of segregated white society. Their democratic qualities came from their "publicness," the interplay of a diversity of views and interests. We found analogous spaces for open intellectual life and civic and political learning at the heart of all broad democratic movements in American history, including the women's organizations that created the foundations for women's suffrage, community-grounded labor organizations, and farmers cooperatives, the basis of the populist movement of the 1880s and 1890s in the South and Midwest. We wrote about these in *Free Spaces: The Sources of Democratic Change in America*. A starting point in Public Achievement is the need for such spaces where young people have room to self-organize and develop skills and public identities.

The improvisational quality of Public Achievement also creates challenges. As Michael Baizerman, Robert (Roudy) Hildreth, and Ross Roholt, who evaluated Public Achievement for the Kauffman Foundation over four years, put it, "Innovative philosophies and practices [like Public Achievement] which do not fit the classroom or 'program' model rub against everyday practices, rules, procedures, policies, individual preferences and whims." Such challenges are intensified by the short amount of time young people are involved. In a school that runs on trimesters, there are usually only ten meetings. In schools where Public Achievement spans the year there may be up to thirty meetings. This means that teams have between ten and thirty hours for the coaches to get to know team members, for members to know each other, for work to get accomplished, and for the team to process what they've done. For all the challenges, the Baizerman team also found striking results. They interviewed 282 youth participants, 204 coaches, 25 teachers, 24 principals, and others in seven schools in the fourth year of an evaluation. "That it is not fully invisible, submerged, twisted out of its shape or sabotaged is a testament to its inherent soundness and to the vitality it invites in its advocates and leaders," they concluded. "We found that young people experience PA as a place where they were efficacious, had a voice, became skillful, did meaningful work, and learned." For almost all, it provided "an invitation and an opportunity . . . to expand their everyday, small, and private worlds" and to contribute to school and community.[4]

Several vignettes give a sense of the range of places, students, coaches, teachers, and other civic leaders in these years of growth and adaptation.

Andersen Schools, Minneapolis

In the fall of 1997, I made coaching in Public Achievement one of the options for a public work requirement in my graduate politics class, Politics of Public Affairs, at the Humphrey Institute. I asked Joe Groves, assistant principal at Andersen Elementary School, a largely black and Hispanic school with the highest percent of low-income students in the city, to speak to the class to help recruit coaches. Joe was blunt. "We don't need missionaries. If you want to help these students at Andersen, stay away. They've been helped to death by do-gooders. What they need is adults who will stay with it and be open to learning. I can guarantee you will learn a lot."

Joe challenged and inspired young people in his school and in my class. After visiting Saint Bernard's and talking to teachers and students there, he was convinced that Public Achievement could bring needed skills and confidence to Andersen. "My passion for Public Achievement comes from experiences I had growing up in Chicago's Henry Horner Projects," he explained. "Conditions there were very harsh and hardly anything was done about them. People, including myself, became comfortable with the horrible conditions or they simply didn't have the confidence and skills to do anything about them." I asked him what he saw in Public Achievement. "Students gain confidence, leadership, and problem-solving skills. They learn how to work independently and in groups. [They have] the opportunity to express themselves and have their voice heard. It gives them a sense of purpose." Without such confidence, he added, "kids fall prey to the many ills of society. Instead of becoming agents of change they simply perpetuate a cycle of crime, poverty, and illiteracy."[5]

A diverse group of seven students chose to coach that fall. Their final paper conveyed their hopes. "In order for Public Achievement to succeed on a grand scale," they wrote, "it is necessary to develop a public school model to complement the success of St. Bernard's. Andersen Elementary School is a highly diverse public school in the troubled Phillips community of South Minneapolis." In their view, "Success at Andersen will demonstrate that Public Achievement can work in *any* school and in *any* neighborhood." They learned how to work with young people in a different way. "The temptation to direct the team members rather than to inspire them to action can be quite strong. However it is very important that the coach play the role of facilitator . . . help identify the public tasks and *catalyze* the team to action. We help develop leadership skills and encourage the students to take responsibility for their actions." They were inspired. "With so much hopelessness and despair in the world many of our country's youths have given up. As Public Achievement develops, the sense of hope is reborn, the students gain a sense of ownership and worth." They added, "We know democracy can work!"[6]

My students learned this lesson despite the failure of Andersen to prove that "Public Achievement can work anywhere" in a sustained way. Several years after it began, Barb Shinn, the principal of Andersen Elementary School, left. She had a commitment to revitalizing the civic purposes of education and to cultivating cross-cultural engagement among students. With her departure, Public Achievement soon ended at both Andersen Elementary and its paired school, Andersen Open. The Andersen experience illustrates the difficulties we have often seen of sustaining public work politics in schools without institutional leadership committed to its vision and practice. But the years Public Achievement operated in the Anderson schools also showed the impact that public work has on those involved.

The first year, teams addressed teen pregnancy, violence prevention, computer enhancement, police-teen relations, saving the rainforest, and community cleanup. In addition to being coach coordinator for the coaches, which involved leading the debriefings every week and getting to know staff and teachers in the school, I sometimes helped coach the rain forest group. The group researched the issue and found out about a nature conservancy in Brazil that was raising money to purchase acres of the Amazon rain forest, thus preventing the land from being razed for commercial development. The group members decided they wanted to solicit money from shoppers in the vast Mall of America. In those years my son, Craig, who was a DJ in a nightclub in the Mall of America, had an ongoing battle with the mall management over whether he could play "crossover music" that attracted a black clientele. I told the team about Craig's experiences, adding, "I think the management may be racist. I don't think you're going to be able to get them to agree. Why don't you find a shopping center with a more liberal management?"

A sixth-grade team member, Jenayah, a political natural, responded. "Excuse me, Dr. Boyte, you're wrong," she said. "They have a public relations problem in the way they treat black kids. We're going to use that to get their support." Confirming her insight, the team got an appointment to discuss their idea with the community relations director. Team members practiced what they would say, with different arguments for why disappearing rain forests posed a global crisis. After several minutes, Jenayah told the group, "None of this is going to work. We can't tell them why we think they should let us do it. We have to figure out why they want us to do it." Jenayah convinced the other team members that the management's self-interests—getting better publicity from allowing a racially diverse group of young children to undertake a visible project—were not the same as the team's, but they were useful in achieving the team's goal.

The community relations director agreed they could raise funds in the mall. They made a deal with a store to lend them animal outfits and spent a day raising money from shoppers. They were able to help the conservancy purchase four acres. The *Star Tribune* covered the project, accompanied by a photograph of an exuberant Jenayah in a gorilla outfit.[7]

AmeriCorps members served as coaches at Anderson Open School, in the same building complex. Jamie Minor was skeptical. "I'm thinking, the kids are going to run this? It took me about a year to realize how narrow my thought process had gotten by being in education. I automatically went to the negative. I never thought big." Seeing the excitement of the young people, especially Spanish-speaking immigrant kids, turned her around. "All day long they're probably understanding 10 percent of what's going on. Public Achievement was the part of the day when they had some control. Public Achievement got them to school, happy to be there." She also saw the students gain a sense of importance to others. "They mattered to someone outside their family, someone outside their neighborhood. That's one of the most impactful things about Public Achievement. Kids see not only that they can manipulate their environment but that the work matters and adults care. The confidence that these kids develop is irreplaceable."[8]

One team of eight boys, including Mexican immigrants, Native Americans, and European Americans, expressed anger at the state of their bathroom. The stalls had no doors. Toilet paper and other supplies were missing. The walls were covered with obscenities. They named themselves "the Bathroom Busters" and decided to remedy the mess. Two coaches helped them to understand the issue in public terms larger than the bathroom itself. They decided, after discussion, that the issue was twofold: students' disrespect for common property and the school system's disrespect for students. The coaches also helped them to map the power and politics around their problem. They were dealing with a highly inefficient bureaucracy, and the principal had been unable to get the central school district to paint the bathrooms for four years. Unions had to give approval. Funds had to be found. Furthermore, the group had to learn how to make themselves understood. Half of its members had difficulty speaking English. Yet youthful determination mixed with good coaching got action that many adults thought was impossible. The team allied with administrators, teachers, and parents. They contacted district officials. The walls were painted and the stalls repaired.

The next year, graffiti again began appearing on the walls. Caesar, involved the year before, chose to work on the problem again. His team met with other children. "This is our property. What can we do to prevent graffiti?" they asked. Drawing from many kids' ideas and suggestions, they developed a plan to create a mural. As the mural took shape, the bathroom became graffiti-free. It turned into a symbol of school pride. A string of visitors—Congressman Martin Sabo; Jim Scheibel, by then vice president of the Commission on National Service in the Clinton administration; and other political and civic leaders—came to see the school that year. All were taken to the bathroom. They heard from Caesar, known for his eloquence: "This is our property. We have to take care of it!"[9]

Meanwhile, across the state in Dakota Middle School in Mankato, Minnesota, students, coaches, teachers, and Joe Kunkel, a professor at Mankato State University, began Public Achievement.

Dakota Middle School in Mankato

"As Thursday lunch ends at Dakota Meadows School in North Mankato, Minnesota, hundreds of seventh and eighth graders tumble back to their afternoon classes," wrote Joe Kunkel and Clarke Johnson, professors at Mankato State University, and Heather Bakke and Jason Miller, two teachers at Dakota. "A large van pulls up and out jump a dozen university undergraduates and their political science professor. After a quick check-in at the office, they disperse throughout the building. For the next forty minutes, each university student will coach a team of middle school students. Even though they call themselves coaches and teams, this is no game; the activity is practical democracy."

The teams worked on a dozen issues—a lunch-waste recycling program, teen pregnancy, legalizing fireworks, and others. "In a hallway the Tobacco Hackers design a certificate to award to nonsmoking restaurants. The child abuse prevention team finishes a poster advertising Abuse Awareness Day. The End Racism team is with the principal videotaping a TV public service announcement. The Pet Patrol is disappointed . . . no one is bringing items for its Humane Society supply drive. The Paper Pixies group is creating a school newspaper in a school that had none." Kunkel, Johnson, Bakke, and Miller, authors of an article for the National Council for the Social Studies bulletin, connected their Public Achievement site to "visionary activists and educators trying to implement and improve PA at thirty or forty sites in the Midwest" and described it as a "national movement."[10]

Public Achievement began in Mankato as a collaboration between Jane Schuck, principal of Dakota Meadows, and Joe Kunkel, a professor of political science, with support from teachers in the school. At first Public Achievement operated only in seventh grade. The initiative in Mankato was largely self-supported, with training from the Center for Democracy and Citizenship in Minneapolis, ninety miles way, and participation in several regional and national Public Achievement conferences.

At the end of the first year, Dakota Meadows teachers petitioned Schuck to expand to eighth grade as well. The second year there were not enough coaches for the large numbers of students who wanted to be involved. From 1999 on, participation was capped at 180, with the number of coaches ranging from twenty-six to thirty. Public Achievement in Dakota Meadows created a buzz. "The student excitement put pressure on other middle school electives scheduled at the same time," wrote Kunkle and his coauthors. "The teachers and principals creatively adjusted the school schedule to resolve these problems."[11]

Building on a chart developed by the Center for Democracy and Citizenship describing different paradigms of civic education, Kunkel and his colleagues show Public Achievement is an approach to civic education different from civics and service.

"Civic education," they explained, "usually means that students learn about the Constitution, the legislative process, and the role of interest groups, parties, and elections." In their view, "this model conveys valuable information, but its limitation is the implication that democracy is the work of public officials and a few hard-core political activists." The "alternative vision of citizenship is volunteer or public service. Scouts are encouraged to 'do a good turn daily.'

Church groups do service projects and go on mission trips. Many schools require service. . . . All of these efforts aim to overcome the selfishness in our culture. . . . They teach the valuable lesson that the good citizen is responsible and caring. The limitation is that while involvement is encouraged, it avoids politics and controversy."

In contrast, in the public work model, they said, "citizens work collectively to build and maintain their communities. . . . It is work because it is important and difficult and requires skills that must be learned. The work is public in that it is visible and open, concerns the larger population, and is done by the public, not just by public officials and political elites." They explain that "the public work model bridges the gap between government courses and craft of public problem-solving. . . . Students choose public issues and problems that arise out of their own experience and interests. They are not pretending or practicing. They are doing real public work. Because of this they show a remarkable degree of passion and are usually highly motivated. What students do feels real and important. They make a difference."[12]

The two Dakota Meadows teachers described ways their students' learning changed. "Initially I thought that there would not be a connection between Human Heritage, a survey course on ancient cultures, and Public Achievement," wrote Heather Bakke. "For many students the development of civilizations was a non-issue: civilizations had always existed and they didn't question when or why it happened." After students participated in Public Achievement she saw a change. "I was surprised to find some students who used words like 'community' and 'ownership.' They talked about how life was better when people worked together. They pointed out that people living in Mesopotamia had some common challenges and resources. They had to figure out a way to grow food, and although they lived near two rivers they needed to make this water useful. These common needs and resources and how people responded to them led to civilization." When the class later studied Greek democracy, students were able to clearly distinguish democratic government in Greece from government in the United States. "Curious, I finally asked these students why they knew so much about government and many of them replied, 'Public Achievement.'"[13]

Jason Miller saw Public Achievement as helping to address common challenges of teaching middle school students. "Middle school students are famous for their inconsistency," he said. "But they are able to commit to a project that means something to them personally." Miller draws on Howard Gardner's argument that education for understanding comes when students work in environments that challenge them. "Involvement in significant projects and regular discourse with one's peers increase the possibility that one's own stereotypes and misconceptions will be challenged and that a more realistic and comprehensive perspective will begin to emerge," wrote Gardner. Miller believed that "the skills learned through PA are skills that will carry over into other areas of their lives and will stay with them in the future."[14]

Looking at larger patterns, I found that seventh and eighth graders in Dakota Meadows chose issues similar to those chosen by students in other suburban school sites (for instance, in 2001–2002, after 9/11, there were eight teams working on teen depression and teen suicide). Kunkel used two forms of assessment to explore the students' skills and views of politics. He surveyed what he calls political and professional skills practiced by kids. In 2001–2002, 54 percent made a phone call to an adult in authority, 80 percent interviewed adults, 43 percent used a power map to identify people to contact, 50 percent chaired meetings, and 72 percent spoke in public.

Public Achievement in Mankato illustrated the power of a jazz-like citizen politics. As Public Achievement spread to Missouri and Kansas, Saint Gregory Barbarigo School, a Catholic school in the small rural town of Maryville, Missouri, was a pioneer. It helped birth a citizenship movement across the heartland.

Saint Gregory Barbarigo School

The Kauffman Foundation supported the expansion of Public Achievement to the Kansas City area. Saint Gregory Barbarigo School in Maryville, a town north of Kansas City, also began Public Achievement. Over time it proved to be the wellspring for a significant citizenship movement across the region. At the end of 1998, Saint Gregory's celebrated a new swing set on the playground, brought to the school by kindergarten students. "I will never forget the day that the students came into my office. They were very upset," remembered the principal, Sue Dorrell. "They said there is not enough time, not enough space, and there are not enough swings." Dexter Barmann, a kindergarten student, elaborated. "There were only two swings and there was a long line."

The kindergarten students organized. "We went around the school with petitions. We had people who wanted a swing sign them," said Dexter. The video that the Kauffman Foundation supported, "We the (Young) People: Public Achievement and the Changing Face of Change," told stories of teams in Kansas City, Saint Paul, Milwaukee, and Maryville. One team was the kindergarten students. Some had petitions they took around the school. Others timed older kids using swings with stopwatches. The group had fundraisers. And they got their swing set. "The day it arrived it was wonderful," said Dorrell. "They were on a mission." Dexter added, "We were really young so it was hard for them to believe we could do something that great."

Public Achievement at Saint Gregory's began with fifth through eighth graders in 1996 after Dorrell and Shelly Robertson, whose son attended the school, heard Dennis Donovan speak at the conference of the National Catholic Educational Association. They recruited coaches from Conception Seminary College, New England Business Systems (NEBS), and Northwest Missouri State University. Shelly took on the job of coach coordinator. Principal Sue Dorrell was site coordinator. She created a culture of action akin to that at Saint Bernard's. When the kindergarten students came into her office, she asked them, "What are you going to do about the problem?" Like Dennis Donovan at Saint Bernard's, Dorrell posed the same question to teachers and parents when they raised problems, asking what they could do about them. She witnessed how students changed in the process. "People who are involved in Public Achievement develop the skills that are needed. They will challenge adults and also they'll shame adults into saying we need to do something. We can't just sit and take this. When they become adults Public Achievement will become a part of who they are. They'll continue to be involved in making change, saying we have to do something about this."[15]

The local paper, the *Nodaway News Leader*, reported on the swing effort, which was celebrated in a student assembly in February 1999. Dennis Donovan came, as did Mishkat Az-Zubair from the United Way of Wyandotte County, Kansas, and Elizabeth Budd, an organizer hired through Kauffman Foundation support. Mishkat expressed hard-headed realism. "A lot of people will say they like Public Achievement," he said. "You have to weed out the pretenders."

Dennis and Mishkat congratulated the teams. The list of projects included Indoor Recreation Center, building community support for a recreation site; Youth N' Action, creating a trail from Maryville to the nearby Mozingo Lake for walkers, bikers, and joggers; Ecology Team, beautifying the environment; Outdoor Recreation, working to create a safe play area outside; Cignified Lighter Fighters, educating the community about smoking hazards and encouraging businesses to become tobacco free; Falcon Press in the Nest, creating more communication between the community and the school; K-4 Animals, fighting animal abuse; and Spirit, which started a cheerleading team to encourage students. The Cignified Lighter Fighters, who continued their work over several years, succeeded in passing the first no-smoking ordinance in the state of Missouri.

Then there was the Kindergarten Team. "No other Public Achievement site has kindergarten students involved," said Dennis Donovan. Miskat Az-

Zubair shook each kindergarten student's hand. Dorrell congratulated Shelly Robertson, who had helped the group learn organizing skills.[16]

In 2001, Betty Bush, a civic and educational leader in the region, encouraged Judy Sabbert, chief operating officer of Heartland Foundation, to check out Public Achievement at Saint Gregory's. Heartland Foundation had begun in 1994 to engage citizens in northwest Missouri and adjacent counties of Kansas, Iowa, and Nebraska "in building new pathways for community and regional sustainability." To this end, the foundation created a "healthy communities" initiative based on a broad vision of health as much more than treatment or even prevention. They started with a series of community forums bringing together local leaders, lay citizens, and young people. "It became very clear to us that young people really believed they could make a difference but really felt disenfranchised from their communities," explained Sabbert. Three out of four young people said they planned to leave the region when they graduated. "It was a pretty big wake-up call that we needed to begin to engage young people." Foundation leaders saw Public Achievement projects as a way for young people to develop a sense of ownership and pride in rural communities.[17]

Betty's husband Bob, healthy communities director for the Heartland Foundation, volunteered as a coach at Saint Gregory's to experience Public Achievement firsthand. In 2003 Shelly Robertson began to work with Heartland Foundation as the Public Achievement organizer across the region.

Shelly organized Public Achievement for the next eleven years, creating a partnership involving Heartland Foundation, Northwest Missouri State University, and Missouri Western University and strengthening the Public Achievement partnership with Conception Seminary College. Public Achievement spread across twenty-five schools and community organizations in eleven counties. Projects ranged widely, testifying to young people's concerns for fairness and illustrating their eagerness for knowledge about the world.[18]

In Saint Joseph, a joint project on child safety brought together students from a Catholic school, Saint Patrick's, and Neely, a public elementary school. The team got donations of "beanie babies," stuffed animals from Ty Corporation. Working with Child Protective Services, team members passed out the stuffed animals to children who had been abused with messages saying "You are precious. It's not your fault."

Another project, gaining recognition in several national youth conferences, was called Realizing Accessible Health Care, or RAH!! RAH began when two seventh-grade students in a Public Achievement team concerned with affordable health care visited a soup kitchen and homeless shelter. They surveyed those at the soup kitchen, asking about their thoughts on health care, and found that affordability was not a concern—a local free clinic was available. Most didn't seek out health care because they didn't trust the system. The team contacted Heartland Health and discovered that a mobile health clinic, traveling to schools for wellness checks, was idle one day a week. The team partnered with the Social Welfare Board, Heartland Health, Open Door Food Kitchen, the Salvation Army, and the homeless shelter. They organized biweekly visits to a place in the community where homeless people lived. A paramedic and a nurse practitioner from the free clinic provided care while the girls did patient intake, conducted evaluations, and delivered supplies.[19]

In yet another innovative effort, Heartland Foundation made an agreement with the Buchanan Fifth Circuit Court to allow forty-seven juvenile offenders, with an average age of fifteen, to participate in Public Achievement in 2009 and 2010. This involved letting Shelly Robertson do a study for her master's degree at Northwest Missouri State University on the impact, if any, Public Achievement experiences had on participants. Protecting confidentiality, Heartland Foundation's Civic Surveys were used. There were challenges— some participants moved away, others went deeper into the court system, and some of the families didn't want to participate. But teens accomplished a good deal nonetheless, and the impacts were evident. They made play areas safer and installed improved equipment. They successfully got schools to provide vending machines with healthy food alternatives. They created a homeless youth advocacy program with peer-to-peer support for youth who were homeless.

Shelly's thesis, "Effect of Public Achievement on the Resilience of School Aged Youth at Risk," combined Public Achievement theory with positive youth development and resiliency theory, fields that emphasize young people's talents, strengths, interests, and potential. "Resilience is a strengths-based construct . . . focused on providing the developmental supports and opportunities (protective factors) that promote success, rather than on eliminating the factors that promote failure." She hypothesized that experiences in Public Achievement would substantially improve participants' feelings of empowerment. Findings are described at the end of this chapter.[20]

Heartland Foundation established the Public Achievement Democracy Council with participants from different PA teams to help allocate foundation funds to support Public Achievement projects. In 2007, the council undertook a project across seven counties to study poverty. They gave out cameras, using a method called "photo voice" to make poverty visible. Then they brought their findings to policy makers and presented them at the Healthy Communities Summit in Saint Joseph, Missouri, to several thousand community leaders.

Attitudes changed considerably among community leaders and PA members. Some of the children and teens involved in the project came from low-income backgrounds themselves. According to Shelly, the project helped remove stigmas. "They started thinking about people's stories, not what was wrong with them for being poor." Shelly Robertson believes that participants in Public Achievement also saw their own communities differently. "They came to see themselves as contributors, as co-creators. They modeled for adults how to work together. They were examples for the whole region."[21] Cathy McKinley, a citizen activist who led a fight to save Neely School from closure, became a PA coach coordinator in Saint Joseph. She identifies "respect" as well as practical political skills as the heart of young people's learning. "They realize you can't simply sound off about an issue; you have to do research and develop a plan," she says. "You learn to be respectful to your peers and to others in the community."[22] Bob Bush is convinced that Public Achievement experiences created stronger sense of ownership and responsibility for community life. "I see many adults today who have taken these lessons of citizenship into their careers," he observes.[23]

Meanwhile, Judy Sabbert and others at Heartland Foundation strategized about how to expand the approach to make a difference in young people's relationship to communities across the region. The foundation created an ongoing civic education effort called emPowerU. "Though Public Achievement is no longer a stand-alone project, its concepts are now woven into Heartland Foundation's full range of programs and initiatives," she wrote in *Come Together, Think Ahead.*[24]

When I interviewed Judy, she explained the connections. "We loved PA, but it reached only a couple of hundred kids a year. We serve the region of northwest Missouri and adjacent counties in Kansas, Nebraska, and Iowa." Judy included elements of experiential learning, "a process of learning what it means to be a citizen, helping young people understand the opportunity they have to contribute to communities. We believe in our young people and want them to see a future here."[25] The emPowerU initiative promotes ideas of empowerment and citizenship as public contribution. It has worked with more than twenty schools. It also includes an actual site, where students come from across the region to develop a plan for taking action on an issue they identify. They present to a council of local civic leaders, including political officials, businesspeople, university faculty, clergy, and others. "The council serves as sounding board. It asks them tough questions," Judy says. In her view it has proven successful in helping thousands of young people imagine themselves as change makers.

Like Public Achievement, emPowerU includes team-based work in schools and community sites with coaches, called facilitators, who are certified after a weeklong training program and paid modest stipends for their work. Heartland offers teacher training and other support for schools who want to bring it into the curriculum. As in the earlier Public Achievement effort, emPowerU teams have an opportunity to apply for foundation grants for larger projects. In all cases, Sabbert believes, the skills and capacities young people develop are at least as important as whether or not they achieve what they set out to accomplish. Effects have been dramatic. "Over the last ten years we've served over twenty thousand students. Young people come to understand that they are valuable and important to the community." She sees empowerment, or agency, as akin to voice. "In the first evaluations and surveys, we asked young people, 'Do adults listen?' A majority said they do not. Knowing this, we wanted to help them discover the power of their voice." In later surveys, students who completed emPowerU were compared to those who did not. Heartland Foundation found a striking difference. "Students told us they were being listened to, and two out of three said they were interested in staying in their communities." Judy sees the relevance of emPowerU to citizenship, education, and future careers. "Our mission is to champion education and to empower people. We see this also as workforce development: teaching team building, critical thinking, researching. These are skills businesses see as critically important."

Marie Steichen has evaluated Heartland Foundation youth empowerment efforts for more than ten years. She observes that the experiences expand young people's identity to include a civic dimension. "They have been told they were just kids. They learn they are citizens."[26] Her evaluations show significant changes even from the one-day experience of presenting to the council. The evaluation team benchmarked emPowerU student responses against the 40 assets in the Development Assets Profile developed by the Search Institute, a model for positive youth development. Participants in Heathland Foundation efforts showed a strikingly different profile. Among Heartland participants, 80 percent reported positive family communications, compared with 28 percent on the national survey. Fifty-eight percent reported a "caring neighborhood" and 63 percent reported a "caring school climate," compared with 37 percent and 29 percent, respectively, on the national survey. In terms of academic goals, 57 percent of Heartland participants reported commitment to homework, compared to 47 percent nationally, and a striking 64 percent reported reading for pleasure, compared to 22 percent among students across the country.[27]

Each year an emPowerU Scholarship is given to alumni of Public Achievement, Public Achievement Democracy Council, and emPowerU to honor a young person "who has demonstrated commitment to improving the quality of life within the region."[28]

Meanwhile, Public Achievement also began in a Buddhist institution, Naropa University, in Boulder, Colorado.

Spreading to Colorado

Eric Fretz began Public Achievement at Naropa University in 2004. Naropa, America's leading Buddhist university, describes itself as "dedicated to contemplative education." As Thomas B. Coburn, president of the school, put it in *Naropa Magazine*, "The movement from wisdom to compassionate action . . . lies at the heart of Naropa's mission, the linkage of peace within and peace without." The same issue of the magazine featured Fretz, a fierce social justice advocate inspired by the community-organizing tradition of Saul Alinsky. "I want to set up free spaces in my classroom where the gifts of my students can flourish," he explained. He argues for the importance of creative conflict in facilitating that process: "If you don't have conflict, you're not working together."[29]

Fretz, while director of the Communities Studies Center at Naropa, created a class called Democracy, Education, and Social Change. Students became coaches at Centaurus High School in nearby Lafayette, Colorado. Naropa is in the heart of Boulder. Centaurus is a different world. When Public Achievement began there in 2004, a quarter of the students were Latino. Twelve percent were English language learners. Many were from immigrant families. Thirty percent were eligible for free or reduced-priced lunch.[30]

In 2006, Naropa student coaches created *We Are the Ones We've Been Waiting For*, a student guide to Public Achievement. The short book offers a wealth of insight into their own interests and experiences.

Susie Aquilina, in the introduction to the guide, described their starting point. "How can our academic writing have a tangible public purpose?" The coaches wanted to write a document that was not aimed at the professor, describing instead "the skills that we were developing through our involvement with Public Achievement . . . a toolkit for students like ourselves who were just beginning to become practitioners in culture making." Aquilina also made the link between the contemplative education at Naropa and political work in the world. "A great deal of the 'Naropa journey' consists of the inner work of knowing the self. The Naropa Public Achievement program serves as the optimum vehicle to utilize the inner work . . . and put that work to use through involvement with the larger community." She noted that the "cultural jump is no easy task." But she also said it made for rich learning. "Breaking out of the comfort of familiarity and working with these students was rife with opportunities. Helping these students to realize their passions, hopes, and abilities taught us a lot about our own self-interests and capacities to play active roles as culture makers in our communities."[31]

The guide describes seven issue groups: Fighting Racism; Raza Helpers, concerned about the lack of bilingual education at the school; Anti-War in the Middle East, based on the belief that lack of understanding across religious divides causes hostility and violence, which planned a speaker series of different faith leaders; Parking for Unlicensed Students, which changed Centaurus's policy requiring a driver's license for the school parking lot; Ending Segregation through Diversity, concerned about the self-segregation of students; Bilingual Support at Centaurus, concerned about the limited bilingual capacity of staff; and Public Perception of Centaurus, which addressed what students felt were the misperceptions "that Centaurus is not a good school in the public eye, especially when compared to 'wealthier schools'" in the county.

Leanne Bird wrote a "Letter to a New Public Achievement Coach." In her view, the role of the coach "is to guide students into finding a public voice by providing them with an opportunity to engage in work that matters to them. This is done through the creation of a space where students can develop public skills and engage in public work." Like my Humphrey student coaches, she stressed student initiative and independence. "It is extremely important that the students take the lead in what happens. If this is successfully done they will then own the experience of developing the project themselves. This is what makes the PA program unique." This does not mean a hands-off approach. "As a new coach, your role is to coach these students while holding them accountable." But the end goal is student independence, "for the students to develop the confidence and the skills to do public work independent of a coach." Drawing on what the Industrial Areas Foundation calls "the iron rule," she stressed "never, never do for others what they can do for themselves." She "struggled with this idea throughout the semester." But in her view it is crucial for empowerment, especially in our time. "Today social change generally runs on the model of 'experts' telling other people what to do and how to do it." She quotes the organizer Ernie Cortes, who said that "when people have a charismatic leader who does all their thinking they become dependent. They become passive. They lack initiative."

She coached two groups, one working to change school policy on drivers' licenses and the other increasing dialogue and understanding around the school's diversity. The latter group included an Armenian immigrant, an

African American, a Latino student, an immigrant from Turkmenistan, three European American students, one of whom was an out-of-the-closet lesbian, and a student with a disability. In both groups, she said, students' self-interests were key to their passion. She felt it was crucial to get to know each student's strengths while also addressing the student's weaknesses. "In both groups I coached it was not nearly as important that the students were successful with their issues as it was that they developed the skills and confidence to realize their hopes." She observed the benefits of participants rotating through different roles. Roles included a recorder (taking notes), timekeeper, facilitator (holding the group accountable to the agenda), encourager (boosting morale), and evaluator (looking at what can be improved).

Bird stressed the central importance of building "public relationships," drawing on the idea of the late Ed Chambers, then director of the Industrial Areas Foundation. Chambers emphasized the need to balance and hold in combination love and power. "Love means sustaining relationships in which the interdependence of one's own and the others' interests is recognized and respected." Power is the capacity to act. "Power without love is tyranny, and love without power is sentimentality," said Chambers, quoting Martin Luther King. Bird got to know each student. "An easy way to begin to develop relationships with students is by asking them questions." She and her cocoach, Rachel Paine, took time to tell the students about themselves. And she stressed the importance of students developing public relationships with those in powerful positions. "When we created a power map in our first group," she said, "the person the students felt had the most power over this issue was their principal, Dr. Pilch." So the students held three meetings with Pilch over the semester, developing a serious public relationship. "Through [these conversations] the students and the principal realized they had the same self-interest: wanting to help undocumented students feel less segregated." They worked together. Pilch agreed to a change in school policy. Leanne Bird concluded by encouraging new coaches to be open to life-changing experiences. "I adored my students. I thought about them when I wasn't in their school, and I got excited to see them every Wednesday. I'll leave you with this: have fun while coaching, build relationships and trust with your students, and cherish your time with them. . . . Enjoy! Public Achievement is an incredible journey."[32]

Elaina Verveer took over the directorship of the Naropa Community Studies Center, intrigued by Public Achievement and its connections to the community-organizing tradition. Raised in the heart of national progressive politics, she shared Eric's commitment to social justice. Reflecting on her experiences in Washington, she said, "It was impossible to turn a blind eye to the profound injustices that were literally on every street corner."

Elaina liked the idea that young people can learn organizing skills and habits. She began integrating Public Achievement methods and concepts into the work she was doing. After serving as interim director of the center at Naropa, she developed a yearlong practicum course at the University of Colorado Boulder that focused on PA's curriculum, theory, and practice. Over the years the course trained more than five hundred college students as coaches working with teams of younger people in area schools.

Elaina has had many experiences seeing young people of diverse racial and income backgrounds work across differences to take effective action on issues from immigration to homelessness. They regularly surpassed the expectations of others and at times her own expectations for them. They negotiated bureaucratic hurdles, mapped power, built partnerships with diverse groups, and deliberated. She has also spread methods and concepts from Public Achievement elsewhere, for instance, teaching power mapping to a youth advisory committee in Lafayette. "The committee initiated a campaign to establish a Lafayette Skate Park in 2007," she recalled. "I thought, 'We're talking about a $900,000 undertaking. How does a group of eighteen young people tackle this?'" Using a power map, they found the support they needed for the skate park, which was built in a year and a half.

When I asked Elaina in 2016 about her view of politics, she stressed the importance of developing capacities to shape the world in open-ended ways. She has become convinced that citizen politics, in which people learn the skills of working with others of different partisan views and backgrounds, is far more effective than polarizing politics or protest.

Beyond Service and Ideological Politics

Public Achievement reframes youth engagement and civic education, addressing the controversy between what are called the "service" and "political" approaches to young people's active learning and engagement in communities by promoting a different kind of politics.

The controversy is detailed in a well-known study by Joseph Kahne and Joel Westheimer of ten nationally recognized programs to engage young people in community-based experiences aimed at developing democratic values. Service and service-learning programs, they find, are "structured for success," designed to make sure young people succeed. These also make up the overwhelming majority of youth community engagement efforts. A study by the Department of Housing and Urban Development found that of 599 college service-learning projects, 50 percent provided direct service (tutoring, serving food, organizing clothes drives, and the like), 42 percent provided technical assistance such as computer training, and 7 percent emphasized improvements to the physical environment such as tree planting. Only 1 percent involved students in "political advocacy such as drafting legislation or building tenant councils." Service projects are generally apolitical. They do not address "what role is played by power, by interest groups, and by politics in structuring responses of key institutions to those who seek reform." Students come away with the feeling they can make a difference, but also "learning that citizenship does not require government, politics, or social action." In contrast, those few programs designed to engage students directly with power systems and politics often leave students feeling powerless and cynical, though sometimes more interested in public affairs. "I think it's really hard to get things done that count for anything," explained Kara, failing to get action on a women's health center. Kahne and Westheimer use the concept of a "service/politics" split developed by Tobi Walker, who concludes that most engagement teaches "a great deal about how to serve but little about affecting political change."[33]

Darwyn Fehrman and Aaron Schutz were involved in Public Achievement's expansion to Milwaukee, where they worked in a public charter school. They situate Public Achievement between the two. "PA appears to fall somewhere between charitable and apolitical service-learning and the more politically contentious form of social action embodied in non-school-based youth organizing," they write. Fehrman and Schutz, coming from the mobilizing tradition described in Chapter 1, are critical of Public Achievement for presenting politics "as mainly collaborative in nature." In their own efforts in Milwaukee, they sought to shape Public Achievement projects so young people would have a politically contentious experience, what they call youth organizing. "Youth organizing confronts oppression more directly, using often contentious tactics developed by Alinsky. A central theme in organizing efforts is that the powerful rarely offer anything of real value voluntarily to the less privileged. Only through collective action, confrontation, and conflict can the less powerful demonstrate that they are a force to be reckoned with and 'win' concessions from elites."[34]

Fehrman and Schutz's critique of Public Achievement for not being sufficiently confrontational has a counterpart from the other side of the political spectrum, the conservative National Association of Scholars (NAS). In its report, released in January 2017, *Making Citizens: How American Universities Teach Civics*, NAS portrays Public Achievement at the heart of "a major new movement in higher education" intent on radicalizing America's youth, according to David Randall, its author. The movement, he argues, is made up of service learning, community involvement projects, internships, and other student educational experiences outside the classroom. "We call this movement the New Civics," writes Randall. "By pretending to be old-fashioned civics, the new civics has captured an extraordinary amount of university resources and student time that's supposed to be devoted to civics education." Randall argues that the New Civics has a hidden agenda. "The movement is one of the most successful tactics by radical left activists from the 1960s to revolutionize America." From NAS's perspective, Public Achievement represents the leading edge. "The ideas of Saul Alinsky have entered into higher education," says *Making Citizens*. "The most serious such transfer occurred in the late 1980s and early 1990s, via [the] Public Achievement movement." Public Achievement, it proposes, is smaller than service learning and other forms of community involvement, "but with a harder political edge. Service-learning generally works to forward progressive political ends. Public Achievement works toward these ends with more focus and organization, via the Alinskyite method of community organizing. The Alinskyite tactical model of Public Achievement is what makes the New Civics formidable." Public Achievement is "camouflaged Alinskyism." It "relies on the Alinskyite emphasis on power, which reduces politics to the use of force to defeat hostile opponents."[35]

Both sides misconstrue the citizen politics of Public Achievement, which neither aims at a predetermined ideology such as anticorporate progressivism, nor focuses mainly on the machinery of government, the version of civics championed by NAS. Public Achievement's public work approach is political in the democratic but nonideological sense of politics described in Chapter 1. It engages people who are different in constructive ways, without violence and with respect. It recognizes the importance of government as a resource and a partner but does not locate politics only in government. As a result, its citizen-as-co-creator concept does not revolve around a vertical relationship with government. Public Achievement does not present power as the one-directional ability to get others to do one's bidding. Power mapping, one of the core practices, illuminates multiple sources and kinds of power. Finally, while citizen politics pays attention to patterns of inequality, its emphasis on *creating the commonwealth* in public work surfaces the importance of collaborative projects across differences of class, race, faith, and partisan belief to co-create solutions and public goods with wide support and ownership.

Public Achievement's politics is unconventional not only from the vantage point of politics-as-usual but also from the perspective of funders. In March 2001, several of Public Achievement's major funders—the Kauffman Foundation, the Pew Charitable Trusts, the Surdna Foundation, and the Bradley Foundation—hosted a roundtable in Kansas City with ten community foundations from across the country that work from a "donor services" model, meaning they identify donors who might support an initiative and connect them to projects reflecting their interests. The aim of the consortium was to explore possibilities for national expansion of Public Achievement. The community foundation representatives listened to a remarkable panel of Public Achievement participants—children, coaches, and teachers—describe their work. Staff from the Center for Democracy and Citizenship gave an overview of the infrastructure needed to promote and support PA in communities. But Public Achievement, more like a "network" animating groups doing citizen politics and public work than a "program," simply did not fit the logic model traditionally used in funding, a linear account of how particular inputs produce predictable outputs. We received little interest. In retrospect, I realized we needed to create a sustained way of working with the community foundations for them to understand that Public Achievement can be spread, but it cannot be "replicated." Issues, projects, partnerships, outcomes, and cultures are different in every place.[36]

As unconventional and unpredictable as it is, there is considerable evidence that Public Achievement develops civic and political talent, knowledge, and values that are widely seen as desirable among young people. RMC Research Corporation did a two-year evaluation of Public Achievement in 2005 and 2006, supported by the Carnegie Corporation. The evaluators used qualitative and quantitative methods, gathering information from 556 students, 55 coaches, 8 principals, and 12 site coordinators in the Twin Cities, northwest Missouri, and Mankato, Minnesota. RMC found many positive impacts. "Participation in Public Achievement gave students wider perspectives on the world and better skills in working with others. It gave the students better ways to justify their opinions with evidence, and helped them to work better with others by listening to differing opinions, balancing their needs with those of others to complete projects, and see how their actions impacted others in their communities." RMC found specific effects in different grades. "Elementary school students who had sustained participation in Public Achievement were more likely than their peers to acquire civic skills and to believe that young people can make a difference in the world. Sustained involvement in Public Achievement was associated with strong increases on measures of civic dispositions, civic skills, and civic engagement outcomes." Middle school students "were more likely to take responsibility for helping their schools become positive learning environments." High school students "acquired multiple communications skills, including oral persuasion and listening skills." School administrators also had positive views. "They noted that students who participated . . . were more engaged in their communities, had improved behavior, developed communications skills, became problem solvers, helped others in need, and gained self-confidence. Public Achievement brought positive recognition to their schools and helped to develop school-business-community partnerships."[37] Shelly Robertson's study of the effects of Public Achievement on adjudicated ("at-risk") youth in Missouri had similar findings. Public Achievement participants "reported a sense of empowerment and persistence in their contribution. They believe that they can help solve community problems. . . . They reported an increased interest in the importance of participating in school and community activities." She concludes that "youth who participated in . . . the Public Achievement process gained confidence in their abilities to resolve conflict, make decisions, organize and work in teams. They reported that they increased their ability to listen for understanding and for common ground on issues where there are many perspectives."[38]

Roudy Hildreth, part of the Baizerman evaluation team, found that Public Achievement enriches the concept of free spaces. And Joe Kunkel's student papers, collected over the years, show that when an explicit language of politics and democracy are part of the regular learning in Public Achievement, it transforms students' perceptions.

Free Spaces

Roudy Hildreth was a graduate student with the Center for Democracy and Citizenship who worked closely with us on Public Achievement for several years. In the evaluation, he found that "the [Public Achievement] group is a space and place where young people can 'craft' themselves in a new way . . . outside their identities or roles as a particular type of student or member of a peer group." In school settings, young people feel highly constrained by grade as well as by categories of class, race, family, and teachers' perspectives of their talents. "Public Achievement is experienced as an alternative sociopsychological and political space where group members do not have to take on the social roles grounded in their reputations," he observed. Students often made comments such as "'Public Achievement is a chance to be different'; 'I can be myself'; 'I can take my masks off in Public Achievement'; and 'others see and treat me differently.'" Hildreth called Public Achievement a "space of freedom" where children labeled as behavior problems or low achievers often thrive.[39] Hildreth also found significant impact on young adult coaches. They "often describe Public Achievement as one of the most frustrating and most rewarding experiences they have had." Coaches have roles that are much more fluid and multidimensional than most adult interactions with students. They face multiple and contradictory tasks, such as dealing with kids who act up, helping children learn, facilitating project work that includes everybody, using a language of politics, and not acting like a teacher. Though such varied roles and tasks can be demanding and confusing, coaches are often deeply affected by their experiences. "One of the great ironies and delights of Public Achievement is that the undergraduates often come to see the youngsters as role models [whose] passion, dedication, thoughtfulness, and practical efficacy often inspire undergraduates to reconsider their own political convictions, sense of involvement and even career choices."[40] Indeed, I often saw graduate students at the Humphrey Institute *unlearning* formulaic ways of dealing with youth while coaching Public Achievement.

Redefining Democracy

Each year Kunkel assigned his college students an essay reflecting on their experience with Public Achievement. He asked them what the teams learned and also what they learned about "democracy, citizenship, politics, and working in groups." A few quotes illustrate their reflections: "Coming into PA I thought that citizenship meant to live in the United States and that politics was something only politicians were involved in," said one. "As the year went on I could not believe how big a role politics played even in a Middle School. The kids and I had to deal with the principal, workers at Hy-vee [supermarket], and people at Echo [a local food shelf]. I am proud to say the kids handled this all themselves, but I know exactly how big of a role politics will be playing as I enter the teaching world."

Kunkel's student papers show the latent political energies of young people. "I am amazed by what I have learned," one student noted. "Not only did I learn to be an effective coach, I also learned about what it means to be an active citizen. We as coaches are renewing democracy for future generations. It has become clear to me through this course that the concept of democracy in America has lost much of its luster and it must be restored." Another also described learning from the experience: "I learned something fundamental about democracy. Democracy is only what we make it." A third explained: "No longer do I just sit back and let this crazy democracy machine roll by. If we do not like something we can take steps to make the situation better."[41]

Table 4.1. Civic Education in Different Frameworks

Frameworks	Civics	Service	Public Work
What is democracy?	Free elections	Civil society and elections	Way of life built through public work
Citizen	Voter	Volunteer	Co-creator
Citizenship	Voting	Community involvement	Public work
Politics	Who gets what?	Search for harmony	Engagement across differences to solve problems and build the commonwealth
Power	Power over	Power with	Power to

Comparing Paradigms

Democracy, politics, citizenship, and power are understood differently in Public Achievement than in other youth civic education programs and efforts. The public work framework doesn't propose that civics or service are "wrong"—both have strengths. But citizen politics and public work greatly expand the concepts of democracy, citizenship, power, and politics itself. They convey a generative experience of politics. And they point to a much deeper story about democracy. The chart in Table 4.1 is one of the several versions developed by the Center for Democracy and Citizenship in collaboration with Marie-Louise Ström of the Institute for Democratic Alternatives in South Africa (Idasa) and Elinor Ostrom, a cofounder of civic studies. I developed the original version for the Poynter Institute in 1994. Journalists proposed three models of journalism: watchdogs for civics, Seeing Eye dogs for service, sled dogs for public work.

The public work frame expands people's political imaginations. It generates "commonwealth" projects, creating shared resources and cultural change. In 1998 I analyzed more than one hundred PA projects in half a dozen communities. About one third were justice-oriented struggles against authority (for example, student rights and struggles against structural racism), 17 percent were service projects (for instance, food shelves and tutoring), and 50 percent were commonwealth projects, creating material goods (playgrounds, recycling programs, and the like) or cultural change (such as working to change norms around bullying) in which all have a role.

When students in other colleges and universities have the opportunity to explore these broader ideas of politics and citizenship tied to work of public significance, they very often show passion about changing the narrow stories and definitions in the public culture. The power of a public work approach was made even more abundantly clear as Public Achievement and co-creative politics went abroad, to thirty countries.

5

Public Work Abroad

Harry C. Boyte with Tami L. Moore
and Marie-Louise Ström

In the spring of 1998, twelve Protestant and Catholic educators from Northern Ireland visited Saint Bernard's Grade School in Saint Paul, Minnesota. Sponsored by the country's Civic Education Network, the group was touring the United States to see whether they could find examples of the "best of local and international practice" that might help the country move beyond the long-standing religious conflicts between Catholics and Protestants. "Whilst in America the group visited Minneapolis and St. Paul in Minnesota. Among the programmes they saw was Public Achievement," their joint statement read. "It was agreed by the whole group that this was the most impressive programme . . . one which they felt could easily be adapted and used in Northern Ireland."

Several aspects of Public Achievement stood out. Primary school children took part in the civic education work in a way the group had rarely seen. Erin Lothian, a thirteen-year-old, chaired the meeting with the Irish visitors. Children talked about their public work in building a playground, campaigning against land mines, commemorating victims of violence, and other projects "off the script," and young people were honest when they didn't know the answers. This broke the scripted pattern the group had seen elsewhere. They saw Public Achievement as having the potential to help prepare young people to be active citizens in Northern Ireland at a time when their energies were needed. As Angela Matthews, a youth leader from Belfast traveling with the group, put it, "I disliked the philosophy that young people are 'tomorrow's future' rather than an important part of today's society. I feel that Public Achievement is a vehicle to harness the energy and enthusiasm of young people in a positive way." The next year Public Achievement began in Northern Ireland.[1]

One year later, in 2000, Dennis Donovan went to a meeting called the

Salzburg Global Seminar at the suggestion of a Humphrey Institute colleague who told Dennis, "I think they need to hear about your work on Public Achievement." The seminar's chief program officer, Clare Shine, describes the seminar's purpose as a networking site, "bring[ing] together partners and people of different backgrounds who forge breakthrough collaborations to bridge divides on the key challenges of our time."[2] Dennis saw it as an organizing opportunity. As he put it, he was "interested in who was there" and especially wanted to know "who might be interested in collaborating" in the spread of Public Achievement.[3] Dennis's purpose fit the bill, and he took advantage of an offer for seminar participants to share their work in morning workshops. He presented on Public Achievement.

The audience included Ala Derkowska and Julie Bourdeaux, both active in the School Plus Network, a post-Soviet effort "to promote democratic educational practices and pro-active learning" throughout Central and Eastern Europe.[4] Over the next several years, that seminar proved to be the launching pad for the expansion of Public Achievement beyond the United States and Northern Ireland to sixteen former Soviet-bloc countries, Turkey, Israel, and the Palestinian territories.

Meanwhile, in 2001–2002, Marie-Louise Ström, director of the democracy education program of Idasa, an independent democracy institute working across the African continent, came to the Humphrey Institute on an international fellowship. She worked with the Center for Democracy and Citizenship, bringing a wealth of knowledge and experience in the adult popular education pedagogies described in Chapter 6. When she went back to Africa, Marie took the philosophy of public work and citizen politics, which she and her colleagues adapted in Idasa's Citizen Leadership Programme and community-based democracy schools working mainly with adults.

Adaptations of the Public Achievement pedagogy and the philosophy of public work, now tested in thirty countries, offer lessons for revitalizing democracy. Collectively, they also point toward a new approach to development, discussed in the conclusion to this chapter, in which citizens are co-creators, not only rights-bearing individuals. Here we describe experiences and insights from Eastern and Central Europe and Africa.

Citizenship in the Post-Soviet World

In post-Soviet countries the organizing of Public Achievement, as well as its philosophy of citizen politics and public work, is rooted in a freedom struggle, just as it is in the United States. Alicja "Ala" Derkowska worked in the Solidarity resistance movement against communism in Poland. She was underground from December 1981 until 1989, when martial law that had been imposed to counter the rising power of unions finally ended as communist regimes collapsed.[5] Ala calls her participation in Solidarity the catalyst for her involvement as "an active citizen within the political system of Poland."[6] In the resistance years she envisioned the day when "martial law would come to an end and we would need to be ready to start again."[7] For her, starting again after the fall of communism included establishing democratic forms of governance, reinvigorating civil society, and shifting to a market economy. It also included democratic approaches to education.

Ala, formerly on the Faculty of Mathematics at the University of Łódź, was especially interested in the potential role of schools in teaching young people the skills necessary for a democratic society. Shortly before the end of the communist regime, a small group of parents and educators in Nowy Sacz, Ala's home, formed Malopolskie Towarzystwo Oswiatowe (MTO), the Educational Society of Malopolska, "to provide a different, alternative, civic-minded education better suited to the changing reality of Poland in the period of transition."[8] Under the new government, schools administered by nongovernmental organizations were allowed in Poland for the first time since the Second World War. Building on months of planning, MTO established an independent school called SPLOT in 1989, with Ala serving as the director for its first decade. In 2017, celebrating its twenty-eighth year, SPLOT served 155 students from primary grades through high school. Its mission emphasizes asking "good questions" over offering "ready answers." In Polish it reads "SPLOT jest miejscem, gdzie sztukę stawiania pytań."[9]

In the late 1990s, Julie Boudreaux, from the United States, joined the faculty at SPLOT. She was to become Ala's main partner in bringing Public Achievement to Eastern and Central Europe. She shared Ala's passion for shaping schools as sites for fostering civic engagement. Ala and Julie tapped into an existing network of schools and educational organizations across Central and Eastern Europe, organized under the umbrella of the Open Society Institute. This led to the creation of the School Plus Network, linking parent-teacher organizations like MTO. By mid-2002, the School Plus Network included members in Serbia, Kosovo, Albania, Bulgaria, Romania, and Moldova. Organizations in the network registered as nongovernmental organizations connected to existing schools, thereby allowing them to accept grant funding for their schools to support "a democratic, open, civil, creative, and entrepreneurial society."[10] The network was lively and people maintained regular contact with one another, also acting as magnets for others. It functioned as a vehicle for spreading new initiatives, with Julie, Ala, and their partners at

SPLOT working through MTO to support small groups in making meaningful change.

When Ala and Julie heard Dennis in Salzburg, the two women immediately recognized Public Achievement as a valuable tool to advance their goal of "making schools a center of civic engagement in the community." Ala remembers his presentation. "We were looking for ways to make school more interesting, active, engaging rather than a dull, boring and passive experience," she explained. "Along comes Dennis with this really engaging, active, interesting program."[11] In 2003, Dennis received an email from Poland with a request: "We are ready for Public Achievement. Can we send someone to you for training?" Agata Kita, a teacher at SPLOT, came to Minneapolis for a week. Dennis sent her home with the same advice he gives new coaches today: "Just do it. It's never going to be perfect. Just start." Dennis recalls the first PA project at SPLOT. Students coached by Agata "did a wonderful project based on kids' concerns about horses on trains going to be processed for meat." Raising funds, the students rescued a horse from its fate, handing her to a therapeutic riding program.[12]

That was the start. As of June 2017, the School Plus Network had introduced Public Achievement pedagogy and philosophy in Albania, Azerbaijan, Bosnia and Herzegovina, Bulgaria, the Czech Republic, Georgia, Hungary, Kosovo, Macedonia, Moldova, Montenegro, Poland, Romania, Slovakia, Serbia, and Ukraine. Partners in the network embraced Public Achievement as an alternative narrative of how democracy can and should work, different from the more conventional framework promoted by most NGOs and aid agencies in the region. Rather than simply focusing on citizens as voters, as state-sponsored democratic reforms generally did, or emphasizing the stronger but still limited idea of citizens as volunteers who "help out" in scripted roles, the public work philosophy promotes the idea of individuals engaging with one another in a self-organizing way to do serious civic work, much of which was previously understood as solely the role of the state.

MTO has trained more than seven hundred teachers, and nearly two hundred Public Achievement groups have formed across the region over the years, ranging in size from five to twenty-eight participants. The philosophy of citizen politics and public work and the pedagogy of Public Achievement fit well with MTO's interest in "trying to build democracy around school." Bringing schools and democracy together made sense, Ala explained, because "almost everyone's life is connected with school. In a natural way, people are interested in what's going on in school. And if the school is open and goes out and does something for the community . . ." Julie finished the sentence, "the community reciprocates."[13] It is important to add a caveat: if people have the confidence to take the initiative.

Challenging Fatalism

Believing in one's capacity to effect change and working with others to make change requires a transformation of attitude in post-Soviet societies, going against dominant narratives of what is possible for everyday citizens to do. Ala points out what she sees as a significant difference between the mindset of typical Americans, who believe in their capacity to make change, and people who live in a country with an authoritarian legacy. Change in mindset to get beyond fatalism is not simply an individual process but a broad cultural one. "In this part of the world, it's important to convince people not just by training them, but by creating an environment," she explains. "People actually don't believe that they can make the change."[14] As an American citizen who still lives part of the year in the United States, Julie points to cultural norms that reinforce a sense of agency. "In the United States, people at some level do believe that they can do something, especially at the community level."[15] In post-Soviet societies that sense of possibility is missing. MTO trainers identified the most difficult job for a coach as "convincing PA members that they really could influence how things turned out and *really* have an impact—at least partial—on the resolution of situations."[16] This challenge of overcoming a sense of fatalism about the possibilities for ordinary citizens to make any substantial change runs throughout the Public Achievement experiences in the region.

MTO worked with a partner organization in the Republic of Georgia to assist internally displaced persons from the destabilized regions of Abkhazia and South Ossetia in the north. The refugees were still in shock after leaving most of their possessions behind. They were starting their lives anew in difficult conditions, in a camp with limited access to water and lack of sewage systems, and facing daunting problems of unemployment and an uncertain future. Eight Public Achievement groups organized to address different issues in the camp, using strategies that ranged from protest to community service. Many petitioned the municipality or regional government to solve problems. But team members demurred when Julie and Ala suggested approaches by which they could make real changes themselves. The teams said such approaches may work in the West but not in Georgia. Julie now anticipates this sentiment with every group by saying, "There is no country—no matter how well organized or how rich—where the government is able to solve all the problems. If you don't do it, it will not be done."[17] Over the years, Julie and

Ala have seen shifts in this mindset, with many people learning to understand that "they are responsible for making the community they want to live in." Not only are they responsible, but they also have the capacity to co-create tangible contributions to their communities, from museums and speed limit signs to systems of running water.[18]

Public Achievement flourished in the Crimean region of Ukraine. The "Rostok" ("Sprout") group consisted of thirty-six primary school students who developed a project to address the needs of elderly people in Bakhchisaray. Starting work in October 2006, team members discovered that the Tartars, historic residents of this area, had suffered deportation and forty years of exile under the communist dictator Joseph Stalin. In the 1990s, some elderly survivors returned to Crimea. Many needed assistance around their homes. Rostok group members exchanged their help for artifacts and documents of Tartar culture and history. They negotiated with school officials to use two empty rooms for a museum about Tartar culture and history, in the process learning from the elders about Tartar culture and also sharing that information with the wider public. Soon community leaders located a larger space for the collection.

Beginning in January 2007, another group of eleven teenagers at Bakhchisaray Special School organized to address the lack of shade and resting space near their school. They worked with the school director, forest manager, and community members. A ranger in the local forest allowed the group to dig fifteen saplings at no cost. Concerned about caring for the trees over the summer holiday, the students reached an agreement with a neighboring restaurant to water the saplings during the holiday. Their mentor-coach later reported the "trees are growing happily! The group has a sense of success and has started a new project."[19]

Beyond Volunteering

Neither "working for the common good" nor volunteering are new concepts in these post-Soviet countries, but, as Ala remembers from her youth, the practice was more like "forced volunteerism" rather than the self-organizing citizen politics of public work. "We were brought up in the spirit that we *should* work for the common good," she explained. "You should go out and clean the park, or help in a hospital." It was voluntary work because no one was paid. But the country's leaders identified what "common good" meant. In schools, the head teacher or the school principal would decide, and students were not involved. To Ala, self-directed cooperation was missing. This, she says, is "the part that we actually value most in Public Achievement."[20]

It is often a challenge for coaches and students participating in Public

Achievement to move beyond older models of volunteering and charitable giving. Fundraising projects to help those in need are common. In one case, wealthy students in a private high school in Kharkov, Ukraine, decided to forgo their end-of-year dance. For three years they donated the money they would have spent on dresses, tuxedoes, flowers, and special dinners to a local children's heart hospital in a campaign they called "Give Your Heart to Kids." Initiatives like this are well intended, but Julie and Ala wonder whether they address deeper problems in the community.

An example of taking action with short-term results for the common good without paying much attention to the long-run impact was a project in a city near the borders between Ukraine, Hungary, and Slovakia. A team cleaned a local park. The mentor-coach was thrilled with the outcome. Julie paraphrased her enthusiastic report this way: "They [the team] didn't clean it for themselves. They cleaned it for the public, right?" she asked. The coach responded, "They achieved something. So by definition it's a public achievement."[21] During an MTO monitoring visit later in the year, the coach was surprised when Julie and Ala expressed some dissatisfaction with the project. From their perspective the problem with this kind of action is that it doesn't necessarily create lasting change. "If you clean [the park] once, it will be littered the next day. So what kind of achievement is that?" asked Ala.[22]

MTO trainers added a process to Public Achievement. They call it "Roots, Action, and Results." This approach has generated discussion and debate across the region. It is common, they explain, for a Public Achievement group to focus simply on taking action. But as Julie puts it, "They don't ask, 'If we do this are we really going to the roots of the problem?'"[23] Nor do the teams always think sufficiently about longer-term results. The satisfaction of taking some kind of positive action can seem sufficient: experiences that "feel good" without making real change. This highlights a number of tensions. Addressing root causes of problems in the community takes time. Students need to develop an understanding of complex dynamics. This complexity in itself can cause them to feel discouraged and lose heart. It is unreasonable to expect quick results, let alone striking successes. With this in mind, Julie and Ala emphasize the *process* of learning the skills and achieving the mind-shift of co-creation and public problem-solving. The development of skills and the belief in people's everyday power gained through Public Achievement are meaningful results in themselves. In fact, they can matter more than the product.

Students in Cahul, Moldova, showed something of what is possible when Public Achievement integrates school work and public work, allowing students to grasp the roots of a problem more deeply. A team working with their chemistry teacher and other coaches cleaned up a section of the polluted River Prut. They also collected water samples to test for the source of the pollution. Students had a strong sense of mission in their research, showing that they wanted to understand the causes of the problem and actions they might take to address it. In the course of their project, they learned about related material in chemistry and also explored further applications beyond the classroom. The experience underlined the point that learning about democracy and citizenship through Public Achievement is not simply about political work, nor does it exclude academic content. It can be both together.[24] For this to happen, however, Public Achievement needs to be embraced as an integral part of the school curriculum, not treated as just an extracurricular activity. There are many institutional challenges that make this difficult.

Public Achievement participants in an Albanian school took on a problem that brought together issues related to town history, economic development, health, and the environment. The citadel in Kruje, Albania, the famous site of a stand against the invading forces of the Ottoman Empire, is today a major tourist attraction. It is an important economic resource for the city. And it is covered by black soot from nearby lime factories. In addition to the blight on this national heritage site, the smoke presents a major health hazard. The high school students tried different approaches to getting the soot removed themselves but settled on raising public awareness through a letter-writing campaign to government officials and community members, increasing public awareness of the interrelated problems. A lot remained to be done to clean up the air in Kruje, as well as to clean the citadel itself, but the students created an opening for more to happen. Realizing the *need* to change something is a starting point in Public Achievement. The more challenging aim is for people to see themselves as co-creators of change and to develop the skills and confidence to take action to address public issues.

Sustaining Public Achievement

From interviews and documents, a picture emerges of what makes Public Achievement attractive in the post-Soviet countries. It presents powerful concepts that offer to reshape radically the way people see society and their role in it. However, the concepts are not necessarily easy to grasp because they counter dominant thinking. The legacy of communism generated what Elemer Hankiss calls a "second society," fatalistic and skeptical of cooperation with others on public projects, as well as of the values of transparency and accountability.[25] Whether or not Public Achievement becomes a sustainable, regenerating initiative in a particular place is shaped, to a significant degree, by the attitudes of the teachers and mentors trained by MTO.

The distinction between co-creative public work and following someone's directions "is a hard concept to get across," in Julie's experience.[26] Teachers in the participating countries have been trained as one-directional leaders, with their students as followers. When a student names a problem, the teacher's conventional response is to provide an answer, not to help students take action to solve the problem themselves. The approach of Public Achievement "goes against what the Soviet system programmed people to be, people who follow instructions and do not have their own ideas." The idea of co-creation "works actively against that mindset." Julie and Ala emphasize repeatedly the challenges of facilitating this shift in thinking, adding that it is more difficult to achieve with the teacher or mentor than with students because students have been less socialized by authoritarian norms. Because of this, spreading Public Achievement successfully involves finding the right people. Typically, teachers who become committed and effective in Public Achievement are deeply interested in education and don't have an authoritarian bent, whatever their age.

Beyond identifying teachers who can grasp the principles of citizen politics, the success of the initiative comes down to the level of institutional support in formal settings such as schools or the capacity of group members to move on their own toward a second round of problem-solving. Today, adding to challenges from the legacy of communism, many countries in Central and Eastern Europe are experiencing a revival of more authoritarian politics. In Poland, for instance, ministers seek tighter control of educational curricula by the state. Economic and political uncertainties also contribute to upheaval and movement among people in the region. Many teachers are restless, seeking opportunities for better paying positions in another school or outside education. Those with strong English language skills often pursue employment or advanced education in Western Europe or the United States. Starting Public Achievement in schools has not been too difficult, but sustaining it beyond the first year is often a challenge. While projects such as those in Moldova and Albania described above lend themselves to sustained work over several years by successive teams of students, the mobility of teachers and coaches also makes this difficult.

Integrating Public Achievement into the culture and academic life of schools is particularly hard to achieve. It requires sustained commitment and collaboration among teachers, both of which are undermined by high turnover. Team projects are typically extracurricular activities, not part of the school day, and involvement in Public Achievement is not part of the teacher's usual job description. Teachers are thus not paid for the work and are not necessarily eager to continue year after year without compensation. The physical demands of teaching itself are difficult. Teachers work very long hours. Those who teach in more than one school also spend time moving from one place to the next. Teachers often share classrooms, leaving no space where PA groups can meet. Overcoming these practical obstacles takes determination and resourcefulness.

There are also lessons about what contributes to growth and sustainability. For example, Public Achievement had considerable successes in Azerbaijan prior to the suspension of NGO activities in that country in 2014. Both the quality of the work and the propensity of groups to continue Public Achievement beyond a single experience and to grow new groups were noteworthy. In Ganja, under the leadership of Shahnaz Salmanova, creating time for the coaches to work and learn together proved particularly helpful. During these meetings, coaches brought problems from their Public Achievement groups and reached out to others who might have had experience with a similar situation. Thus, coaches in Ganja gained perspective from others who knew the city, local resources, the local political situation, school politics, and the culture and traditions of the area. Young people commonly moved to a second round of problem-solving after their first experience with Public Achievement. Coaches and students felt confident in bringing together a new group of people to address new issues.

While many Public Achievement groups in Azerbaijan were originally based in schools, Halima Fatullayeva worked with a group of adults to build community relationships, beginning with seemingly apolitical activities. She had a sense that such relationship-building could provide foundations for civic agency and public work in a society long subject to communist rule. The older generation of women in particular had had fewer opportunities to engage in public life in this region of the world. While young people in Ganja were active in social activities such as riding bicycles, swimming, and going out to restaurants, their mothers were not doing such things. "They live a routine life. They are not going to make a public achievement," said Halima. "Even though it is the twenty-first century, you would think it was half a century ago."[27] The private orientation of older women's lives even extended to someone like Halima's mother, who worked outside the home for thirty-eight years as an accountant. She put her remaining energy into caring for her family. Moreover, old attitudes sometimes placed pressure on young women. For example, one woman interested in becoming part of Public Achievement could not participate because her mother-in-law would not grant permission.

Halima and her colleagues began Public Achievement by creating a yoga club with the goal of "help[ing] women to be more social." Thirty people came to the first meeting. The sponsoring group initially recruited young women, and many brought their mothers. A movie club and a book group grew out of the first initiatives. All became "important intergenerational opportunities, where older people are learning from the greater activity of . . . younger people," Halima said.[28] Her own mother got involved in these social gatherings. These activities were free spaces where people learned how to socialize outside of their private domain and developed skills and confidence for acting in the public world. One group of women identified a public project: bringing reliable, running potable water to the homes in their neighborhood for the first time in ten years. They began by literally digging into the topic, seeking physical evidence of the challenges that had to be overcome in order to provide running water. With Halima's coaching, group members learned about government structures pertaining to water systems and municipal infrastructure. Equipped with this knowledge, they wrote letters to the appropriate officials, requesting attention to crumbling water lines. Eventually, the women succeeded in getting the lines repaired and the water supply restored. This same group then identified a second project and continued their work.

Nearly ten years later, Halima describes herself as strongly affected by these experiences of being a Public Achievement coach. She developed confidence and a sense of satisfaction that "what I was doing was good for others. I felt better and wanted to do more." She also gained recognition beyond the role of teacher. "Through Public Achievement I could do more things," she said. "Learning all these things about how the process works, I applied these lessons in my life and I saw that public work is not only something I do myself. I can do it with other people." People frequently asked her if she was paid to facilitate the yoga club that began as part of Public Achievement. When she said she did it for the intrinsic rewards of the work, they urged her to find private, paying students. Halima says this is a typical mindset, "seeing everything as an opportunity to make more money." Halima's motivation is different: "Whatever [I] learn now, [I] exchange it. Not with money, but with love." For her, civic empowerment became the key motivation. Halima understands that she is contributing to the larger project of democracy. She gets her main satisfaction not from money but from the experience of agency and public creation.[29]

In Azerbaijan today, after sharp restrictions were imposed on nongovernmental activity in 2014, civil society is hobbled by the threat of arrest and active repression of public demonstrations. Many of those active in Public Achievement, including Halima, were forced to leave Ganja. But as a teacher of English language to university students in Baku and as a teacher trainer working with other English as a Second Language teachers, Halima now structures her courses as democratic learning spaces. Her students make decisions collaboratively. She constantly reinforces for them the idea that they will be part of a new society, different from the one in which they live. She sees in those students who have had experiences with Public Achievement more openness to self-directed work and other democratic educational practices.

Throughout the region, Public Achievement can be seen as an early stage of a long-term movement. It may take one or two generations or even longer for people's thinking to change on a wide scale across former Soviet societies. Public Achievement leaders hope that the skills and habits of thought that participants gain will spread on a large scale among adults as well as youth.

Public Work in Africa

A world away, while Public Achievement was spreading in Eastern and Central Europe, citizen politics of public work began to take root in South Africa and then spread to other African countries.

In 1992, during the tumultuous transition from apartheid, the Institute for a Democratic Alternative (later Institute for Democracy) in South Africa, Idasa, created a new Training Centre for Democracy, based in Johannesburg. Idasa, which had been established in 1987, was well-known for playing a critical role in the transition by promoting a "politics of engagement" different from partisan politics.[30] The politics of engagement, similar to the citizen politics described in Chapter 1, involved many thousands of South Africans in interracial dialogue and learning, especially aimed at educating white South Africans about the lives, interests, and frustrated aspirations of the black majority. Idasa brokered conversations at the highest levels between black and white leaders to imagine and plan the future, and it also played a key role in bringing the far right wing into the election. Idasa work created many foundations for a workable alternative to violence.

Ahead of the election of 1994 when Nelson Mandela became the first black president of the country, Idasa's training center helped to organize a vast process of voter education across the country, emphasizing work in communities with low levels of literacy. The Idasa training materials included a poster of farmers working their fields with diverse crops, some thriving and some not. It conveyed the idea that a vote is like a seed. Democracy requires the ongoing and patient work of all citizens, not only elected leaders, to bear fruit. After the election, Idasa promoted broader civic and constitutional literacy focusing on themes such as active citizenship, good governance, community development,

and women and democracy. Through the 1990s, Idasa's most important contribution in the field of democracy education was to introduce large numbers
of community educators and leaders to participatory training methodologies
for building democracy. Building on these experiences, Idasa established a
lasting partnership in 2002 with the Swedish adult education organization
Studieförbundet Vuxenskolan. The partnership allowed Idasa democracy educators to become more familiar with the Scandinavian folk school tradition
(described in more detail in Chapter 6), as well as the Swedish study circle
tradition. This shaped the evolution of Idasa's strategy to create nonformal
schools for democracy.

Inspired by Marie Ström's experience with Public Achievement (she
coached in 2002) and her study of public work philosophy, Idasa democracy
education program made a paradigm shift to stress that citizens, not government, are the foundational agents and co-creators of democracy. "Democracy in its strongest form is really about citizens actively shaping their world,
not just thinking about it and talking about it but getting out and doing
something about it," explained *Youth Vote South Africa*. This Idasa-authored
newspaper supplement was distributed as a series over twenty weeks to all two
thousand high schools in the country in 2004. It continued with many examples, exercises, and stories to encourage young people to participate in "the
public work of democracy." Supplement 4 argued that "regular elections and
the freedom to vote are usually seen as the most basic criterion for determining
whether a country and its government are democratic or not. But . . . how
citizens participate in public life and how government exercises its power are
more important tests. . . . The real test is whether citizens are able to act and
help to shape what happens in society on an ongoing basis."[31] The supplement
also observed that such a work-centered understanding of democracy marked
a shift from conventional European and American models of democracy. "If
we deepen our definition of democracy to include the ongoing public work
of citizens, then there are [other] traditions we can draw on." It also described
relating to government as a partner rather than simply as a deliverer of services.
"To protect and promote democracy, citizens need to work together with government, holding it accountable but also providing energy, intelligence, talent,
and resources to create things that are of value to the whole community."[32]

Idasa adapted public work theory and aspects of Public Achievement to
create an extended "citizen leadership" training program for community leaders. This allowed the core concepts and practices of the alternative model of
democracy to be taught face-to-face on a large scale in workshops for adults.
The Idasa democracy education team conducted training for citizen leaders

in poor communities in the provinces of Mpumalanga, KwaZulu-Natal, the Northern Cape, North-West, Gauteng, and Limpopo. The training course had a significant public work component, with participants working in project groups ("teams" in Public Achievement language) between workshops to take action on issues of common concern. The course also stressed the importance of developing "relational leadership" by equipping trainees to become involved in collectively planning, implementing, and evaluating solutions to local problems. Over the years people tackled many issues: water quality and conservation, funeral costs, care and respect for the elderly, teen pregnancy, violence in schools, improvement of local infrastructure (from sanitation to public spaces), and many others. Many outstanding leaders emerged from the program. For example, Nomthandazo Skhosana, upon graduating from the program, developed an after-school support program for one hundred AIDS orphans in her township, training out-of-work youth to assist and developing a pool of highly motivated young leaders. She attributed its success to skills she had learned in the citizen leadership training. "With a power map I can do anything!" she told an evaluator, giving one example.[33]

Translating Public Work

From the mid-2000s until Idasa ended its citizen education work at the end of 2011 because of dwindling funding, the organization spread its citizen leadership training program to other African countries including Mozambique, Angola, Malawi, Zambia, and Burundi, with a vision that echoed Septima Clark's vision for the citizenship school movement in the American South. Idasa set out to create nonformal "schools for democracy" with local trainers running the citizen leadership program in association with local organizations. The Idasa educators strategically sought out partners who were interested in initiatives for rethinking the meaning of democracy and citizenship and for developing civic agency on a large scale.

After the end of her work at Idasa, Marie Ström continued to work in Burundi until 2015, collaborating with the Burundi Leadership Training Program (BLTP) and their funding partner, the Netherlands Institute for Multi-Party Democracy (NIMD) to create village-based schools for democracy. BLTP had originally focused its work on training elected politicians and leaders in political parties. After a period of relative stability following the election in 2005, the political situation in Burundi again began to deteriorate and the ruling party became increasingly opposed to multiparty collaboration. BLTP decided to make a strategic shift to developing capacity for democracy among citizens at the grassroots level.

Marie trained a group of Burundian trainers and worked with them to develop a citizen leadership curriculum adapted specifically for the Burundian context.[34] The process of adaptation and translation allowed local trainers to take strong ownership of the training materials. They first created a French version and then worked on translating the materials into the local language, Kirundi. This was a collaborative process often eliciting much debate among the Burundians themselves as they struggled to translate or, more precisely, to find adequate ways of conveying core concepts for which no equivalent words could be found. The formal language of democracy is largely absent from Kirundi. Thus, the process of translation ceased to be only about words and became much more fundamentally about culture. The course offered by BLTP's School for Democracy was entitled Training for Responsible Citizenship in a Democratic Society.

The first training at the community level was implemented in Gitega Province in the village of Giheta, known for the relatively high level of political and cultural engagement among its citizens. The second pilot project took place in Cibitoke Province in the village of Buganda, a more unstable and impoverished border area, still deeply scarred by the civil war. In both cases, participants in the course were selected primarily for their interest in working with fellow citizens to resolve local problems rather than merely complaining about them. Diversity among the participants was carefully balanced in terms of gender, ethnicity, political affiliation, and age. Most were peasant farmers with an average of six or seven years of schooling to complement their practical and cultural wisdom. A few were elected members of their *conseil de colline* (hill council), roughly equivalent to a residents' association. Almost all were members of community-based associations: loosely organized groups of market women, displaced persons, volunteer HIV/AIDS caregivers, as well as youth and cultural groups, savings groups, burial societies, agricultural co-ops, and the like. All participants were active church members, and most were openly affiliated with one political party or another. Together, these diverse groups learned skills of civic organizing and gained a new understanding of democracy as they tackled local problems with their fellow citizens.

The course was conducted over a period of five months, with a two-day training workshop each month. Drawing on public work theory, it stressed the citizen as a co-creator of a democratic society, based on the conviction that ordinary Burundians, regardless of social status and education level, could play a role in solving problems and rebuilding democracy. Within the highly unstable political environment of Burundi, the course promoted the idea that citizens themselves could take responsibility for development at the local level, working with local institutions and elected leaders whenever possible. Course participants adopted the title "catalysts of democratic development" for themselves.

The five training workshops focused on the following themes:

1. Community, diversity, and a view of people as storytellers and meaning-makers
2. Power, understood multidimensionally as the capacity to act, not the ability to dominate others
3. Citizen politics, understood as the everyday work of ordinary people negotiating different self-interests to solve problems and create common resources in their communities, not mainly the work of "professional" politicians
4. Civic organizing and civic agency, the collective capacity of citizens to organize themselves and shape their environments
5. "Responsible citizenship" and mutual accountability, both horizontal (among citizens) and vertical (between citizens and government)

The course also involved an important practical component, with participants organizing their fellow citizens in the community to take action on a shared problem. Problems addressed in the villages included soil infertility due to overexploitation, production of strong alcoholic liquor (moonshine), teenage pregnancy, polygamy, disputes between herders and crop-growers, and the absence of latrines. Most problems turned out to have strong cultural dimensions. As part of their organizing projects, groups of trainees interviewed their fellow citizens to find out how they understood the problem at hand. They learned to map the self-interests and power relations around the issue, to build relationships with public officials, and to plan and implement, together with other people in their community, a strategy to address the problem.

These organizing projects formed the experiential foundation of the course. Much of the "classroom" activity involved reflection on these experiences. Participants learned the core concepts and skills by putting them into action and analyzing their effectiveness. There was a strong emphasis on mutual accountability throughout, from everyday tasks for which people held each other responsible to the presentation of formal, public reports. Participants learned skills of public speaking, overcoming shyness in order to act as citizen leaders on a public stage. Here the learning also drew on cultural practices that form an integral part of people's lives, providing resources for leadership and public action. Such practices include conducting or singing in choirs, participating in family negotiations around weddings, making speeches at formal celebrations, and animating informal discussions in bars and taverns. As these experiences were drawn into the learning process, participants developed confidence in their agency, seeing themselves and, just as importantly, each other as co-creators of knowledge, capable of shaping their environments. Instead of being daunted by the expertise of trainers who come from the capital city, they claimed their own knowledge and talents, building on skills they previously took for granted. They indeed became catalysts of democratic development.

Impacts

The idea of citizens organizing themselves to solve community problems—and in the process developing public relationships and public goods—challenges the idea of politics as a partisan battle or simply a struggle against oppression. The public work approach can be conceived as "developmental," a term sometimes used to describe such citizen politics, in several ways. First, it moves people beyond a stance of victim and supplicant based on the expectation that someone else—usually the government—has to provide solutions to their problems. Rather, co-creative citizen politics involves people in devising and implementing lasting solutions to their common problems, sometimes on their own and sometimes in collaboration with government, contributing constructively to creating public resources and building better communities. At another level, citizen politics consciously strives to transform citizen identities, develop citizen capacities, and build citizen power. It goes beyond the mass action of protest politics, which often leaves people feeling angry and righteous but with little ability to reshape their everyday environments. Such politics highlights multiple sources of power, including relational power, the distinctive power of young people and women, the power of cultural traditions and practices, the power of local knowledge, and the power of imagination, to name a few.

Marie saw participants in the Burundi training program demonstrate significant shifts in understanding. They were surprised and energized by the real, tangible successes they achieved and the resources they created through their organizing projects. In an evaluation meeting some months after the conclusion of the pilot project, the Burundian trainers spoke enthusiastically about the impact of the course on the participants, in spite of doubts they had initially harbored. Emmanuel Manwangu commented, "I was afraid that people at village level might get lost in the training, but even if it was a little challenging for them at the beginning, their minds were awakened and they very quickly came up to speed. Democracy started to become *concrete* for them—the power to take action on issues right where they live." Juliette Kavabuha admitted, "I wondered whether we would really manage to achieve results, but I have seen that each citizen really does have value and can contribute something. [The participants] have lost their fear of approaching the authorities. Citizens are now the initiators of change. This is a huge change in the context of Burundi." Eusébie Nzorijana described a striking relocation of "politics" that decentered the concept and the practice: "At the beginning, some participants were uneasy about conducting interviews. 'This is politics,' they said. Later a participant said proudly, 'I can do politics myself now!'"

Trainers reported remarkable personal change and growth in themselves as well. Julienne Mukankusi said, "I have been deeply touched. I had done research and training on democracy before this, but I had not *lived* it. Now I have seen that a skilled citizen has more power than one can imagine." Marie-Paule Ndayishimiye commented, "The course has transformed me. I know that I myself am capable of being an agent of change." Manwangu described shifts in the meaning of democracy and citizenship: "This course changes one's understanding of democracy itself. Our language has changed. Citizens are at the center."

In the villages many people initially expressed the view that democracy in Burundi created more problems than it solved. They saw it as something imposed on them by "intellectuals," a category of nameless people toward whom they felt considerable scorn. Politics was understood as the sole preserve of politicians. The thought that ordinary citizens could—and should—learn political skills was novel and initially uncomfortable. But this changed as they gained the skills to read the "politics" of any situation—that is, the play of interests and power—as well as the skills to navigate these often tricky waters. They developed the capacity to engage in *constructive* action beyond zero-sum struggles. For instance, participants often approached their parish priests to assist them with their organizing projects, based on the premise that they held authority and resources that could help.

In one village, a group chose as its project the need to resolve long-standing tensions between elected leaders in their community, diving right into the difficulties of politics as conventionally understood. The trainers worried that the group had set itself up for failure, but the villagers succeeded spectacularly. After they confronted the leaders with concerns that their disagreements were blocking development in the community and threatening cohesion more

broadly, the elected officials agreed to bury the hatchet. The local priest pre-
sided over a public ceremony of confession and reconciliation. The group then
organized their community around another issue, confident that space had
been created for a productive partnership between villagers and their elected
leaders. Another group approached their priest to request wooden poles for the
construction of latrines in the area. The group had no money to buy the poles,
but the parish owned a large eucalyptus plantation. With their new confidence
and belief in local collaboration, they easily convinced the priest to support
the latrine project. Village inhabitants rolled up their sleeves and assisted with
digging and building, knowing that improved sanitation would have public
health benefits for the whole community.

After the first phase of BLTP's School for Democracy project, a new
initiative was launched in October 2014 to involve the police. The Burundi
National Police, working with BLTP, embarked on an effort to introduce a
development-oriented community policing strategy. It aimed to eliminate the
distance between police and communities and to encourage collaboration by
proactively addressing a range of local development issues rather than focusing
only on conventional, reactive approaches to security. The three-year training program, which concluded in December 2017, was implemented across
the country. The slogan of the course was "Security is everyone's business." It
brought together community police agents, known as *police de proximité*, and
representatives of the villages where they were based. The primary focus was
on developing a *shared citizen identity*, where citizens were understood to be
co-creators of safe and secure communities and where police saw themselves
first and foremost as citizens of the place where they work.

At the beginning of the pilot training workshop, police and other members
of the community lined up on opposite sides of the room. The unease was pal-
pable. Given the country's long history of insecurity, Burundians tend to view
the police at any level with suspicion, and police in turn are guarded in their
interactions with the people. Marie witnessed remarkable changes as police
and lay citizens joined in pairs after only a few days, leaning toward each other
in intense, respectful conversation, identifying shared concerns and imagining
how they might address them collaboratively. "I have seen this man in the
street, but I never thought that we could talk like this and solve problems
together," said one police officer. Another commented, "I cannot believe how
clever this woman is; we can make a real difference if we work together." The
words were positive, but even more profound was the evidence of new respect
for neighbors who, not long before, were seen as useless and having nothing

to offer. The detached stance of the police began to dissolve. A new commitment to working collaboratively with local residents emerged. As the course unfolded, trainers and the police top brass repeatedly expressed amazement when seeing the energy unleashed among citizens in far-flung villages and the steps they took together to become agents of change in their communities.

Such institutional and professional change is inspiring to see, but also precarious. The releasing of civic energies can easily provoke suspicion and even fear. Such energies cannot be scripted or controlled in a heavy-handed manner, nor do they lead to predictable outcomes. In citizen politics people embark together on a journey whose twists and turns cannot be discerned at the outset. In a public setting with diverse actors, unpredictability and risks are magnified. A training program such as the democratic development course for the Burundian police is thus riddled with risks and challenges, as Marie had also seen in other contexts with different kinds of professionals, such as health workers. Trainers sometimes lose their receptivity and responsiveness as the work becomes routinized. Trainers, participants, and newly empowered community members can be tempted to abuse their power, reverting to the conventional understanding of power as control over others. Those in existing positions of power frequently attempt to reassert themselves as they feel challenged by the emergence of new leaders in the community. Citizen-driven responses to local problems based on local knowledge and capacities are often seen as inadequate. At other times, officials try to take promising local solutions "to scale," resulting in a rapid return to top-down, one-size-fits-all approaches. It is all too easy for imaginations to narrow, stifled by conventional ways of thinking that place human beings in static categories. It is also a challenge for those who have graduated from the course to stay active. In sum, community policing—a real example of how citizens can enact what it means to be co-creators—is a fragile strategy.

During the implementation of the program for the *police de proximité*, Burundi experienced increasing political instability and violence. The program continued in the face of these obstacles, with trainers and local police alike insisting that it was more urgently needed than ever. BLTP displayed great political agility, but growing repression in the NGO sector, as well as the many other risks mentioned above, point to the fact that sustained citizen politics needs local institutional allies such as churches, educational institutions, businesses, and others.

To sustain such institutional partnerships citizen politics must democratize the cultures and work practices of schools, congregations, and businesses;

professions such as journalism, teaching, health, and government service; and electoral politics. It presages a long process of reintegrating professionals and institutions into civic life.

"Developmental Democracy"

> Too often transformation has come to be seen
> as a way of compensating previously disadvantaged
> people rather than creating opportunities for all
> citizens to contribute their talents, experience, and
> skills to the process of developing our country.
> Development can't be done "to" people. People have
> to become the agents of their own development.
> —Mamphela Ramphele, *Laying Ghosts to Rest*, 2008[35]

The spread of public work abroad, with relatively modest funding and often struggling against large cultural and political obstacles, is limited compared to development efforts using other paradigms with far more extensive donor support and other kinds of institutional help. But the case studies in this chapter show that the public work framework holds potential to strengthen emergent trends in development and its academic counterpart, development studies, that emphasize the empowerment of poor people. The public work framework makes explicit themes and concepts that are often implicit but largely unnamed: citizens as co-creators, democracy as a way of life, and citizen politics. Such politics involves work that builds common resources ("the commonwealth") across lines of difference in income, institutional contexts, ethnicity, religion, and party, creating new strategies and ways to also address questions of distributive justice and exclusion.

Contemporary public attention to development, in practice, policy, and academic theory, is often traced to the inauguration of Harry Truman as president of the United States in 1949. "More than half the people of the world are living in conditions approaching misery," said Truman. "Their food is inadequate. They are victims of disease. Their economic life is primitive and stagnant. Their poverty is a handicap and a threat both to them and to more prosperous areas." Truman also challenged hopelessness. "For the first time in history, humanity possesses the knowledge and the skill to relieve the suffering of these people."[36] While he drew attention to questions of poverty, the condescension of Truman's language ("victims," "primitive," "stagnant") also conveyed the top-down approach that generally has dominated in development work.

In her quote above, Mamphela Ramphele, a former leader of the Black Consciousness movement in South Africa, later vice-chancellor of the University of Cape Town and then vice president of the World Bank, challenges such condescending top-down thinking and practice. Many development advocates argue for movement away from top-down approaches in which the poor are rescued or saved by others, sometimes with the best of intentions, to a paradigm that supports bottom-up citizen action. The idea is elaborated in the collection *Culture and Public Action*, based on experiences of the United Nations Development Programme and the World Bank. As editors Vijayendra Rao and Michael Walton put it, "Although there are disagreements stemming from different paradigms . . . there is broad agreement that [we need] a shift from equality of opportunity to 'equality of agency' . . . creating an enabling environment to provide the poor with tools and the voice to navigate their way out of poverty."[37]

In 2008, Dutch development aid organizations supported an effort called Civic Driven Change, organized by the International Institute of Social Studies in The Hague. The initiative highlighted citizen-driven development efforts and the concept of civic agency.[38] Another major citizen-centered effort, a ten-year study entitled "Citizenship, Participation, and Accountability" (generally referred to as Citizenship DRC) details many of the themes that are common in development approaches focused on empowerment. Organized by the International Development Research Centre, directed by John Gaventa (formerly with Highlander Folk School) and supported by the British donor agency DFID, as well the Ford and Rockefeller Foundations, Citizenship DRC used participatory research methods to examine 150 case studies of citizen action in nearly thirty countries. Researchers took what they called a "seeing like a citizen" approach. Conventional approaches, they argued, assume that "if markets, elections, legal frameworks and civil society organizations are working, then citizenship identities will evolve as consumers, users and choosers, voters or legal entities but rarely as drivers of political and social change in their own right." Citizenship DRC, in contrast, started "with the perceptions of citizens themselves and ask[ed] how they interact with and view the institutions that serve them." They also challenged conventional definitions of citizens as simply voters, consumers, users of state services, and rights holders. In these cases citizens are cast in narrow or passive roles that "impose rigid constraints." In contrast, authors said that citizens should not be simply defined in relationship to the state. "Citizens . . . also have rights and duties with relation to non-state actors—their families, local associations, trade groups, religious communities," they wrote. A citizen "also connotes someone who belongs to different kinds of collective associations and defines their identity from participation in activities associated withthese different kinds of membership." This definition supports "people's aspirations for justice, recognition and self-determination as a driving force for development."[39]

Such an agency-focused approach overlaps with the public work framework. Both recognize that effective democratic change is most often led by lay citizens, not experts or elected officials. Both stress attentiveness to local cultures and institutions. Both have a relational understanding of power, understanding, for instance, that collaboration as well as contestation with government is important. Both realize that effective action takes time, involves developing people's skills, habits, and knowledge of how to make change, and requires building relationships. Both view people, including poor and marginal people, as having great untapped and unrecognized talents. Both stress the need for constructive public discussion. Moreover, like Public Achievement and the Idasa work, Citizenship DRC's "seeing like a citizen" approach is realistic in its assessment of projects, recognizing that some initiatives turn out poorly. Of the initiatives Citizenship DRC studied, 75 percent had positive effects and 25 percent had negative impacts, though they use measures of success that are far more subtle and multidimensional than most project evaluations. Many of the positive effects, such as developing confidence, building skills, and thickening civic networks, are not visible in conventional assessments.[40]

The public work framework also points toward a new paradigm beyond the "rights-holders approach" that focuses on the rights of citizens but not their productive roles. The language of citizens as "rights holders" and governments as "duty bearers" is currently widespread in development work that aims to be empowering. Public work holds citizens to be co-creators of democratic societies, not simply members of different communities or people who have rights. The case studies in this chapter show that such reframing can generate a sense of responsibility and ownership, is attentive to the overall civic health of communities, and fosters awareness of the larger idea of democratic society not emphasized in a rights-bearing point of view (though perhaps implicit in some of the Citizenship DRC case studies). The development of enlarged civic identities and an ethos of care for democratic culture and civic life is evident in stories from post-Soviet societies, such as Halima's creation of intergenerational social gatherings as the prelude to broader public work and also her intrinsic motivation for public work. The stories from Burundi of villagers who successfully challenged the elected officials to "bury the hatchet," in the process taking responsibility for dysfunctions in formal politics, and of the project that created "citizen police" show large civic aims and civic responsibility in one of the world's poorest countries.

It is worth revisiting the chart about paradigms of democracy, citizenship, and politics. In political theory, representative democracy emphasizes rights-based citizenship and free and fair elections. It is a great achievement in human history, deepened through the struggle for "the right to rights," to use Hannah Arendt's phrase, and also through the development of international codes of human, economic, and social rights, as well as civic and political rights. But a rights-centered view of citizenship alone fuels the metastasizing consumer culture in which an omnivorous "I" takes center stage. The second paradigm, embodied in what is called "communitarian" theory, emphasizes citizen voice and strengthening communities. Jonathan Sacks, the British rabbi, gives wise expression to this view in *The Politics of Hope*, a book that inspired Ramphele. Sacks contrasts the hopeless circumstances of many poor people today with his own family's background, economically impoverished but rich in cultural and relational resources. "Every age has its characteristic preoccupations," he writes. Since the Enlightenment, intellectuals have been concerned to create space for individuals "to be themselves" against the weight of constricting tradition or totalitarian systems. "[Today] it would be fairer to say that we stand in the opposite situation. In today's liberal democracies, it is not that we are too much together but that we are too much alone and seek to learn again how to connect with others." Ramphele echoes such views in the South African context, calling for a conception of citizenship that involves sacrificing self-interests for the common good.[41]

Both the state-centered and the community-centered frameworks have insights, but they are usefully supplemented by the public work framework. It adds new dimensions to voluntary associational life and social movements. Citizenship DRC identifies these two settings as well as officially established public participation forums as sites of citizenship. Public work relocates citizenship across the full sweep of society, not simply in government or community life. It harnesses self-interests for work with public benefit. It includes not only struggles for justice and inclusion but also the creation of shared resources and public problem-solving. And it identifies work roles and work settings as civic sites, stressing the long, relational, cultural change process involved in "making work more public," a theme developed in Chapter 8.[42] This chart compares three frameworks of democratic theory that build on each other.

Table 5.1. Frameworks of Democracy and Development

	Representative Democracy	Communitarian Democracy	Public Work Democracy
Who is the citizen?	Voter, consumer, rights bearing individual	Community member	Co-creator
What are the main tasks?	Representing voters, fairly distributing rights and services	Inclusion, participation, communication	Developing civic agency, negotiating a common life
What is the method?	Mobilizing	Strengthening social capital	Organizing
What is the government?	Service provider	Facilitator	Civic partner, organizer, catalyst
Self-interest?	Seen in consumer terms	Usually submerged and neglected	Integrated with making work more public
What is power?	Power over	Power with	Power to

Hidden Patterns of Power

Finally, a public work lens draws sustained attention to challenges that are underemphasized in other empowering approaches to development. In particular, its work-centered, political view of civic agency highlights how cultures of technocracy, what Pope Francis identifies as the "technocratic paradigm" pervading professional systems erodes people's civic confidence and development.[43] Professionals have come to focus on people's deficiencies rather than on their assets and capacities. The South African public intellectual Xolela Mangcu, writing from the Black Consciousness tradition, calls this "technocratic creep." In the United States, technocratic creep has been accelerating for many decades. Higher education bears a significant share of the responsibility, educating professionals to be mobile individualists who are detached from the communities in which they work and the cultures from which they come and who see people in terms of insufficiencies, as demanding customers or needy clients. The historian Thomas Bender calls this a shift from "civic professionalism" to "disciplinary professionalism." Expert-knows-best views also dominate in African, Latin American, and Asian universities.

Technocracy, control by experts, is accelerated by the efficiency principle and the digital revolution.[44] It reifies settings that once served as sources of civic learning, turning not only schools but also congregations, local businesses, unions, nonprofits, and government agencies into service delivery operations. This dynamic renders civic life an off-hours activity in civil society, usually through volunteering or community service, which are experienced as oases of civic idealism and decency in a degraded world. A great challenge of our time is to develop a politics to enlist the broad energies of all citizens to address our multiplying challenges. To use an ecological analogy, just as conservation work involves the restoration of complex habitats such as wetlands, the long range task of democratic development requires an understanding of change as a dynamic, interconnected whole, emphasizing the influences of the parts on each other and the way they function together. We need to regrow the "wetlands of democracy," revitalizing cultures of citizenship in whole communities. These themes are developed in Chapter 9. Democratic development in a time of growing challenges to democracy itself must not only address the symptoms of civic decline but also must go upstream to address their invisible roots in higher education, a topic taken up in Chapters 7 and 8.

6

The Power of Big Ideas

Harry C. Boyte with Marie-Louise Ström

With catchy rhythms and an exuberant rap, four children in Fridley Middle School start the YouTube video "Public Achievement in Fridley—Transforming Special Education."[1] They were likely unaware that they were taking part in an ancient debate.

"What's PA?" shouts one. "Working together to change to our world," all repeat three times. In a well-choreographed scene, Michael Ricci, their teacher, begins a boring lecture. "Now in Public Achievement, there are core concepts, help you keep it together step by step." With a good-humored shove, a girl bumps him out of the way. "Don't need no teacher, learning's up to me. Today we will start with one, two, three." "Like freedom," goes the group. "Tell me freedom," says one.

A handmade sign conveys their ideas. "We are free to live under the law, society, or world we make for ourselves," they sing. Power is next. "We got power." "What is power?" "The ability to influence people, institutions and how things work." Accountability and responsibility follow. "Do what you say you're going to do for the group," they sing three times. All gather together with the teacher, an assistant teacher, and a student coach. "Working together to change our world—that's PA!" They clap, and the screen cuts to the video's title: "Real Power—Using Public Achievement to Transform Special Education."

The YouTube production, directed by Humphrey student Jen Nelson, tells the story of Public Achievement projects organized by middle school students in what is called a "Level Three" EBD (Emotionally and Behaviorally Disturbed) class. It also conveys something of the craft of the teachers, Michael Ricci and Alyssa Blood, who changed their pedagogy to create an empowering culture of civic education. Their students took leadership in shaping their learning. They also learned to think of themselves as citizens in the process. Level Three EBD in special education means the children are segregated from other students in the school. The video is the story of how they "went public," breaking out of their segregation, with projects like an antibullying campaign and a mural to encourage healthy lifestyles. They gained public recognition in the school, throughout the Fridley community, and on Minnesota Public Radio.

Conventional special education pedagogies, described in Chapter 7, crystallize in stark form the technocratic assumptions of efficiency education. The children placed in special education are labeled with disabilities that teachers strive to remediate. They are like "canaries in the mine," whose extreme difficulties in school and troubles after graduation provide a cautionary tale for education as a whole. The special education children's obvious enthusiasm for using big concepts and their willingness to take leadership in their own learning through a pedagogy of empowering citizenship refute conventional assumptions.

The students' hip-hop production illustrates the submerged side of an argument that descends from Plato's famous allegory of the cave. Most people lived in a world of shadows. Only the rare philosopher could exit the cave and the reality beyond the shadows. The young people show that even those marginalized and stigmatized have potential to become enthusiastic about education, to use "big ideas" like power and freedom, and to develop civic identity in the process. "It is not that simple people like to hear about little things," wrote the educator Jane Addams in 1899, whose views are detailed later in this chapter. "They want to hear about the large and vital, great things simply told." She was talking about adults, not children, in the Chicago neighborhood where she cofounded the Hull House settlement dedicated to teaching citizenship to poor and working-class immigrants. She contrasted lectures about science at Hull House that presented ideas "large and vital" for immigrants and connected the subject to people's actual lives with subsequent lectures by academics whose pedantic, dry style "annihilated" the audience.[2]

Addams's educational philosophy contrasts sharply with dominant Platonic approaches. Belief that people who are not "intellectuals" might care about big ideas goes against conventional wisdom in education and philosophy alike. "Only a very limited group of people in any society engages in theorizing," argue Peter Berger and Thomas Luckmann in their classic work, *The Social Construction of Reality.* Similarly, Isaiah Berlin, the famous British liberal philosopher, argued that "men cannot live without seeking to describe and explain the universe. The models they use in doing this must deeply affect their lives." Yet, in his view, "ordinary men regard [the work of thinking] about these models with contempt, or awe, or suspicion, according to their temperaments."[3] Today, not only special education students but also poor, working-class students and students from racial minorities are often seen in this way. Moreover, progressives often describe conservatives in ways that make them seem like poster children for Berlin's view. There is little attention to ways the abstract and condescending knowledge flow of educational methods in schools and the public culture fail to speak to the lived realities of large parts of the population.

Public Achievement builds on four strands of pedagogy based on the premise that co-creative citizenship and its skills, values, habits, and identities have to be *learned* and that deep democratic learning requires significant reflection about people's experiences as well as the purposes and meanings of action. People are not born knowing how to be "citizen co-creators." These pedagogies all teach empowering citizenship through active learning experiences based on respect for the intelligence, energies, and talents of children and adults. They aim to "awaken the spirit," not simply to convey knowledge and skills. The pedagogies feeding into Public Achievement include Jane Addams's approach at Hull House; the citizenship schools of the civil rights movement; Danish folk schools and their educational philosophy, which influenced these movement schools; and the reflective process of the Industrial Areas Foundation, a broad-based community organizing network. The training of Public Achievement coaches often incorporates a brief orientation to such pedagogical histories. Participants in Public Achievement also benefit from understanding the pedagogical roots of the program in earlier popular movements, creating continuity with citizen-driven initiatives for change.

The Hull House Philosophy

Jane Addams cofounded Hull House with Ellen Gates Starr in 1889 in Chicago to teach citizenship to poor and working-class immigrants. Addams and Starr were, most immediately, inspired by the example of Toynbee Hall in London, a learning site that brought together graduates of Oxford and Cambridge Universities with poor and working-class residents of the East End neighborhood. Gioia Diliberto describes Toynbee Hall as a "civic community" that embodied "the distinctive reform spirit of the Victorian era—an earnest combination of self-improvement and duty toward others . . . a conviction that all people, regardless of class, birth, or wealth, have the capacity and indeed the duty to 'evolve' into their best selves." It teemed with courses, projects, and meetings. In one month, Diliberto found, there were "classes for writing, math, chemistry, drawing, music, sewing, nursing, hygiene, composition, geography, book-keeping, citizenship, and evening courses in geology, physiology, botany, chemistry, Hebrew, Latin and Greek, European and English history, and literary subjects from Dante to Shakespeare to Moliere."[4]

Addams and Starr also applied their philosophy to public education in general, recalling the American tradition of the "Little Red Schoolhouse," schools that were sources of community pride and centers of civic life. They deepened the democratic purposes of this tradition by tying education for citizenship to a process that might be called "awakening the spirit and energies" of whole communities, not simply school students, as Nick Longo has described in *Recognizing the Community in Civic Education*. Addams reflected on what public schools might look like if they followed the methods of Hull House. "We could imagine the business man teaching the immigrant his much needed English and arithmetic and receiving in return lessons in the handling of tools and materials so that they should assume in his mind a totally different significance from that the factory gives them." She envisioned Italian immigrant women learning English in kitchens and teaching their instructors "how to cook the delicious macaroni."[5]

In "Educational Methods," Addams argued that the educator has a role far beyond "informing" students: "We are gradually requiring of the educator that he shall free the powers of each man and connect him with the rest of life. We are impatient to use the dynamic power residing in the mass of humankind, and demand that the educator free that power."[6] Like Toynbee Hall, Hull House overflowed with different kinds of educational experiences, based on a deep belief in everyone's potential and also in the cooperative nature of education. "Addams believed that democracy required true reciprocity," wrote Ellen Lagemann, her biographer. Addams saw education as much broader than what happens in classrooms or within the walls of schools. "She focused on whether and how social relationships (domestic, familial, occupational, political, intergenerational and intergroup) allowed and promoted free expression for all parties."[7] Hull House was "something of an open university where a constant flow of talk about politics, ideas, public events, art, philosophy, and the immediate problems of a destitute family or a gang of neighborhood boys provided constantly evolving and lived meaning to such abstract concepts as citizenship, culture, assimilation, and education."[8] The pedagogy powerfully challenged more typical academic approaches. "The Settlement recognizes the need of cooperation, both with the radical and the conservative, and . . . cannot limit its friends to any one political party or economic school," wrote Addams, contrasting settlement house philosophy with the cloistered disciplinary cultures of academia. Residents of Hull House, she argued, "feel that they should promote a culture which will not set its possessor aside in a class with others like himself, but which will . . . connect him with all sorts of people by his ability to understand them as well as by his power to supplement their present surroundings."[9]

John Dewey's famous lecture in 1902, "The School as Social Centre," described in Chapter 2, theorized Hull House as a model for all schools. The school, in his view, was a space for the face-to-face mingling of diverse populations in urban areas. He contrasted such a space with the forced, destructive "Americanization" in urban settings. In factory-like schools, he argued, where children are instructed according to a strictly prescribed curriculum and rote learning methods, they have little chance to interact. As a consequence, young people "are frequently left floating and unstable between the two [their immigrant cultures and the dominant culture]. They even learn to despise the dress, bearing, habits, language and beliefs of their parents." In contrast, at Hull House "the younger generation [learns] something of the skill and art and historic meaning of the older generations. . . . Many a child has awakened to an appreciation of admirable qualities hitherto unknown." Schools like Hull House were creating a "means for bringing people and their ideas and beliefs together in such ways [that] lessen friction and instability and introduce deeper sympathy and wider understanding."[10]

Themes from Jane Addams's philosophy informed Public Achievement's style of citizenship education from the beginning. "All are teachers, all are learners," was a founding principle. Public Achievement incorporated Addams's view that children, as well as adults, can be engaged with "big ideas simply told." Finally, as Chapter 3 described, after the disastrous hat strike at Highland Park High School, Public Achievement incorporated Addams's insight that civic empowerment depends on preparing people to negotiate diverse cultures. Similar themes run through the citizenship schools of the civil rights movement.

Citizenship Schools

Myles Horton cofounded Highlander Folk School in Grundy County, Tennessee, in 1932, with Don West, an educator, and James Dombroski, a Methodist minister, as an educational site intended to "free the powers" of poor people in Appalachia. Longo describes how Horton drew inspiration in part from Jane Addams and Hull House, which he had encountered as a student in Chicago.[11] Decades later, following a trip to the school by Esau Jenkins, Highlander became the incubator for a citizenship school movement that spread across black communities in the South as the foundation of the civil rights movement.

The citizenship school movement grew from a conversation Alice Wine had with Esau Jenkins, who operated a regular bus service from Johns Island, off the South Carolina coast, to Charleston. Jenkins, a prominent civic leader in the black community—president of the Johns Island parent-teacher association, superintendent of Sunday schools at Wesley United Methodist Church, and president of the Citizens Club, a community betterment group—was an outspoken critic of segregation. Wine asked him to help her learn to read— she had not finished third grade—so she could meet the literacy requirement used to prevent blacks from voting. Jenkins passed out copies of the state laws on voting to Wine and other passengers. He began teaching literacy and discussing the meaning of the laws—creating what historian Katherine Charron calls "a rolling voter registration school." In the long ride between towns, "the autonomous space of the bus afforded Jenkins and his passengers an ideal opportunity to engage in rudimentary voter education, unbeknownst to white people," writes Charron.[12]

The first official citizenship school class took place on January 7, 1957, on Johns Island. Ten female and four male students gathered in the backroom of a store. Septima Clark, who had brought Jenkins to Highlander and was the chief architect of the school, argued successfully with Horton that literacy needed to be part of the curriculum. In that first group of students on Johns Island, eight read "very poorly." Three could not read or write at all. She and Horton had chosen Clark's cousin, Bernice Robinson, a beautician with an activist history in New York as well as South Carolina, to be the teacher.

Robinson was not a professional educator, but she had strong relational skills and was a good listener. Although Clark herself had four decades of exemplary teaching experience in public schools, she and Horton decided not to recruit professionally trained teachers to pioneer the citizenship schools. While Clark had learned how to teach in an empowering way, she also knew that most teachers were likely to be too focused on content, too middle class, and too prone to want to be the center of attention. The two cousins engaged in long discussions to clarify an alternative approach. Robinson began by erasing the normal hierarchy in the classroom. "I'm really not going to be your teacher," she said to the students. "We're going to work together and teach each other." She asked them what they would like to learn. Some wanted to read the Bible, others to read letters from their children, still others to fill out a catalog form or a money order. "I started off with things that were familiar," said Robinson. "I'd have them tell me stories about what they did in the fields and what they did in their homes." She copied these down and used them to teach. Men, she discovered, were especially interested in learning arithmetic. How much gasoline would it take to drive from the island to the city? How much material would it take to build a fence? Robinson, again following Clark, also combined the everyday with the visionary. "I tacked up the [United Nations] Declaration of Human Rights on the wall and told them that I wanted each of them to be able to read and understand the entire thing before the end of school."[13]

Public Achievement began with the core mission of the citizenship schools: to teach citizenship to everyone, including children. The importance of drawing on people's personal experiences and interests was central. When teenagers in the 1990 listening sessions for Public Achievement suggested "coach" as the role for adults working with teams, it made sense and resembled the role Bernice Robinson had played. A good coach listens, gets to know each team member and their interests, builds on their experiences, and is committed to developing their talents. Coaches are concerned with developing the confidence and courage of team members to act collaboratively in public. The team is "on the field."

In sharing the origins of Public Achievement, the importance of beauty parlors in the citizenship school movement was often part of the narrative. Myles Horton in 1977 had pointed out that black beauty parlors were a prime example of free spaces.[14] They were not under the control of the white power structure. They were community centers where diverse people socialized beyond immediate family and friends. Clark and Robinson had understood that beauticians could incorporate civic education into their everyday work. They had good relational skills. They sustained important community sites. They were well positioned to inspire others. Clark and Robinson recruited fifty-two beauticians from Tennessee and Alabama for a workshop at Highlander Folk School held in January 1961. At the meeting, Eva Bowman, a former examiner of the Tennessee Cosmetology Board, called her colleagues to see "civic service as a responsibility of the Beautician." Beauticians from Fayette County, Tennessee, organized a group, created a board of directors, and decided to organize a health center for the homeless.[15] They became what can be called "citizen beauticians."

Clark had also learned to be a "citizen teacher" from decades of organizing for change in the segregated schools of South Carolina. Clark had learned that citizenship schools needed to be about agency, capacities for self-directed effort, and work with others to change one's environment. "Your creative ability [as a teacher] is the thing you need to pull out of these children their creative ability," she counseled other teachers. Citizenship schools were based on the premise that agency begins with the practical and concrete. "Those who learned to read, write and figure felt more self-sufficient and less vulnerable," recounts Charron. "More important, they had the means to preserve their independence." Bill Saunders, a citizenship school leader on Johns Island, observed that sometimes whites would claim to pay black landowners' property taxes and then not follow through, so blacks would lose their land. Through the citizenship schools, "folk were learning that they can go and pay their own taxes. . . . They had the receipt."[16]

Clark knew that citizenship schools needed to be part of community life. Congregations and civic groups, PTAs, beauty parlors, barbershops, and a host of other settings all provided educational resources and opportunities outside the classroom. At the very beginning of her career, when she worked on Johns Island, Clark had also learned to involve rural children's families in the life of schools. She was building on a rich heritage of schools as civic centers in the African American community. For instance, local black communities had done the lion's share of the work in creating more than five thousand "Rosenwald schools" in the South in the 1910s and 1920s, catalyzed by the Rosenwald Fund, a foundation created by a Jewish immigrant, Julius Rosenwald, that provided seed money for black schools.[17]

Finally, Clark saw the need for citizenship schools to be part of a larger movement for democratic change. As Charron observes, she had helped to build "a growing army of black teachers [who] forged an activist educational culture that had long-term political consequences. Shaped by improvisational pedagogical strategies and underscored by commitment to local people, [they learned] success depended not on confrontation but on driving a wedge, gaining ground an inch at a time and holding it."[18]

When the Southern Christian Leadership Conference (SCLC) took over the citizenship schools from Highlander in 1961, they were renamed the Citizenship Education Program (CEP). Clark and Robinson joined with Dorothy Cotton, who was on the SCLC staff, and Andrew Young, a twenty-eight-year-old minister then working as associate director of the National Council of Churches' Department of Youth. Young returned to the South—he had grown up in New Orleans and was eager to join the movement—with the belief that what "the masses hunger for most is some form of ideology that can hold them together as a movement. Somehow the 'classes' and 'the masses' must be brought together in this struggle. My job is to find out how." Clark, sixty-three years old, soon enlightened him. In her view, citizenship schools, like the movement, taught citizenship with a larger purpose: "To broaden the scope of democracy to include everyone and deepen the concept to include every relationship."[19]

The next several years were a time of explosive growth for the CEP. By

1969, more than five thousand people had passed through the weeklong training program offered by SCLC, and tens of thousands of local leaders had been involved in local citizenship school classes across the South.[20] This expansion also created challenges. The citizenship schools on the Sea Islands off the South Carolina coast worked because, as Clark put it, "I was literally a Charlestonian . . . and knew the people on the island and in the city." Earning people's trust meant building relationships. It also required adaptability. Citizenship schools were not standardized. "You expand the citizenship idea in a new place in the way the needs and problems are considered by the potential leaders in that particular situation," she explained. "The pattern is the same and yet different."[21] Public Achievement retains a similar commitment to flexibility within local contexts. Clark fought to keep attention on the local relationship-building and grassroots education of the citizenship schools, in the midst of a whirlwind of demonstrations and a focus on passing national civil rights legislation.

SCLC leaders moved rapidly from one community to another, following the strategy of the March on Washington, which had sought support from the American mainstream. Yet, as Clark realized, "had not an educational organizing structure been in place . . . SCLC would not have generated the sustained protest that so starkly portrayed segregation's injustice. . . . Along with the church, the CEP provided SCLC's grassroots institutional base." Clark and other citizenship school leaders also knew that empowerment is a molecular process, not something that comes from marches and demonstrations. It required overcoming ingrained patterns of deference and developing the courage to "go public." As Victoria Gray, coordinator of the CEP in Mississippi put it, "Until you free a person mentally, emotionally, and spiritually you can't accomplish very much." While marches could publicize injustices, the challenge was to create lasting change. "Those left behind [after the demonstrations] still had to find a way to negotiate concrete change in their hometowns," observes Charron. "The CEP provided many of these people with the courage and practical proficiency required for that task, though that did not mean they always succeeded."[22]

The immense impact of the citizenship schools across the South is an insufficiently recognized aspect of the freedom movement. Beyond hundreds of thousands of new voters, CEP alumni took leadership in other efforts, from the Mississippi Freedom Democratic Party, which gained national attention in 1964 at the Democratic Party convention for its challenge to the segregated official delegation, to rural cooperatives and federal antipoverty efforts.[23] Today, the long-term goal of the citizenship schools still remains to be enacted. In 1962, Clark had envisioned "a learning society made up of educative communities." Clark, Young, and others conceived of a network of permanent learning centers across the South with parallels with and differences from the schools that the American Missionary Society (AMA) had established a hundred years earlier to educate newly liberated slaves. "My criticism of the AMA has always been that it devoted itself to the theory of the 'talented tenth,'" wrote Andy Young. "[It] did not develop an approach to aid the masses."[24]

One source of these and other ideas that inspired the CEP can be found in a nineteenth-century movement—the Danish folk schools—and their philosophy of popular education.

Danish Popular Education

The Danish folk school tradition had its roots in the philosophy of N. F. S. Grundtvig, a nineteenth-century Danish Lutheran theologian and philosopher. It had considerable impact on American adult education practices in the 1920s and 1930s. Intellectual historian Andrew Jewett discovered that 80 percent of rural sociologists surveyed in the 1930s saw Danish folk schools as the leading model for democratic education. Alain Locke, a driving force behind American adult education and widely seen as the philosophical architect of the Harlem Renaissance, was also impressed with the approach.

Extension agents based at land-grant universities, including the historically black colleges and universities established in the segregated South in 1892, also drew on the Danish popular education tradition, in their work in agriculture, home economics, and 4-H. Mary Mims of Louisiana State University, founder of the "community organization movement" in cooperative extension, traveled through Denmark in the 1920s to study the folk school philosophy and the schools inspired by Grundtvig's philosophy.

Similarly, Myles Horton visited Denmark to learn about the schools and their philosophy before establishing Highlander. He was taken with the combination of the practical and immediate, the world as it is and the vision of what could be. In his last year as president, Barack Obama paid tribute to Grundtvig's little-known influence on the civil rights movement in a tribute to Nordic presidents on May 13, 2016. "Many of our Nordic friends are familiar with the great Danish pastor and philosopher Grundtvig who . . . championed the idea of the Folk School, education that was not just made available to the elite but to the many. Training that prepared a person for active citizenship, that improves a society," said Obama in his toast. "Over time the Folk School Movement spread including here to the United States. One of those schools was . . . Highlander Folk School [where] a new generation of Americans came together to share ideas and strategies for advancing civil rights, for advancing equality, for advancing justice. . . . They ended up having a ripple effect on the Civil Rights Movement."[25] In South Carolina, Wil Lou Gray, another key leader in adult education, espoused the folk school philosophy, particularly its emphasis on cooperative living, community problem-solving, and spiritual and cultural revival. Clark collaborated with her.[26]

Grundtvig's educational philosophy was integrated with his understanding of human life and Christian life. The folk high school was to be a "school for life," awakening young people to their reality, with all its troubles and promise. It enabled them to solve real problems in everyday life and readied them for a life of practical faith.

Reacting against the cultural colonization of his country by other dominant European cultures, including what he called the "Roman yoke" of the classical Latin curriculum, Grundtvig developed a passionate commitment to awakening the identity of the Danish citizen in order to build a flourishing, authentically Danish society. On superficial reading, his work might appear to have an overly nationalistic flavor. However, as Niels Jensen observes, "Though no one has declared his love of his fatherland with greater warmth than Grundtvig, he recognized that man was necessarily born into a particular nation and would grasp and understand life in this mold and in this tongue."[27] For Grundtvig the vernacular language with its proverbs and idioms, and traditional culture with its ballads, myths, and histories, offered deep resources for building a good society. Although his homogenous cultural context was vastly different from today's diverse societies, including twenty-first-century Denmark itself, his understanding of the citizen and the role of education still holds wisdom for our time.

The overarching aim of Grundtvig's educational philosophy was "enlightenment for life"—*livsoplysning*. Holger Hansen explains that Grundtvig was concerned about "making people aware of their own identity and possibilities in their own setting and within their own way of life, of putting man at the center in his historical, national and religious context."[28] For Grundtvig, the surest route to such popular enlightenment is through living interaction among people from different backgrounds across the whole society.[29] For this to happen, he believed that a particular kind of "people's education" was needed. Popular enlightenment or awareness would not come about automatically. People from *every* occupation—farmers, small merchants, sailors, and others—all needed education "other than that which is gained behind the plow, in the shop, climbing the mast of a vessel or in the place of business."[30] In his view, "public servants and professional men" needed the same education.[31] He described the folk school as providing "an indigenous, general education, on a continuous basis, [to] enable [people] to understand the structure of our society and also help them to weigh the advantages and disadvantages of the various vocations as contrasted with one another."[32]

Grundtvig believed that folk high schools needed to teach people from every walk of life to see themselves as *citizens first*, "to become Danish human beings in all vocations."[33] In so doing, they could discover a civic dimension to their work and gain an understanding of how their vocation fits into the society, what other vocations contribute, and how they can interact usefully with each other. The aim is for the people together to build a thriving society through their *daily work*—in effect anticipating the idea of citizens as co-creators—not only through voluntary, after-hours civic effort, which is often how "civic engagement" has come to be understood. This is an extraordinary vision for democracy education: unleashing the powers and capacities of every citizen, or, as Grundtvig put it, "the fostering of all our vital efforts."[34] In the contemporary context, this can be taken as a challenge to citizens in every setting—whether school, sports club, neighborhood, factory, office, town, province, or nation—to understand their role as doing the practical work of building a better society.

Grundtvig's educational philosophy anticipated public work and its pedagogies in other ways as well. He did not pit the poor against the rich, but believed that all needed a "people's education" so that they might be capable of solving real-life problems together and building a better, more egalitarian society. He wrote, "The same potential for educational and cultural achievement is discoverable in both cottage and manor house."[35] In other words, every citizen, whether peasant or wealthy landowner, held essential capacities and resources to create a flourishing Danish society. Today, the folk high school movement birthed by Grundtvig, as well as the cooperative movement that it nourished, is considered to have played a vital role in the democratization of Denmark and the emancipation of its rural populations, as well as in the country's commitment to the welfare of all its citizens.

In today's world, a scarcity mindset and rampant individualism undermine efforts to foster civic collaboration. The culture of competition is reinforced by deeply entrenched patterns in education inasmuch as traditional classrooms are competitive arenas that pit individual students against each other. This competitive ethos is reinforced from an early age by testing. Grundtvig, already in his time, was alert to how damaging such a competitive culture was to the spirit of citizenship. Not only was he determined there should be no tests or exams in the folk high school, but he also thought it should have an open-door policy that would admit students from any station in life. The idea of "living interaction" across lines of difference was his foundational pedagogical principle. He believed it could result in "an increased joy in the community of the people."[36] He was not naive and recognized the inevitable tension in communities. "In a human community there is always the obvious danger of inner dissolution, increasing conflict, and growing dissatisfaction with one's lot in life," he observed.[37] But for Grundtvig, deepening citizen identity through folk school education was the solution to this problem. By 1872, the year of his death, "grundtvigianism" flourished in many different movements. His followers formed or joined political parties on both the conservative and liberal sides of the political spectrum. Bjørnson, a Norwegian admirer, praised Grundtvig for his "'spiritual capaciousness,' his ability to see friends amongst enemies and make full friends of half-friends by showing confidence in them."[38] What is striking, from the vantage point of citizen politics, is Grundtvig's profoundly *public* sensibility. The folk high school was not simply to be a place where citizens would become friends. The purpose was to look outward to the work of building a good society. Working toward this goal could unleash the potential of citizens. Though he didn't use the term "co-creator," Grundtvig understood the creative power of the vocation of citizen expressed through everyday work. The working group that founded Public Achievement did not know this history in detail, but these themes infuse its pedagogy and philosophy.

The final stream that fed into pedagogies of public work is community organizing with a reflective dimension, which found its richest expression in the Industrial Areas Foundation.

Reflective Practice

A number of organizations emerged from the "backyard revolution" of citizen action that began in the 1960s and that the *Christian Science Monitor* called "the invisible story of the 1970s." They shared many similarities, but there were also differences, including different pedagogical approaches.

Consumer and environmental groups and other progressive organizations typically adopted the mobilizing approach described in Chapter 1. This approach fails to develop people's public capacities, especially their philosophical and intellectual life. As the late Paul Wellstone, a community organizer, college professor, and populist senator from Minnesota, observed, "Organizers are under a strong pressure to ignore this development process." Huge pressure from funders—church groups, foundations, liberal contributors, and the canvass—emphasized results, not discussion of ideas or deeper purposes. Organizers themselves felt pressure to have concrete victories they could point to. They felt "a compelling need to keep up the morale of the people by having early successes."[39]

Absent strong intellectual and philosophical dimensions, the mobilizing culture of citizen activism tends toward a focus narrowly on skill development: how to write a compelling leaflet that avoids jargon and dense prose, how to hold a press conference, how to chair a meeting, how to give public testimony, how to use social media to turn people out. These skills are important parts of civic action, but they neglect the reflective habits of learning and the consideration of "so what" questions. Ends are taken as a given and narrowed down to specific outcomes on issues. This reflects the pressures of a society where the priority is to get things done quickly, without thought about how the activity contributes to democratic change.

Organizing in the 1930s and 1940s often entailed more reflection about democracy. Thus, for instance, Saul Alinsky's first book, *Reveille for Radicals*, published in 1946, codified the principles of Back of the Yards and other democratic organizing efforts by emphasizing the rich democratic tradition and philosophy in America. Alinsky also stressed the need for popular organizations to be rooted in and to work through local community life, a lesson Public Achievement learned after the hat strike in 1991. "The foundation of a People's Organization is in the communal life of the local people," he argued. "Therefore the first stage in the building of a People's Organization is the understanding of the life of a community, not only in terms of the individual's experiences, habits, values and objectives but also from the point of view of the collective habits, experiences, customs, controls and values of the whole group, the community traditions." The organizer "should have a familiarity with the most obvious parts of a people's traditions." Organizers might disagree with local traditions, but efforts at democratic change must always be undertaken in the terms of a place and its history. "The starting of a People's Organization is not a matter of personal choice. You start with the people, their traditions, their prejudices, their habits, their attitudes, and all of those other circumstances that make up their lives." To know a community "is to know the values, objectives, customs, sanctions, and the taboos of these groups. It is to know them not only in terms of their relationships and attitudes toward one another but also in terms of what relationship all of them have toward the outside. . . . To understand the traditions of a people is . . . to ascertain those social forces which argue for constructive democratic action as well as those which obstruct democratic action."[40] Leaders in the freedom movement such as Ella Baker, Myles Horton, Septima Clark, and Bayard Rustin, like Alinsky, had roots in the popular movements of the 1930s.[41] A deep appreciation of culture also was at the center of Danish popular education.

The Industrial Areas Foundation organizing network that Alinsky founded expanded the emphasis on culture and intellectual life after his death in 1972. Workshops conducted by IAF, which now has affiliates in Great Britain, France, Germany, South Africa, and elsewhere, described organizations themselves as "universities of public life," in the language of Ernesto Cortes. This meant engaging big ideas and questions of purpose in a sustained way. It also meant taking seriously people's interests and intellects, doing one-on-one relational meetings to find out "who people are"—their interests, stories, and motivations—and creating a constant process of reflection on their experiences. In contrast to organizations that are based on relatively passive constituencies and that use mobilizing methods such as the canvass, the Internet, or direct mail, IAF groups ground their work in an ongoing conversation. Sister Margaret Snipe, in a parish connected to the East Brooklyn Churches, described how preparing lay leaders with skills of listening and face-to-face meetings worked a dramatic rebirth in the community. People became more sensitive to others' points of view, more skilled in interpersonal communication, and more aware of their own needs and interests.[42] Public Achievement's core practices, such as one-on-one relational meetings, power mapping, and collective evaluation, all came directly out of these IAF experiences.[43]

The reflective bent of the network also meant that leaders and organizers took the resources of faith traditions far more seriously.[44] The result of this relational and intellectual culture was a growing consciousness of what IAF leaders and organizers called "the values war" with the dominant American culture. As the document *Organizing for Family and Congregation*, largely authored by organizer Mike Gecan, put it, the question is "who will parent our children? Who will teach them, train them, nurture them?" For most people today, "parenting" takes place in a "strictly secular setting where the system is said to be the solution, time is money, profit is the sole standard of judgment." IAF organizations sought to create an alternative.[45]

The IAF educational process not only teaches specific knowledge about government policy and skills about negotiating the system but also involves a sustained and vibrant discussion of political *concepts* such as "power," "interests," "politics," leadership, and public relationships, which are different from private relationships among family and friends.[46] Public Achievement continues this practice of sustained discussion of core concepts, and we have found that even children are excited about "big ideas."

The process is illustrated by the idea of "public and private," a distinction that is valuable in Public Achievement. The difference between public and private relationships clarifies key contrasts:

Private	Public
Family, friends, and self	School, workplace, religious group, and politics
Sameness	Diversity
Loyalty	Accountability
Givenness	Fluidity
Private love	Public love (see Chapter 1)
Need to be liked	Need to be respected
Purpose is intimacy, personal support, recreation	Purpose is public creation, problem-solving, public power

The seemingly sharp distinctions are framed by the argument that there are a few "universals" to political life, applying across widely varying cultural and community contexts, but nothing is ever "either-or." As Gerald Taylor puts it, "We're the same people after all, whether we are in a public or a private setting." These concepts are best understood as fluid and influenced by context. Different settings such as a church service or a school or a geographical community, take on varying public and private qualities. A church, explained Arnie Graf, a long time IAF organizer, is more personal than a political convention.

Differentiating between public and private relationships has proven to be very useful for students learning public work approaches. It forms the basis of the collective evaluation that Public Achievement teams conduct at the end of every meeting and action. This fosters a culture and habit of mutual accountability and joint responsibility for the work of the group. It follows the pattern of experiential learning, drawing lessons from the ups and downs of a team's life and the successes and challenges of a team's work. Collective evaluation can be a difficult practice to implement initially—being held accountable can be uncomfortable—but when conducted in a supportive way it is transformative.

The concept emphasizes a public world of diverse interests, views, and backgrounds where the main point is to create public relationships for public work, not to find personal love or intimacy; this framework is often missing in schools with a focus on therapeutic approaches. In Dennis Donovan's undergraduate class at the University of Minnesota, which distills lessons of Public Achievement, students say that learning the difference between private relationships and public relationships is extremely helpful in negotiating many settings. "Before this class I was constantly trying to impress and get praise from everyone in my life whether it was a teacher, boss or coach," said Max Thommes, a UMN football player in Dennis's class. "That was a very stressful and demanding way to live my life. Does my teacher like me? Why does the head guard always pick on me during training?" Learning to distinguish public from private relationships was a revelation. "This class really taught me about where to get my loving from, my friends and family. With public relationships politics plays a huge role in a person's decision making. This does not mean you shouldn't do your homework or not be on your coach's good side. Instead you just need to understand that those relationships do not make or break you."[47] As special education students learned this distinction in Public Achievement, they developed what Alyssa Blood calls a "public persona," a citizen identity, as Chapter 7 describes.

7

Tackling the Empowerment Gap

Harry C. Boyte with Susan O'Connor
and Donna R. Patterson

In 2011, according to the American Community Survey, forty-three million Americans, 14 percent of the population, lived below the family poverty level of $11,500. For Native Americans, 27 percent live in poverty; for African Americans, 26 percent; and for Latinos/Hispanics, 23 percent. Behind these grim figures are too many lives haunted by misery and powerlessness. Poverty endures, and so have public concerns about poverty. A Gallup survey in 2014 found that 76 percent of Americans worry a great deal or a fair amount about those who do not have enough to eat or a place to sleep—more than worry about the size of the federal government, the possibility of a terrorist attack, or illegal immigration.[1]

A growing number of observers point to the close links between poverty, race, and education.[2] Both issues were evident on February 27, 2014, when President Obama spoke persuasively about the intertwined realities. While noting the "larger agenda" of economic insecurity and stalled mobility for Americans of all racial backgrounds, he also described "the plain fact [that] there are some Americans who . . . have had the odds stacked against them in unique ways that require unique solutions." Leaders from more than a dozen foundations attended the White House event. They pledged at least $200 million over five years in a search for solutions to the problems that black males face with early childhood development, school readiness, educational opportunity, discipline, parenting, and the criminal justice system.[3]

Public attention to the issues of poverty and race is welcome. But when the issue is education, the problem is misdiagnosed as a *distributive* and *remedial* challenge called the "achievement gap," focused on the gap in test scores between minority students and students of European American background. If achievement in conventional high-stakes testing is the challenge, then the solution is to do a better job channeling resources to poor people and preparing them to work in a meritocratic society. In this world, each student's success is measured by income levels, formal credentials, and career paths of upward mobility.

There is considerable evidence, however, that such norms themselves contribute to economic disparities. They require poor people from strong community and cultural backgrounds to make a choice between who they *are*, their cultural identities and support networks, and the demands of individual achievement.[4] In these terms, the problem of chronic poverty and racial disparity can be better diagnosed as the absence of individual and collective agency. Educational systems disempower racial minorities and the poor. Empowerment, creating spaces and generating tools for people to manage their lives and co-create their educational experiences, is an alternative strategy to remediation, but because such empowerment is rare, it is more useful to talk about "the empowerment gap" than "the achievement gap."

Atum Azzahir, a prominent African American philosopher of health and education in Minneapolis, sees acquiescence to individualist, meritocratic norms in African American communities as an enduring, tragic amnesia about the communal solidarity and mutual aid generated by generations of struggle in the African American community. "With a more open society, we began to pursue outside jobs and schooling and learn outside values," she says. "The movement for human dignity became a movement for equal rights. The black psychological, social, cultural, and emotional infrastructure that had endured through the unprecedented brutality of slavery and Jim Crow was not valued." Freedom came to be redefined as individual success. "We sang free at last," she says. But what did freedom entail?[5]

If the deep problem is the "empowerment gap," those who fail in today's educational system are like "canaries in the mine," signaling hidden dangers for everyone. Damaging effects of individualist norms and pedagogies and pervasive feelings of powerlessness in education among both students and teachers are worsened because high-stakes testing pushes out other experiences. As Diane Ravitch observes, "In response to the federal and state pressure to raise test scores, school districts across the nation have been reducing the time available for the arts, physical education, history, civics and other nontestable subjects."[6]

In the Twin Cities, Minnesota, since 2010 faculty and students in special education at Augsburg University, working with partnering schools and communities, have undertaken an experiment to address the empowerment gap.

The Beginning in Fridley Middle School

Like other founding moments in Public Achievement's history when schools were at the center—Saint Bernard's in Saint Paul, Saint. Gregory's in Maryville, Centaurus in Colorado, SPLOT in Poland—the Public Achievement movement to change special education began in a school, in this case a school within a school. Alissa Blood-Knafla described the scene in the segregated "Level Three EBD" special education program in Fridley Middle School, in a northern suburb of Minneapolis.

"The room is full of noise and controlled chaos," she wrote. "Middle-school students are mixed in with athletes from the University of Minnesota and they are all focused on measuring, cutting, and tying the fleece material to make blankets. Adult coaches from Augsburg College are divided up amongst the tables providing instructions and engaging everyone in conversation." Jen Nelson's video crew was filming "Public Achievement in Fridley," the YouTube video beginning the last chapter. Alissa, then a teacher in the school, was "in awe of how well it [was] going." She turned as the superintendent of the school district walked in the door. "I try to hide my astonishment as the superintendent remarks that it is difficult to tell the middle school students from the college students."

Confusing college students and middle school students may seem unusual, but this confusion was more remarkable. "Almost all the middle school students in the room are a part of the self-contained program for students with Emotional Behavioral Disabilities (EBD)," writes Alissa. "Students with EBD are noted for frequently displaying externalizing behaviors such as aggression, internalizing behaviors such as anxiety and depression and impaired relationships with teachers and peers. How are these students, who have struggled in so many social situations for so many years, able to handle such a situation with such poise that they are mistaken for college students?" She has an answer: "Public Achievement."[7]

The 2010–2011 pilot experiment in special education through Public Achievement in Fridley, launched soon after the Center for Democracy and Citizenship moved to Augsburg College in 2009, began a sometimes exhilarating, sometimes agonizingly slow process to change disempowerment to empowerment for special education students, an effort that empowered many teachers as well.

A Field in Transition

Students are placed in special education programs because they are identified with a disability under one of thirteen state-defined categories.[8] These labels are assigned to individuals because the disabilities are deemed to interfere with students' education. Depending on the nature and severity of the perceived disability, young people may be segregated from the mainstream educational community. African Americans, Native Americans, Latinos, and students of color are disproportionately placed in special education, with far-reaching consequences. For many, the placement leads to a lifetime of mental illness, unemployment, and entanglement with the criminal justice system.[9]

Another challenge in special education is teacher retention.[10] Up to two thirds of teachers leave within the first three years of beginning their careers, a departure rate twice that of general educators.[11] This departure, according to surveys, is mainly because of administrative and systemic factors and because many teachers view themselves as unable to make meaningful change.[12]

The field of disability studies calls for new approaches. The movement reframes disability as a social, cultural, and political phenomenon, in contrast to the dominant clinical, medical, and therapeutic perspectives on disability. "Critical special educators . . . foreground issues such as special education's insular, reductionist approach to research," write Jan Valle and David Connor. They challenge "an overreliance on the remediation of deficits; sustained use of intelligence testing; commonplace segregation based on disability and/or race; the professionalization of school failure; and the continued medicalization of disabled people."[13]

Disability studies adopts the positive youth development approach championed by Shelly Robertson in her work with adjudicated teens, described in Chapter 4. The field focuses mainly on young people's capacities, not their deficiencies. It rejects the perception of disability as a functional impairment, a characteristic that exists "in" the person, or a problem of the person to be "fixed" or "cured."[14] Instead, disability is understood as a construct within social and cultural environments that hides capacities.[15] Rather than segregation, disability studies advocates for the inclusion of students with disabilities into the school community.[16]

Disability studies scholars have found that self-determination skills and individual and collective (or civic) agency play important roles in better academic and social outcomes for students labeled with disabilities. For instance, because students in special education often exhibit problems with peer relationships, they need opportunities to learn skills of cooperative action, initiative, and self-determination. Parallel research from the field of executive function has established that people who "act out" with what are labeled behavior problems suffer from a misperception of others' motives, not from a lack of impulse control, which has long been considered the problem.[17] From the public work perspective, misperception of motives is a *political* problem that can be addressed through practices such as one-on-one meetings and power mapping.

Preservice teachers in special education need preparation to help develop such skills, habits of mind, and concepts. Yet, as education scholar Michael Gerber observes, few teacher education programs prepare teachers to create capacity-affirming pedagogical cultures that help students with varying talents, learning styles, and life stories to develop their unique gifts. Gerber asks whether the meaningful and productive inclusion of students with disabilities might require a "wholly different kind of expertise."[18]

Since its beginning in 2000, the Augsburg University special education program has focused on preparing a different kind of teacher by implementing a disability studies approach. The program asks preservice teachers to question the system they are being prepared to practice in with such questions as these: Why are so many students with disabilities still excluded from general education? What type of education do students who are labeled receive? What are teachers doing to include successfully their students in the general education setting? Though these questions were constantly discussed, theory and practice remained disconnected from each other. Faculty felt the Augsburg teacher-training program fell short of providing the experiences needed to prepare preservice teachers to make needed connections and to employ pedagogies that could change the system.

Fridley Middle School

The Center for Democracy and Citizenship moved from the University of Minnesota's Humphrey Institute to Augsburg College in 2009. The move was partly motivated by the belief that departments and programs in a medium-sized liberal arts college like Augsburg—with a citizenship mission, the spirit of an "urban settlement" woven into the fabric of a diverse immigrant neighborhood, and a conscious effort to resist the pressure to admit "the best" students defined by standardized test scores—have more freedom for innovation than colleges or universities intensely concerned with national rankings. Dennis Donovan soon began working with the special education preservice program to experiment with Public Achievement as an answer both to the disability studies critique and to the movement's call for action.

Dennis and two faculty members, Susan O'Connor and Donna Patterson, partnered with Michael Ricci and Alissa Blood-Knafla, graduates of the special education program at Augsburg who were teaching at Fridley Middle School. Their goal was to design an alternative class in the school using a Public Achievement approach. Over three years, they produced dramatic results. "Problem" students, most of whom were racial minorities and low income, students who in many schools would be strictly confined to their special education classes, became public leaders on issues such as school bullying. They built relationships and received recognition in the school and in the larger Fridley community. Their Public Achievement work brought them into contact with school administrators, community leaders, elected officials, and media outlets such as the local paper and Minnesota Public Radio.

For her master's thesis on the impact of Public Achievement, Blood used a qualitative methodology, conducting face-to-face conversations with five individual participants and making detailed observations of young people's behavior and interactions, which she recorded on videotape. She found substantial effects on students' self-image, sense of empowerment, and behavior. "They believed that they were more capable than they had ever thought they were in the past," Blood writes. "The students believed that they could be positive citizens and that the people who believed differently about them were wrong. This is a very powerful belief for any student in middle school."

Many expressed new pride and confidence. "I feel more mature and happy," said one. Another commented, "It makes me think I can do stuff that I haven't [before]." "I feel like we can change a lot of things in the world," said Katie.[19] "The kids get to decide." Blood observes that participants "began to express their feelings of power beyond the realm of Public Achievement." Allen commented, "If you set your mind to it, you can do it." Spud described his conviction that "we can change a lot of things in the world [like] Martin Luther King did." Finally, involvement in Public Achievement had notable effects on student behavior. "It is a good way to learn to be more respectful," said one. Katie observed, "We don't normally get to work with each other. It was nice to learn you have to take in what other people want and you can't just insist on doing everything yourself. This is a group effort." Spud said, "I didn't care about nobody but me. But now it makes me open and I care about other people, like my friend. I make sure his little sister gets home from the park okay. The old Spud would have been like, 'whatever.' I have changed. It may be slow, but I am getting there."[20]

The Public Achievement approach also transformed the work of Ricci and

Blood in ways that led them to relinquish control and empowered them. "My role is not to fix things for the kids but to say, 'This is your class, your mission. How are you going to do the work?' Our main task is to remind them, to guide them, not to tell them what to do," explains Ricci.[21]

The teachers became coaches and also partners with their students, who chose the issues and learned to address them effectively. In addition to the antibullying campaign, issues included trying to get a solar panel installed in the school, making murals to motivate peers to exercise, developing a support system for homeless children and another support system for hospitalized children with severe illnesses, launching a campaign to protect tigers, and educating the public about misconceptions regarding pit bull dogs. By tackling such issues, students built citizenship identities, habits, and skills such as negotiation, compromise, initiative, planning, organizing, and public speaking. They developed what Alissa calls "a public professional persona." According to school officials and the principal, the project improved and deepened connections between Fridley Middle School and the Fridley community.

The experiences also had a strong impact on the Augsburg students who coached in preparation for their careers as special education teachers. For instance, they learned how to let students in special education take the lead in projects and also how to better interest them in academic subject matter. Cheryl McClellan, an African American master of arts in education (MAE) student at Augsburg coached a team that sought to install a solar panel to light the school flag and a solar panel to heat school water. She said, "The idea is the students decide who is to be part of the project. They find out how to contact people, send them an email or call, and follow up." By the end of the year, the group, Solar Heroes, had not accomplished the project because of a lack of funds. But they had developed a plan, built public relationships with many people in the school and community, gained recognition for their respectful, knowledgeable work, and developed persistence. "You get a lot of 'no's," said Cheryl, "but they are learning the skills for moving forward." In a forum at Augsburg at the end of the spring semester in 2011, she described the empowering changes she had not anticipated: "At my core I am a better parent, a better citizen, and a better teacher."[22]

The experiences at Fridley shows how disability studies' *theory* can come alive in pedagogical *practice*. Since the three-year pilot, the special education program at Augsburg University has integrated Public Achievement's civic agency approach into its required core licensure curriculum. Twenty-seven students were involved in the first year. Over seven years, preservice teachers have been involved in Public Achievement in fifteen schools across the metro-politan Twin Cities area. Many have graduated and now teach in area schools.

Lessons

Public Achievement experiences over seven years had significant effects on preservice teachers' views of students, on their pedagogical methods, and on their understandings of what it means to be a teacher. They dramatize challenges in integrating Public Achievement into today's education that point to the need for innovations in teacher education. They also suggest the need for a larger citizenship movement that prepares teachers to be change agents, or citizen teachers, and creates "democracy schools" as civic hubs in the life of communities, strengthening values of culture and community and reinvigorating a democratic purpose for education.[23]

From early experiences in Fridley it was clear that coach involvement in Public Achievement could transform the way preservice teachers think about the children, about teaching, and about themselves as teachers. Preservice teachers often enter teacher-training programs wanting to be change agents within the broader education system and within special education. Many are disgruntled when they begin their coursework. Even if they are challenged with new ideas in theory, they enter a system that perpetuates the status quo with few skills to take effective action for change. They see themselves and their students as having limited agency and scope to create change. They often enter the profession with little practical knowledge about specific disabilities, a lacuna that leads them to focus on students' needs rather than their capacities. This reinforces the assumption that children with special needs must be "fixed" before they are part of the general education classroom.

Traditional teacher training conveys tools and techniques for teaching students labeled with disabilities, but it fails to prepare preservice teachers to understand and promote self-determination and citizenship skills, or even imagine that students labeled with disabilities have the capacity to participate in making change. Cheryl described how her attitude about disability was challenged and transformed. "I entered Augsburg not planning to focus on learning disabilities as my specialty area. I could not envision working with students having emotional and behavior disorders. In some ways I bought into the stereotypes that many have about these students." Public Achievement experiences changed her view. "I now have a new understanding of civic engagement as a teaching tool and philosophy capable of bridging the divide between special education and the greater community."[24]

As preservice teachers begin to view special education students differently, they also learn new practices and pedagogies through Public Achievement that enrich their *teaching* and *interactions* with students, other colleagues, and the educational system. They move away from a control mindset to one of builder and coach, from being mere technicians to being co-creators of an education that is empowering for them as well as the children. They also become able to embrace the "messiness" inherent in this paradigm shift, where both teacher and student may experience discomfort as they navigate unexplored possibilities together. New skills include patience. "You might go weeks with nothing great happening and a lot of frustrating things happening," said Courtney Anderson. "You might not have a lot of student buy-in at the beginning because students aren't used to recognizing that even they have questions."[25] Kayla Krebs, an MAE student working with Team Making a Way, focused on homelessness, explained, "I learned to be flexible and to let the students' voices shine." Similarly, Molly McInnis "learned how to let the students make the decisions and drive their own project. I didn't come in [as] a [conventional] teacher. I [learned] to listen and let them lead."[26] Preliminary research by faculty in Augsburg special education has shown an increase in self-efficacy in preservice teachers through their involvement.[27]

Preservice teachers learn to think about teaching and education in multi-dimensional ways. As one put it, "I only thought education was in a classroom, with desks, bells and schedules and the teacher at the front of the room. With Public Achievement I was looking at the classroom dynamics. The culture was student-centered."[28] Another observed, "I think [Public Achievement] pushes boundaries. You don't have to sit in a desk. You can be up and moving around. You can still be meeting standards and doing all you need to do."[29]

In her experiences with Public Achievement, Nora Ulseth built much deeper relationships with students than she had previously known how to do. "Getting to know them," she said, "I can see their potential, what they're interested in, what they love to do, their relationships, what their home life is." This understanding of her students led to a new vision of the classroom. "I want to create an environment in my classroom that doesn't feel like school, that's warm and joyful and in some ways a little chaotic."[30] Nora has come to believe that the foundation of real education is building relationships, not only in the school but in the neighborhood. She brings people in from the neighborhood and larger community, including a person from the school district, a football player, and a school police liaison. She also takes her students outside. "Opening the doors to my classroom, even walking to the donut shop and having my students order, seems more real than having some topic forced on them." When students in special education interact with others, their perception of the kids begins to change. Nora's police liaison officer began by not looking the students in the eye, but he gradually developed a very different view of who they were.

Sometimes simply sharing stories of young people has an impact. "I had a recent conversation with a public school teacher over lunch," Cheryl said. "As I described our PA project, this teacher stopped me. 'Middle school students are working on solar energy?' she asked." Then the teacher continued, "Wait, you mean kids with EBD?" For Cheryl, the exchange showed how Public Achievement challenges the subtle beliefs many have about students labeled EBD.

Courtney recognizes the identity of citizen as a key outgrowth of Public Achievement. It teaches "that students are citizens of this democracy. It's up to you to better it." Courtney believes that democracy "is in a lot of danger right now." In her view Public Achievement also challenges the status quo. Conventional education sustains dominant power dynamics. "All the power comes from the teacher who says this is what we're going to learn, and you're going to do it my way." In such teaching, "some students are going to be successful, usually students who are middle class and white and don't have disabilities. Some students are not going to do well." Recalling the approach Bernice Robinson took in the first citizenship school class on Johns Island in 1957 in which she built a robust learning process on the knowledge participants brought to the process, Courtney changes the power dynamic. "What are we going to learn?" she asks. "How am I going to learn from you and how are you going to learn from me? It can go both ways."

It is possible to connect Public Achievement work with policy demands for academic improvement. Phil O'Neil, a three-year veteran of Public Achievement who was coaching even before he began the master's program at Augsburg, observes that in his PA groups "the young people have used math, science, reading, social skills, social studies, democratic processes, assistive technologies." The different context of their learning makes an enormous difference. "They aren't afraid of not 'knowing' math as it just comes organically in the process." Phil sees this as more than simply education. "It is societal change based on education. Public Achievement is real world teaching."[31]

Public Achievement provides ways for students to become actors in their own learning rather than simply being acted upon, which is a huge paradigm shift. Jess Bowman described how her students, labeled on the autism spectrum and shaped by a system of learned helplessness, develop confidence through what may seem to be small steps. "'Oh my gosh, I can write a letter,' they say. 'I can make a call to someone I don't know.'" Often special education students "are quiet and shy. They sit in the corner. Public Achievement plays into their strengths and shows they can be amazing."[32] Another preservice student, working with students on the autism spectrum, began by thinking, "How can I really do anything with them?" Over time his attitude changed, seeing capacities in the students he had not known were there. Students who did not share eye contact and did not engage with others participated eagerly in projects where they felt ownership. They changed their patterns of social interaction in the process.[33]

In the Augsburg special education program, many preservice teachers coach in pairs as "co-coaches." This also teaches preservice teachers new skills and habits. "We have all gained confidence, not only in our skills as future teachers but also as future colleagues," said Cheryl. "We have had to learn to build and maintain collaborative relationships. In the end, the biggest change I've seen is that we have transformed from being scared of students to seeing ourselves as professionals." Cheryl said her experience carried her beyond the classroom and the school into nonteaching roles. "I refuse to accept any less of myself than what I ask from my students. I am finding my public voice and civic commitment as a result."

Hope and Frustration

Augsburg faculty hoped that by embedding Public Achievement into the special education licensure program they could train "a different type of teacher," one with skills and confidence not only to be effective in special education but also to be an effective change agent within the system. Preliminary research suggests that graduates do understand their students and their own capacity differently. For example, 89 percent see themselves as leaders in their school, program, and department "most of the time" or "sometimes." One hundred percent say they learned practices such as developing positive relationships with students, collaborating with colleagues, and managing disruptive behavior. Sixty percent have used PA principles in their classroom. These include encouragement, creating better environments, facilitating choice-making skills, allowing for organic learning, providing leadership opportunities, using community members as resources, co-creating an agenda, assigning roles to foster ownership of the learning environment, and supporting student-led initiatives. Finally, young teachers express a heightened intention to stay in the field. Intention in early teaching experience is strongly linked to actual long-term retention. Showing teachers' own sense of greater agency, 89 percent strongly agree with the statement "I can effectively make positive changes in my district," and the same percentage say they intend to stay in special education "a long time" or "until I retire."[34]

These stories of civic capacity-building generate a sense of work as far more than mere survival in a bureaucratic system. PA enriches teaching with tools to develop an empowering culture, both for students and for teachers themselves as professionals and citizens. The Public Achievement model provides a vehicle for teachers to awaken intrinsic motivations and move beyond the Pavlovian model of reward and punishment often in place in traditional special education programs. Some might call this shift a radical break with traditional practices; others view it as a desperately needed move from teachers' sense that they are helpless and sometimes hopeless toward a sense of participating in an empowering and hopeful career.

At the same time, preservice teachers who experienced Public Achievement often have major challenges when they begin their teaching careers and are frustrated by school bureaucracies, demands of standardized testing, administrators who have little understanding of the philosophy, and other teachers who see the pedagogy as a luxury or as unworkable. These are precisely the experiences that led Jamie Minor to quit teaching at Andersen Open School years ago, with the observation that teachers themselves "need to do Public Achievement."

Nora believes that "a lot of aspects of school can be arbitrary and disconnected from critical thinking and ownership." She had an especially hard time as a new teacher. "What is my role?" she wondered. She felt fear of being fired or reprimanded.

Becky Hamlin had powerful experiences with Public Achievement as a preservice coach, but she found it difficult to reproduce this when she tried to create space in her own classroom for students who were labeled EBD to take initiative. "I try to do Public Achievement–type things because I know these can work. One day we started talking about camping and they said, 'We want to go camping.'" She challenged them to make a plan, doing research on how much it would cost and what would be required for an overnight trip and figuring out how to present it to the principal. She coached them, but they took initiative in many areas she had not imagined, calling up five different parks, asking questions, going on websites. "Every single one of the kids was involved. Then I got reprimanded because it wasn't in the curriculum. 'How did you know the answer was going to be yes?'" the administrator asked.

Administrators asked questions like "Can we trust these kids out in public?" and "Who is going to want to chaperone this trip?"[35]

Courtney also observed how Public Achievement clashes with conventional school norms. "It's just not the traditional way of teaching. It's process-oriented and it's messy. As a teacher-coach, you have to have training in how to pull out what's inside." She believes that Public Achievement can help students understand "how the school operates, how society operates and give them tools to start changing it," but preservice teachers need a good deal of knowledge, both practical and philosophical, to convey this knowledge. She came back to Augsburg special education after several years in a large corporation. "My job was to make a lot of money. But I asked, 'What am I doing?' It was killing my soul." She decided teaching would be more fulfilling. Based on her experiences in business and also her family members, who were politically active and constantly encouraged her to take action if she objected to something, she has a number of suggestions for how Augsburg's special education's curriculum can be enriched to provide teachers with more political skills. "Others are going to ask questions," she says, anticipating what young teachers will find. "[They will say] this doesn't look like anything we've done before. It's going to cost money. How does it conform to the standards? You have to figure out how to win people over based on what's important to them. If someone is a numbers person, find some data. If they are in management, they are likely to want to do things that make them look good to their boss." She counsels that teachers need to learn how to address the diverse interests they will discover in a school and not become judgmental—an elemental organizing principle that one should always begin with "the world as it is." Courtney believes the key to becoming an effective change agent is understanding self-interests and forming relationships. Teachers also need to get to know the communities in which their schools are located. "What's important to that community? Who are the families? What is life like? What are the issues? Who are the community stakeholders?" She sees such skills and knowledge as essential qualities of a "citizen teacher."

Courtney's insights point to the importance of putting the transformation of special education in a context of democratic change in communities and the larger culture. Schools are not going to undertake significant change without a larger movement that revitalizes democracy and the meaning of citizenship. Intimations of such a movement may be visible at Maxfield Elementary School.

Maxfield School

Over the last several years, Dennis Donovan has brought preservice Augsburg special education students to work as coaches in Maxfield School, alongside coaches from other area colleges and the neighborhood. The story of the Rondo neighborhood that Maxfield Elementary School has helped to anchor for more than a hundred years illustrates in poignant ways the destruction of black communities.

Rondo is named for Joseph Rondeau, who moved to the neighborhood in the 1850s to escape discrimination in a European American community near Fort Snelling where he was experiencing prejudice because of his wife's mixed-race heritage. Rondo was a Jewish settlement area and haven for people of color and diverse immigrant groups. French Canadians followed Rondeau, and later German, Russian, Irish, and Jewish families did the same. Beginning in the 1910s and 1920s, blacks settled in Rondo in large numbers, and the Saint Paul neighborhood came to resemble other famous sites of intercultural and interracial mingling such as District Six of Cape Town and Sophiatown in Johannesburg, both vibrant areas destroyed in the apartheid era in South Africa. By the 1930s, half of Saint Paul's African American population lived in the Rondo neighborhood. "Even during the Jim Crow era, blacks and whites mixed relatively freely, interracial dating and even marriage sometimes took place," said one historian.[36] Rondo was a center of music and theater. Leading African American publications such as the *Appeal* and the *Northwestern Bulletin* gave voice to black community concerns. Roy Wilkins, a student at the University of Minnesota and later national president of the NAACP, helped establish a chapter of the civil rights organization. Hallie Q. Brown settlement created a civic learning center that resembled the Phyllis Wheatley House in Minneapolis. And integrated public schools such as Central High School and Maxfield and integrated parochial schools such as Saint Peter Claver, named after the venerated priest who championed enslaved West Africans for forty years, created a rich education culture that attracted many blacks fleeing racial discrimination in the South.

As early as the 1930s city planners began envisioning a highway to link the business districts of downtown Saint Paul and Minneapolis. After World War II, city engineers chose a route that ran through the middle of the community, located between University Avenue and Marshall Avenue. The Federal-Aid Highway Act of 1956 offered funding. The community fought back, with Reverend Floyd Massey and Timothy Howard organizing the Rondo–St. Anthony Improvement Association to protest the proposed route.[37] The association succeeded in changing the proposed design from an elevated to a depressed highway, with bridges connecting the two parts of the community. But, nonetheless, the community was broken in two. In September 1956, construction began. Police forcibly removed Reverend George David. "Like an unhealed wound, such memories are still raw," said Nathaniel Khaliq, Davis's grandson who was there when the bulldozers came.[38]

In 2016, Maxfield had 346 students, almost two thirds of whom were African American, compared to 25.6 percent in a typical Saint Paul school and 10 percent in the state as a whole. Fifty-seven percent are males and 43 percent females; 90.5 percent of the students participate in the National School Lunch Program, receiving free lunches. On standardized tests in March 2017, Maxfield students had a 17 percent passing rate in math compared to 45 percent in Saint Paul and 66 percent statewide, and a 17 percent passing rate in English language, compared to 40 percent in the district. Only 4 percent of students at Maxfield are in the Gifted and Talented Program, compared to 7 percent across all schools in Minnesota. Finally, 17 percent of students at Maxfield are labeled as "learning disabled," higher than the median in the state. Almost 12 percent of students labeled with learning disabilities were disciplined in 2015.[39]

The challenges Maxfield faces are obvious. So is the determination of teachers, coaches, and participants in Public Achievement. In the 2016–2017 school year, twenty-four coaches from Augsburg, the University of Minnesota, Bethel University, Minneapolis Community and Technical College, and elsewhere began working with one hundred students in fourth and fifth grades. The initial issues were bullying, the environment, racism, healthy living, graffiti and vandalism, relationships between the police and African American youth, animal abuse, homeless youth, children in hospitals, stray animals, the elderly, and anger management.[40] By March, one team had changed its name to Culture and Diversity based on students' perception that people lacked respect for other cultures. They wanted to draw attention to the problem and created a multicultural cookbook as one way to address it. "I think Public Achievement can show other people how to respect other people," said Mukwa, a fifth grader. The cookbook was featured on one of the local television stations. Mukwa felt that while the product was important, he had also learned a good deal. He used to think of himself as a bully, teasing people frequently, but Public Achievement taught him to work with other people, to understand them and their differences rather than to reject them. He also became more "the person he wants to be," understanding the value of teamwork. As he prepared to leave Maxfield for middle school at the end of the year, Mukwa felt confident about giving public presentations.[41]

Brandi Pottle, a fifth-grade teacher, has been a leader in Public Achievement in the school since its beginning, helping it become part of the school culture and developing as a powerful leader and "citizen teacher" in the process. She sees Public Achievement as a way to develop students' sense of agency and also to motivate them academically. "Public Achievement is a valuable experience for my students because it affords them the opportunity to have a voice in positive change," she says. "Too often, adults make the decisions when it comes to changes our school/community needs." Through Public Achievement, students—whom she calls "our scholars"—"learn how to be active change agents by means of selecting topics and then cooperatively working on problem solving and what they need to do to bring about change." She observes that Public Achievement has also strengthened parents' connections to the school.[42] As a result of Public Achievement, writes Elaine Eschenbacher, Maxfield now has security on their back door, recycling bins in each classroom, and master gardeners doing projects around the school and community. "Nothing beats the pride on the faces of our positive change agents," says Pottle. She also believes it impacts adults' views of children, showing that "kids have just as much to teach and learn as adults do."[43]

In Maxfield the Cultural Wellness Center is also active, working with Public Achievement. Its idea is to bring hope by acquainting students and others with the powerful heritage of African Americans, with the intention "to usher in a new chapter of the school's history, bringing it back to the glories of the old Rondo community's proud historical past and heritage." Mary K. Boyd, a leading educator in Saint Paul, described the legacy of preparing "many who have gone on to great power in this community in spite of the odds against them," including well-known leaders such as Michael Wright of Golden Thymes Café, Bill Murray, Curriser Mae Adams, Setchem Thesmaat Steward, and Hatyba Assutinit Massey. Most participate in the Cultural Wellness Center's "School of Elders" at Maxfield. "In the vast majority of cases, students in the predominately African American classrooms of Maxfield in recent years have had tragically low academic performance," wrote Azzahir in an article reflecting on the progress the partnership had made by 2016, the 125th anniversary of the school. "Despite the endless effort and desire of school officials and parents to help the children and to reverse this heartbreaking downward spiral, they were witnessing most of their students fall victim to failure." Convinced that "it is culture that held us to greatness, as we held it *with* greatness," she argued that "only culture can counteract the severity and uncontested wrath of the environments children are experiencing." The Cultural Wellness Center's diagnosis was that "the failure is not in the children.

It is in the curriculum, the methods of delivering the knowledge, and the de-culturalized knowledge itself."

In the last several years, Public Achievement and the Cultural Wellness Center have had an impact. Student suspensions fell significantly from 2014 to 2016. There was also an increase in reading scores by 6 percent and math scores by 9.9 percent in one year.[44] Educators, students, coaches, and community members have a long way to go to overcome "the empowerment gap." But they have made a beginning.

8

Artisans of the Common Good

Harry C. Boyte

**Education then, beyond all other devices
of human origin, is a great equalizer.**
—Horace Mann, Twelfth Annual Report to the
Massachusetts State Board of Education[1]

Augsburg University's special education program, described in Chapter 7, points toward democratic cultural change "upstream," in professional training programs and disciplines that shape the identities and practices of today's leaders. The rich tradition of Catholic social thought, which stresses the priority of the everyday educational *work* of "culture making," has much to contribute to imagining these larger possibilities.

Pope Francis builds on and amplifies Catholic thinking about the public meaning of work, both paid and unpaid. In his homily on New Year's Eve 2017, he expressed "gratitude for all those persons who, every day, contribute with small but precious gestures to the common good." He draws attention, as the bishop of Rome, to those "who live with open hearts in the city," using the example—vivid for denizens of Rome, which has the dubious distinction of being the auto accident capital of Europe—of "those people who move in traffic with good sense and prudence." He praises many others: "Those who respect public spaces, and report things that aren't right; those who are attentive to the elderly and people in difficulty and so on. These and a thousand other behaviors express concretely love for the city," he said. They exemplify, "without giving speeches, without publicity . . . a style of practical civic education for daily life."[2]

In his homily Francis also highlighted the role of educators: "Parents, teachers and all educators who, with the same style, seek to form children and teenagers in a civic sense, with an ethic of responsibility, educating them to feel part [of the city], to take care of it, and to be interested in the reality that surrounds them." These, he said, are "artisans of the common good who love their city not with words but with deeds." In July 2015, Francis, in a speech to the Pontifical Catholic University of Ecuador, had also emphasized the importance of education and advanced a vivid image of citizens as co-creators. "God does not only give us life," he said. God also "gives human beings a task . . . to be a part of [God's] creative work. . . . I am giving you your hands and those of your brothers and sisters . . . the space that God gives us to build up with one another, to build a 'we.'"[3]

Today, as Lani Guinier's *The Tyranny of the Meritocracy*, William Deresiewicz's *Excellent Sheep*, and Lauren Rivera's *Pedigree* detail, higher education's purposes and practices are, in the main, a long way from building a "we." Rather, they are based on individualistic and largely materialistic definitions of success, with cost to the democracy. "When we don't encourage collaboration and the whole host of complementary skills . . . we lose out," Guinier writes. "We choose people who excel at the same, limited things; admit them to the best schools; and send them off to do their own individual work in their own individual careers."[4] Pope Francis's focus on the everyday culture-building roles of higher education through "civic education for daily life" represents an alternative view of education, recalling a rich heritage that shows some signs of revival.

One outstanding example of such revival is the Netter Center at the University of Pennsylvania, which celebrated its twenty-fifth anniversary in the fall of 2017. The Netter Center, founded by Ira Harkavy, has pioneered the creating of respectful, lasting, deep partnerships between higher education and surrounding communities. It has taken leadership in initiatives such as the Coalition for Community Schools, described in Chapter 2, and the Anchor Institution Task Force with more than nine hundred member colleges and universities, exploring ways to strengthen the economic, civic, and social contributions of schools to the communities in which they are located.[5] Such work builds on a history.

Democratic Traditions

The first and most essential charge upon higher education is that at all its levels and in all its fields of specialization it shall be the carrier of democratic values, ideals, and processes.
—Presidential Commission on Higher Education, 1947[6]

David Mathews, who led the process of desegregation at the University of Alabama as president in the 1960s and 1970s before becoming secretary of the Department of Health, Education, and Welfare in the administration of President Ford, describes a conference on higher education at the department in 1977. Earl Cheit, dean of the business school at Berkeley, worried that trends were pushing higher education toward being "whipped into a bureaucratic mold." These threatened to turn colleges and universities into mechanisms that would "process human beings for strictly utilitarian ends," erasing the memory that "our institutions began as movements."[7]

Colleges and universities like Augsburg University, founded in 1869, were founded as part of a movement. Such liberal arts schools were part of an "educational world in which productive, manual labor was valued, egalitarian co-education was emphasized, and the regional culture was open to new ideas," writes Kenneth Wheeler in *Cultivating Regionalism*, describing the proliferation of small midwestern colleges in the nineteenth century, usually founded by religious groups. "Members of small, usually rural denominations were more egalitarian, practical, anti-elitist, and evangelical and their gender ideals didn't emphasize separate spheres or same-sex education." They combined work and learning, substituting labor for the gymnastics that characterized Eastern education and the military drill of the South. They had strong public values that emphasized the dignity and intrinsic worth of workers, "evinc[ing] a 'deep disquiet' with an economic system that valued even humans in monetary terms." They were leaders in abolitionism and women's suffrage.[8]

Public universities played parallel roles in seeking to shape a democratic culture. The University of Michigan in the late nineteenth century was at the center of a movement that aimed to create public universities as civic institutions with a commitment to access for a diverse citizenry and extensive engagement with society. James B. Angell, Michigan's president from 1871 to 1909, believed that public universities needed both to embody and also to help shape the dynamics of a changing democratic society. He built on the pioneering admission of women in 1870 to create a "democratic atmosphere" on campus, full of debate, discussion, experimentalism, and open play of different viewpoints. The seminar was increasingly used as a teaching method to engage students in interactive education. Students also were able to take a wider selection of courses.[9]

Land-grant colleges and land grants, established by the Morrill Act in 1862, and the black colleges and universities created in 1890 emphasized a combination of "liberal arts" and "practical arts." Some used the term "public work" to convey this integration and the work of college graduates. Liberty Hyde Bailey, dean of agriculture at Cornell and a leading horticulturalist who chaired the Country Life Commission, which laid out the philosophy of cooperative extension, the community arm of land grants, often spoke in these terms. He argued the need to connect "public work to the development of democracy, not so much a form of government as a real democratic expression on the part of the people." For Bailey politics was about "political affairs," akin to citizen politics. "It is not sufficient to train technically in the trades and crafts and arts to the end of securing greater economic efficiency," he said. An efficiency focus displaced "self-action on the part of the people." Bailey proposed that education "should . . . function politically. . . . Every democracy must reach far beyond what is commonly known as economic efficiency and do everything it can to enable those in the backgrounds to maintain their standing and their pride and to partake in the making of political affairs."[10]

Land-grant scientists, whom the historian Andrew Jewett calls "scientific democrats," looked at science not as a set of value-free techniques but as cultural practices of free inquiry and cooperative experiment. In the New Deal during the 1930s, scientific democrats gained substantial footholds in the U.S. Department of Agriculture and other federal agencies. In local communities, professionals such as home economics agents in cooperative extension were often "citizen professionals" whose main objective was helping communities develop capacity for self-directed public work. This emphasis challenged conventional yardsticks of success. As Isabel Bevier put it, home economics gave extension work in land-grant colleges "an idealism and a cultural element . . . as well as a new measuring stick. Heretofore, results had been largely in terms of livestock or crops; hereafter, the measure of successful agriculture was the kind of life produced."[11]

Despite the proliferation of civic and community engagement centers, service-learning initiatives, and experiential-learning projects in higher education, this view of colleges and universities as preparing their students to be citizens through their everyday work—citizen teachers, citizen business owners, citizen lawyers, citizen nurses, citizen politicians—has largely disappeared. But here and there a few colleges and universities have begun to revive the concept. This chapter looks at three groups in higher education who are "artisans of the common good": students, whose energy and openness to the future provide wellsprings for change; faculty, whose commitment to their institutions and responsibility for curriculum place them at the center of democratic educational purpose; and administrators and other institutional leaders who are artisans of civic infrastructure.

Students as Artisans of Possibility
University of Maryland, Baltimore County

"Given the rancorous tone of current public debate and the gridlock in government, college students are understandably skeptical about politics and public life," wrote Kaylesh Ramu, a leader in a student movement to create an empowering culture of civic agency at the University of Maryland, Baltimore County (UMBC), in a piece for the *Baltimore Sun*. She coauthored the opinion piece with David Hoffman, the assistant director of student life for civic agency. "This pessimistic view may be the received wisdom, but we see reasons for hope on many college campuses," wrote Ramu and Hoffman. "At the University of Maryland Baltimore County, students are practicing a different kind of politics that bridges differences and strengthens communities." They described many examples. One team of Jewish and Muslim students worked with the administration to bring kosher and halal options to the campus cafeteria. Others redesigned spaces to make them more public, reduced the school's greenhouse-gas emissions, encouraged healthy lifestyles, and sought to boost campus spirit. The Student Government Association (SGA) "long ago leapt beyond the 'let's pretend' model of student government to become a catalyst for students' creativity and engagement."

UMBC was a founding partner of the Civic Agency Initiative that we organized with the American Democracy Project, an initiative of the American Association of State Colleges and Universities. Students and staff picked up concepts and practices of civic agency and public work with enthusiasm. For almost a decade, the SGA, using a public work approach, has been a national model for rethinking its role, which had emphasized the delivery of services to students who were seen as customers. It now recognizes students of different views and backgrounds as full of talents and seeks to support their public work contributing to UMBC. The "BreakingGround" website at UMBC highlights this continuing story, one that is not without conflict. "On a campus with UMBC's diversity, disagreements are inevitable," write Ramu and Hoffman. "The work of building partnerships and allocating scarce resources can be messy and complicated. This is where 'politics' comes in: not as a dirty word or the power-seeking tactics of political elites, but as a set of skills everyone can use to find common ground and to get things done. The kind of generative politics practiced at UMBC . . . brings faculty, staff, students, alumni and community partners together to envision alternative futures and solve problems."[12]

University of Minnesota

The generative politics at UMBC infuses the fledgling Citizen Student Movement at the University of Minnesota. Dennis Donovan's class Organizing for the Public Good has played a key role. "Whether you are conservative or liberal, student or professor, there is a problem on our campus that cannot be ignored any longer," wrote Charlie Carlson, Kat Gehl, and Zach Macon, University of Minnesota undergraduates in Dennis's class, for the publication *MinnPost* in the spring of 2017. They were part of a group of seven who chose to do a public work project on polarization. "The polarization of groups, opinions, and ideas on campus . . . was raised among a group of students who hold all political leanings," they said. "We began our journey as seven students looking to close the divide amongst different opinions and create a conversation as to why every opinion should be valued."[13]

Dennis's interest in each student in his class makes a great deal of difference. "One thing that I took away from this class is just the genuine care that Dennis, our professor, had for all of us," wrote Taylor Morgan, who began the class suspicious of an Italian American professor. She lumped him in with other whites, for whom she harbored deep distrust. But her view soon changed. "Every day he would say hello to us and ask us individually how we were doing and he knew about how the volleyball, basketball and football players were doing in their season. This really meant a lot to me because not many professors genuinely care about a student's day." Dennis also became a model for her. The class "really opened my eyes to the fact that I need to develop better relationships with people and the way that I do that is to ask people how they are and to show that I care." It helped restore her faith in people.[14]

Ali Oosterhuis describes what made the class such a powerful experience for her and others. "Dennis's class works because it makes everyone think for themselves. It creates those free spaces that you don't usually see. A lot of times people are talking in a bubble. Everyone in your bubble agrees. Ideas bounce back. Other people don't feel like they can express what they actually believe. They hide." Ali believes that the method of public narrative, an adaptation of one-on-ones in which people learn to reflect on and tell their own story from the perspective of their public growth, creates a foundation. "It grounded people and let people figure out who they were. A lot of people came to college and are doing things, but they never thought how their upbringing and everything connects to who they are. Having respect for that, and respecting everyone else's story is huge." Like Kaylesh Ramu at UMBC, Ali believes in the importance of a different kind of politics "as a way to deal with people constructively who have different views. [That] was really transformative for a lot of us."

Alumni of Dennis Donovan's class together with Public Achievement coaches in the Twin Cities are creating a "citizen student movement" with three practices: conducting "civic deliberations" in which people learn to talk across differences; training each other and other students, in colleges and high schools, in public work practices such as one-on-ones and power mapping; and implementing public work projects.

One public work project of the Citizen Student Movement addresses incarceration by seeking to make the insights of inmates more widely known. It grows from a Public Achievement project Dennis is doing with Stillwater prison inmates. Dennis regularly takes students from his class as well as teachers and others from Maxfield to the monthly meetings. Steven Vogel described his experience. "We tend to think of prisons as places of downtrodden dreams, deranged individuals, and empty shells of human beings. Yet, my experience at Stillwater Prison last week could not have proved more contrary," he wrote in a report for an independent study. "I met with about 20 inmates in a round table discussion. It occurs monthly, with everyone giving updates on their progress toward getting out, their career ambitions within the prison, and what they hope to change when they get out." Steven was impressed with the examples the inmates were setting for a generation of high-achieving young people who have learned to fear failure. "It's that fear of failure in pursuit of perfection that causes such an unnatural state. We are human: we mess up," he wrote. "When I make my first error, large or small, I feel comfortable knowing that I can only go up from there—afterward there is only minimal pressure because the perfectionist façade has already been broken. By the same token, the inmates had some of the most hope and raw intelligence gathered into one room that I have seen in a long while. Being in prison, the inmates have already sort of hit society's bottom—they don't really have much more to lose." He was also taken with the seriousness of the discussion. "I was highly impressed by the level of professional demeanor and optimism. The guy sitting next to me told me about how he became a programming instructor for the other inmates because he had become so proficient in his 10 years there so far. Another mentioned how he recently got his poems published because a visitor was impressed with his work."[15]

The Citizen Student Movement meetings also incorporate the reflective practices that come from community organizing. In one meeting they recorded their thoughts as they contrasted the relational qualities of citizen politics with the social media world in which young people live today. Julien Kafo, a black football player from Canada, expressed his concerns. "We don't have communications anymore," he said. "There's just people bashing each other because they're behind a screen and they're protected." Julien believes it's crucial to understand "that we come from different places." Sounding like Jane Addams, he argued for a stance beyond "you were raised right and I was raised wrong," stressing the importance of recognizing different stories, experiences, and cultures.[16] The group saw positive uses of social media such as spreading ideas and keeping in touch with friends and family far away. They are also committed to practices, such as one-on-ones, that probe for other people's "self-interests," their stories. "That idea of self-interest really opened my eyes," said Zach. "It's cliché to say we are all human, we come from all walks of life, but I think it's time we take that seriously."[17]

Ali and others in the Citizen Student Movement study examples of citizen professionals. She described how her reading of *Freedom's Teacher*, the biography of Septima Clark, inspired her to become a citizen lawyer. "My goal over the next few years is to create a concrete mission that I can work toward during my career as a citizen lawyer," she says. "This feat will not be easy. However, my vision will propel me on the path of creating change as a citizen professional and making a difference in the world in the years to come. I will use the skills I have learned through Public Achievement, this book, and organizing experiences I have had so far to follow a rich tradition of organizing."[18] It is still too early to assess the fate of the Citizen Student Movement, but it clearly has already had an effect on those involved, teaching the skills and awakening the spirit of civic artisanship.

Denison University

At Denison University, another important school in our public work network, students are beginning to learn how to do public work in their residence halls. Ivy Distle, who is head resident in the Shepardson Residence at Denison University, sees public work and citizen politics as the way to counter students' tendency to retreat to identity-based organizations in times of turbulence.

"Last year after the [2016] election there was a lot of student protest, but there wasn't much relationship outside of like-minded groups," she described. Her residence hall is part of a university-wide experiment to redefine *halls* as residential *communities* where diverse students learn to live together as "neighbors" who develop the skills of building relationships across differences and handling conflicts, whether about loud noises or dirty dishes, in constructive ways. The point is not to depend on intervention by the residence advisors. Ivy is enthusiastic about the experiment but also realistic about the challenges. "When students were faced with political unrest they fell back on organizations that represent their identity, people like themselves. These were a safe and secure space." Ivy, who came up through the ranks of residential advisors (RA) to be head resident of a building with 150 students, likes the concept of residential community because it fits her approach. "In my sophomore year I applied to be a residential advisor and got the job in one of the larger halls. There were between thirty and thirty-two women on my floor, varying over the year." Most were students with very different interests than hers. Ivy is a double major in biology and art. "I learned about how extroverted I am. I like building relationships and spending time with people and finding out who they are. A lot of my job was to figure out people from sororities and from sports. I haven't been involved in either." Her relationship-building skills made a difference. "A lot of time when an RA knocks on a student's door it's not a good sign. There is a lot of negative feeling." But she took a more relational approach than is customary. "I'd invite students to come hang out, and would have ten or fifteen in my programs."[19]

As is true at UMBC and UMN, staff with roots and authority in the institution play key roles in sustaining students' civic learning. Erik Farley, dean of student leadership development, stresses the importance of experiments that teach the skills of living in communities. "'How do communities build community?' is key," he says. "It's a mistake to assume that folks have rapport. But a foundation of knowing each other's stories has real potential to mitigate violence and vandalism. People can learn not only to have knowledge of each other but also to respect the people they share space with." Erik believes that practices like one-on-one meetings and civic deliberations, which Dennis Donovan has been teaching their RAs, hall advisors, and student affairs staff, "are just what students are asking for. Students fumble around with people who are unlike themselves, afraid to make a mistake, be seen as homophobic or something else." Erik points to the potential of weaving different kinds of deliberative spaces into the fabric of everyday life. "The flag pole [in the middle of the campus] has been our Hyde Park, where people can say anything they want. It's a lightning rod for blowing off steam. But it doesn't allow space for meaningful interaction. We need students to develop confidence in their ability to have these conversations, and take these skills into their professional lives." Based on his experience as one of the few African Americans at Denison in the early 2000s, he sees the challenges of an environment where "most people are not like me" as potential opportunities for growth if students develop the skills to negotiate their differences. "You have to understand the culture you're operating in," he says.[20]

Faculty as Artisans of Civic Learning

Maria Avila, born in Mexico, worked as a community organizer with the Industrial Areas Foundation in Los Angeles and other areas of the Southwest for a decade. Then she took a job as director of a newly created Center for Community Based Learning (CCBL) at Occidental College in 2001 because her colleagues in the IAF "helped me see that I could explore this new opportunity to create societal change from a different angle." In the job interview, she also found potential allies among the faculty and others "interested in changing the institutional culture in which civic engagement was viewed as charity and service."[21] I met Maria just as she was taking this position, and we developed a long-standing relationship. She experimented with Public Achievement and has introduced key concepts such as public work, civic agency, and civic professional to those at Occidental.

Occidental is a small, highly regarded residential institution that calls itself the "liberal arts college of Los Angeles." Fifteen minutes northeast of downtown Los Angeles, it is surrounded by poor and middle-income neighborhoods with a diverse racial and cultural mix. Maria came to the work with assumptions drawn from her organizing experience: the college should be treated as a community in and of itself; all communities have existing or potential leaders; long-term transformational and reciprocal engagement must be co-created and coassessed by relevant stakeholders; and engagement should aim at transforming the college, partnering community organizations, and the community at large.[22]

In her first year at Occidental she had more than one hundred one-on-one meetings with administrators, faculty, students, and community partners. "In the early stages of the relational work at Occidental it became apparent . . . that in this institution faculty, and tenured faculty in particular, were key in the power structure." This insight for Maria and the organizing team, which she called a "collective of leaders," did not come formal "power analysis," though her work involved teaching and undertaking such power analysis. "Rather, it came to us in countless individual and group conversations with faculty who were central in developing the charge of the CCBL. . . . We learned that, compared to administrators and students, faculty tend to stay the longest at the college and their tenured status gives them job protection." Further, faculty were key to the mission she and others developed for CCBL: to create a variety of community-based learning opportunities for students grounded in sustained, reciprocal partnerships with community groups.[23] Over a decade of organizing, Maria saw considerable change and development in faculty members, community members, and the culture as a whole.

One highly regarded young faculty member at Occidental, Regina Freer, a founder of the CCBL, had a strong interest in building relationships with community groups. "Civic engagement is not charity," she said. "It's about partnership." The work of CCBL also created new ways for her to deepen her knowledge of and connections to community institutions. Freer had long had relationships with the staff of the Southern California Library in South Los Angeles. Through a series of meetings facilitated by CCBL, she developed a course that involved taking students to the library, teaching them archival skills, and developing ways for them to make presentations throughout the community to encourage young people to explore the collections. Freer drove each week to the library, and the experiences helped build a model for other faculty to emulate. "Constant communication was critical for making midstream adjustments," she said. "I had to adjust my expectations of the amount of time the staff could devote . . . while the library staff had to adjust their expectations of the level of historical knowledge the students brought."[24]

Alan Knoerr, who joined the math department in 1991, was interested in making math education more widely accessible. Earlier he helped to change the curriculum. "Ten years later . . . this program had largely faded," he said. "I realized that I did not know enough about how power and institutions worked to be able to institutionalize changes I had helped bring about." Knoerr became a long-term member of the CCBL faculty committee and learned a great deal about power and politics in higher education and the larger community. Part of his work entailed creating a partnership with the math department at Franklin High School. He and three other faculty colleagues met individually and collectively with math teachers and administrators at Franklin and decided they wanted to collaborate. Together they designed a seminar course at Occidental, Math 201: Mathematics, Education and Access to Power, in which students studied and discussed writings about cognitive science, pedagogy, and the politics of math education. They also worked with students at Franklin and other schools. "Occidental students have found this to be a life-changing course," Knoerr observes. A significant number of students became active in social change and social justice work. Some became math teachers. Franklin also benefited, creating an innovative math curriculum.[25]

Maria has a clear-eyed view of the challenges of organizing in academic cultures in which relationships count for much less than reports and information campaigns. She experienced tension between her emphasis on developing the talents and public skills of others and the expectations that she be the public face of CCBL. In her organizing she often had to deal with conflicts between faculty and administrators, on the one hand, and faculty and student affairs staff, on the other. She also encountered conflicts around institutional culture change and diversity. "Ultimately," she concludes, "this challenge raises the question of how we define institutional culture change."[26]

For all the challenges, Maria's organizing accomplished a great deal. Her experiences are captured in her book, *Transformative Civic Engagement through Community Organizing*. Definitions of teaching and scholarship and the way these are assessed changed across the whole school. New faculty positions incorporated an emphasis on community connections. Formal structures such as the faculty committee of the CCBL became highly valued and recognized. "We created a culture that values and rewards reciprocal civic engagement, throughout the disciplines, on and off campus," Maria explains. "Partly because this culture became institutionalized but particularly because the group of faculty who came to own the work of the CCBL as their own, it continues to exist . . . surviving various administrations and their various agendas regarding civic engagement and my own departure from the college in 2011." She came away from her organizing at Occidental—she continues organizing at other universities and in the higher education network Imagining America—convinced change is possible. "Cultural transformation can happen, but . . . this is a slow, intentional and strategic process."[27]

In sum, the organizing the work of the college and many individuals in the college became more public—filled with public purposes and animated by much more collaboration within the institution and beyond. Maria Avila's reference to the transience and changing agendas of administrators highlights the role of those who have power to be artisans of civic infrastructure.

Artisans of Civic Infrastructure

Denison University

The president of Denison University since 2013, Adam Weinberg has played a key role envisioning, organizing, and crafting an infrastructure of civic change by working with allies.[28] Adam breaks the normal presidential mold. His background in social sciences and humanities prepares him to see and analyze structures, injustices, patterns of oppression, and social problems. But such academic training does not usually equip people to see or know much about civic agency. As the sociologist Philip Nyden observes, academics are problem-oriented, not solution-oriented. Sociology departments have courses on "social problems," not "social solutions." In contrast, Weinberg advances a lived way of knowing in which we learn to see, know, and experience civic agency.

Adam Weinberg comes from a southern Jewish family. His father was a prominent doctor, the first to diagnose patterns of manic depression among adolescents. But his family also experienced discrimination because of their faith. "My father spent a lot of time trying to get schools to understand that the problem wasn't with kids who couldn't sit still but the problem was the structure of schools. If the schools were student-centered rather than administrator-centered the kids would thrive."

Weinberg was mentored by academics in sociology who straddled the line between academics and deep engagement in communities. "They were civic professionals. I loved what they were doing. Their example filled both of my needs, for deep intellectual work and involvement in civic life." He developed a passion about "the ways the sociological imagination can help us both better understand these social processes and act on them to create more space for democratic ways of living." He came to Colgate University as a young faculty member when the college was working with citizens in the community on economic and social revitalization. The experiences showed him ways to be an engaged citizen and a scholar. "People without formal education had a lot to teach me."

When Weinberg became dean of the college at Colgate, in charge of student affairs, he and his colleagues ambitiously organized to change the pervasive consumer culture on campus, which they dubbed "Club Med." They began working with the Center for Democracy and Citizenship on the concept and practices of public work, seeking to transform an entitlement culture into a culture in which students learned to be "innovators, creators and problem solvers." This required shifting from a professional service model "where staff solves problems for students" and required learning new ways to think about where civic learning can take place. "We were sending students out into the community to do community work when in fact the campus was a laboratory of civic learning opportunities." They began to see opportunities "in campus controversies, residential halls, student organizations, and other places where students learn skills, habits, and values of public work."

He brought these interests to Denison, a school long committed to service learning, community service, and community engagement. This foundation has allowed Weinberg to work with faculty, students, and student development staff to push into new territories. Adam's concept of what colleges can contribute to civic life has broadened by rethinking what "democracy" means. "I went into the president's role focused on how students and faculty could do more service learning and fund more investment in the community. But I came to understand that we need a deeper view of democracy, civic agency, and the role that complex organizations like universities play in the local community." Rethinking democracy led Adam to consider new questions.

"Do we encourage faculty to get involved in local causes and projects? Do we support them when they want to blend their teaching, research, and civic work? Do we allow staff to attend civic meetings that take place during the workday? How do we treat faculty and staff when they take public stands that might not benefit the college? How do we respond when students raise important public issues on our campus?" Colleges and universities are large and influential employers and presences. "We play a much larger role in the life of our communities than we think," he reflects. "We can be real forces for developing civic agency. For instance, when important decisions are being made in the local community it's usually the politicians, developers, bankers, and other prominent leaders. As a college president I can get people involved who typically don't get invited to the table when decisions are made." Adam asks, "How do we harness the power of complex institutions to create more opportunity for public work in the local community?" He has an unusual view of the work of presidents. "So often presidents take a traditional political view. They figure out how to move constituencies who are aligned with them to push through whatever agenda they're trying to push through."

In contrast, "if you think about change as a community-building process, you purposively find those who disagree with you and find ways to work together across differences over a longer period of time to get to the right outcome." He also has championed new ways for Denison faculty to become public intellectuals and organizers. For instance, the Between Coasts initiative organized by Jack Shuler, an English professor with journalistic experience, is convening journalists in the Midwest. Its mission is to revive the understanding of journalists as public storytellers as a way for local communities to see themselves and their potential in new ways. It is also aimed at "those of you who recognize that you might be out of touch with what's going on in 'Flyover Country' (beyond the echo chambers of Los Angeles and New York or your Facebook feed)." Shuler calls Between Coasts "a new model of community-based but nationally and internationally focused journalism. We want journalism that's rooted in a place and written by the people who live there."[29]

Adam found allies among the student affairs staff for the idea of seeing campus life itself as a laboratory for experiments in civic learning. A vision of residential halls as diverse neighborhoods where students can learn to be citizens was compelling, but it takes savvy political organizing and grounding in a local culture to make it last. Laurel Kenney, vice president for student development, liked the vision and also realized it had to be grounded in the institution's history and culture.[30] Even before Adam's arrival, the student affairs staff were "thinking much more about our students as unique individuals with different cultural backgrounds, health questions and other qualities." Student affairs sought to make a philosophical shift away from seeing staff as entertainers and residential advisors who maintain order and rules. "We wanted to create a vibrant student life. What does that look like? How can we learn in the process?" They anchored changes in what Laurel calls "Denison legacy strengths," which they identified as leadership development, civic engagement, creative problem-solving or social innovation, and appreciation for diversity of thought. They also identified challenges, especially in the residence halls. "We shifted 'residence life' to 'residence education,' with the hope that education grounded in the concept of student well-being and persistence would create places where students could learn life skills. The truth is we had a hard time getting that off the ground. Residence halls were 'tired spaces' [old facilities with many structural problems] and staff got sidelined on facilities issues." The vision is to "build a model of residential communities that resonates with Denison's unique culture, values, history, and student body." She lists components such as cultivating the skills of democratic living by co-creating communities where students find a sense of home and which are respectful, fun, safe, and interesting. If it works, she adds, "we'll have both lived into the mission of the College and met the exigencies and challenges of the complex world our students are facing."[31] The effort is still in the early stages but has begun to gain wide recognition.

Lone Star Community College

In August 2017, Houston made the news in a spectacular way. Hurricane Harvey was a "once in a thousand year event," according to meteorologists.[32]

Several weeks after Charlottesville, working-class men often reduced to "deplorables" in the centers of intellectual fashion confounded expectations. "The working class, in large part, is being saved by the working class," wrote Manny Fernandez in the *New York Times*. "Recreational vehicles—airboats, Jet Skis, motorized fishing boats—have rushed to the aid of people trapped in their homes, steered by welders, roofers, mechanics, and fishermen wearing shorts, headlamps, and ponchos." Alongside government relief efforts "was an equally giant volunteer rescue effort that operated with little official guidance."[33] The blue-collar heroes of this story rescued people without regard to race, legal status, partisanship, sexual orientation, or income, as if descendants of those who had participated in the Civilian Conservation Corps, as described in Chapter 1, were making a collective statement that they, like their grandfathers in the Great Depression, had things to contribute to communities and the nation but with more tolerance for diversity. Among the rescue brigade were some who had been active in Public Achievement and other public work efforts at Lone Star Community College.

Four months earlier I had participated in the annual Public Achievement celebration in Kingwood, a suburb of Houston, held at Italiano's, a local restaurant. I thought about the pedagogy and co-creative citizen politics as the waters rose after the vast hurricane.

On April 25, the banquet room at Italiano's was full of young people, parents, teachers, principals, and faculty and students from Lone Star Community College, with several political leaders also in attendance. The event highlighted stories about children and teenagers—second graders from Southside Elementary School in Cleveland, Texas; high school students from Splendora; students from Humble ISD MOSAIC, a special education program housed at Lone Star College. Coaches and students described their work on issues such as protecting children from danger on the Internet, bullying, stray cats, and recycling. Parents were amazed to hear about their children negotiating with city officials and school administrators. Teachers and principals voiced enthusiasm about the motivation they had seen over the year. College student coaches said the experience changed their lives.

Public Achievement in the Houston area is organized out of Lone Star College by J. (John) Theis, a partner with the Center for Democracy and Citizenship since the early 2000s when he was teaching at Avila College in Kansas City. John has been both a faculty member (chair for a time of the political science department) and an administrator in charge of civic engagement initiatives across the six campuses of the Lone Star system. In both roles he has proven to be a skilled architect of change. He believes in Public Achievement's effectiveness as a civic education pedagogy. He is also committed to creating civic learning opportunities in many parts of Lone Star academic and campus life. His center organizes civic deliberations, conversations in which people learn to talk respectfully across radical differences even about hot button topics. The center gained local attention when it organized a conversation about pending Texas legislation that would allow guns on college campuses. Many local gun rights champions came to the event, as did opponents. The general feeling was that people respected each other's views. John Theis is progressive, but he is critical of elitist and technocratic trends in today's liberal politics. Most importantly, he embodies cross-partisan civic populist politics in his engagement in the larger community. He has been remarkably skilled in building relationships across partisan divides. In 2013 he and Kyle Scott, a local Tea Party intellectual, coauthored a piece for the *Houston Chronicle* on the importance of citizen agency titled "Power Starts at the Local Level." Seth Howard, who has been assistant director of the center for several years, is a conservative Republican who supported Ted Cruz and later Donald Trump. He also believes "Public Achievement is what this country needs. We have gotten away from doing things on our own. Public Achievement teaches students to gain what their parents may have lost, to be an active citizen, and to be responsible in every area of their lives." Seth has come to believe that Democrats, as well as Republicans, want people to learn more reliance and civic responsibility.[34]

In John's view, schools and colleges have largely abandoned the civic and democratic purposes that once animated them. "When colleges looked at the bigger questions of life—Why are we here and what are we doing? What do we need to be powerful citizens? —we had much better success rates," he says. "Students stayed in school because there was something more to college than just getting a job." But he is not discouraged. He believes that college can be "a transformative experience that makes you think about your most fundamental values and changes who you are as a person." He believes that as schools and colleges recover their public purpose the process will have enormous impact. "Communities are counting on colleges and universities" to be involved in the revitalization of American democracy," he concludes.

One of the outgrowths of the 2012 coalition of colleges and universities called the American Commonwealth Partnership, described in Chapter 2, was the concept called "Citizen Alum," developed by Julie Ellison, also the founding director of Imagining America, a consortium of schools dedicated to revitalizing the democratic qualities and connections of the arts, humanities, and design fields. Citizen Alum is the name for a network of schools experimenting with a multidimensional relationship with their alumni as potential civic resources and agents of change. It is also aspirational, pointing toward the large number of college graduates from schools such as UMBC, Augsburg, the University of Minnesota, Denison, Lonestar, and many others in recent years who have had robust civic engagement experiences—and want to translate these into a civic way of life after college. In fact, research by Richard Battistoni and Tania Mitchell indicate that such alumni are especially concerned with how their careers and work lives can develop civic dimensions.[35] For this to take place on a large scale will require civic transformation of disciplines and professions.

9

A Democratic Awakening

Harry C. Boyte

We have frequently printed the word Democracy. Yet I cannot too often repeat that it is a word the real gist of which still sleeps, quite unawakened. It is a great word, whose history remains unwritten.
—Walt Whitman, *Democratic Vistas*[1]

A strong concept of citizenship is emerging from the networks and examples of public work in *Awakening Democracy through Public Work.* It has potential to tap and cultivate new citizen energies and capacities. To return to the Public Achievement metaphor, it is open-ended, relational, and iterative—more like jazz than a set piece of music. Civic engagement in these terms also has a strong local aspect.

A striking number of young adults are eager to turn their jobs into this kind of public work. As the research conducted by Rick Battistoni and Tania Mitchell and cited in the last chapter suggests, young people who were civically active in college seek to "avoid the bifurcation of their civic and professional lives." They conclude, "We see graduates incorporating civic identities and values into their workplaces, both in terms of their actions and the processes by which they arrive at workplace decisions."[2] Put differently, young professionals, a group with outsized potential for leadership in today's knowledge societies like the United States, want to think of themselves as *parts* of publics and places, citizens working with other citizens to strengthen their communities and connect their institutions to civic life.

But it is useful to begin this final chapter by looking at two large obstacles that create conflicts between aspiration and reality. Professional systems tend to value empirical and academic knowledge and to treat other kinds of knowledge—cultural, relational, local, spiritual, experiential—as secondary. And professionals are trained to think of themselves as detached from local civic life and civic identities. A story illustrates.

"Where Are the Citizens?"

In January 2013, the mayor of Falcon Heights, Minnesota, invited the Sabo Center for Democracy and Citizenship at Augsburg University[3] to moderate a town hall meeting after he saw a Sunday Dialogue in the *New York Times* on the terrible school shooting in Newtown, Connecticut. The Sunday Dialogue was organized in response to a letter I had written arguing that government gun laws by themselves cannot fix the problem and that there are many actions that citizens can take across differences to address gun violence. The Obama White House hosted a meeting to discuss citizen-driven solutions. One solution was to hold civic deliberations in local communities. Another, suggested by Bill Doherty, director of the Citizen Professional Center at the University of Minnesota, was to adapt an Australian program that trains lay citizens in a mental health version of CPR, preparing them to spot warning signs such as angry, isolated teens and to intervene constructively.[4] White House officials agreed these ideas might make a difference. They also doubted they could be advanced successfully in the Washington political scene dominated by hyperpartisanship.

The mayor of Falcon Heights decided to take up the topic, and Elaine Eschenbacher, now the director of the Sabo Center, Dennis Donovan, and I came to facilitate the forum. The twenty-five or so people in the town hall included the mayor, the police chief, the city manager, a few teachers, a local school principal, business entrepreneurs, social agency workers, a University of Minnesota professor from the College of Architecture and Design, four students, and two elderly residents. The elderly residents said they were alarmed about the problem of gun violence in schools. They also expressed regret that "there [were] only two citizens" in the meeting.

There was silence. No one questioned the residents' definition of citizen as volunteer. The idea of citizenship expressed through the professional work of people in the room did not occur to those present. When I raised the question of why those present did not see themselves as citizens in their professional roles, it generated a lively conversation about how much power there might be in the community to address gun violence if people saw their work in civic terms and if work sites became civic sites. I imagined the power of communities to address gun violence—and other complex challenges—if professional programs prepared students for "citizen careers" in government, business, religious life, schools and colleges, and elsewhere. It struck home how much the contemporary world needs a new kind of professional.

The Crisis in Professions

Professional discontent is growing rapidly. According to the Schaeffer Institute, between 60 and 80 percent of those entering the ministry will leave in the first ten years. Over 70 percent of pastors are so demoralized that they regularly think of leaving their profession.[5] The ministry is only one example of professional demoralization among many.

In health professions, the Lucian Leape Institute reports, "production and cost pressures have reduced complex, intimate, caregiving relationships into a series of demanding tasks performed under severe time constraints."[6] According to *Governing* magazine, low morale among local government workers is rampant. Ninety-two percent of state and local government human resource managers rank recruiting and retaining qualified personnel as their most challenging issue.[7] A recent article in *Money* magazine reports on "Five High-Paying Jobs that Will Make You Miserable." Despite the fact that physicians dominate the highest paying professions—with median pay of more than $150,000 a year in 2014—40 percent say they would choose a different career if they had to do it over again. The article also notes pervasive demoralization among junior investment bankers, sales managers, dentists, and lawyers.[8]

Educators in K-12 schools similarly express discontent. Up to 40 percent leave the profession in the first three years. The educational philosopher Doris Santoro has shown that discontent is misdiagnosed as "burnout," a sense of personal exhaustion, despair, and anger. She asked, in contrast, "What if the problem is the structures and constraints within which people teach, not the teachers?" Santoro became convinced that reports about teacher discontentment were blaming teachers for what was, in fact, the way educational systems drain meaning and relationality from the profession. "The burnout narrative comes down to, 'Sorry, you blew it! You couldn't hack it, you didn't preserve yourself,'" she says. She found that, in fact, teachers leave "because they no longer want to be part of a system that is harming students." Teachers talk about administrative confusion and the frustration that comes from being told they are doing it wrong. They feel besieged by technology they see as taking them "away from what they're supposed to be doing as a teacher." When teachers raise such concerns, they are often labeled as narrowly self-interested. In fact, they are worried about larger purposes: "The integrity of the profession, the wellbeing of the students, and whether they are caring for students in the way that they deserve to be treated." Santoro found demoralization not only in inner-city schools but also in the top schools in the *US News* list.[9]

Such discontent was described by Noam Scheiber in the *New York Times*. "Technological developments like the internet have undermined claims to expertise," he writes. "Shrinking budgets have left teachers and other government workers with fewer resources. Consolidation in the health care and media industries has made doctors, nurses, and journalists feel like cogs in corporate machines that don't share their values."[10] In addition to technology, shrinking budgets, and consolidation, changes in professional education play a role in narrowing the identities, sense of purpose, and civic connections of professionals. Professional education has shifted professional identities from "civic" to "disciplinary." This grows, in large part, from hidden assumptions.[11]

Erin Cech, a sociologist at Rice University, has found that despite strong statements by professional associations that engineers are "to hold paramount the safety, health, and welfare of the public in the performance of their professional duties," in fact "students' public welfare concerns *decline* significantly over the course of their engineering education." In her view, "engineering education fosters a culture of disengagement that defines public welfare concerns as tangential to what it means to practice engineering." She traces this culture to three invisible "ideological pillars." These include the idea that engineering is apolitical, "which frames any 'nontechnical' concerns such as public welfare as irrelevant to 'real' engineering work"; a technical/social dualism that assumes technical knowledge is far superior to "soft" skills of human interaction; and meritocratic models of success that emphasize individual stars. She argues that "partly as a result of this culture, students may learn to distance themselves from public welfare considerations in the process of becoming engineers."[12]

Such pillars, with variations, can be found across all types of professional education. Professionals see themselves as servicing citizens or, at the most, engaging citizens through their role as outside experts—not as citizens themselves. Efforts to revitalize a civic identity in professionals requires both a philosophical and a practical challenge to detachment.

Civic Studies

A new framework for professional training and work is not to be found in the angry tide of antiscience sentiments. Neither is the cult of the expert, which holds academically trained professionals to have the answers to complex problems, a workable response. Academics and professionals have a lot to contribute, but they typically lack political knowledge and habits of building public relationships across differences. As Philip Nyden, cochair of the

American Sociological Association's Task Force on Public Sociology, puts it, "Academics may be well trained in methodology and theory, but they are not always trained or experienced in the political process of bringing out change." In his view, their "'problem-oriented' approach—which assumes that the community has a deficit—obscures the fact that *academic researchers themselves may have a deficit* that needs to be corrected by experienced community leaders and activists."[13]

Nyden is part of a new field called civic studies, premised on the idea that professionals and academics themselves are citizens, that asks, "What should we do as citizens?" As one of the cofounders, Peter Levine, puts it, "Scholars [are] citizens, engaged with others in creating [our] worlds . . . accountable for the actual results of their thoughts and not just the ideas themselves." Civic studies was launched in 2007 as a transdisciplinary field, in part to challenge the assumption that academics are outside observers and analysts and professionals are fixers and service providers, not fellow citizens in community life. Civic studies stresses individual and collective human agency and citizens as co-creators of communities at different scales. It seeks to reintegrate what the modern world and its theories of knowledge have split apart—disciplines based on "facts," such as natural and social sciences; disciplines based on "values," such as the humanities; and disciplines based on action strategies, such as the professions. All, from a civic studies perspective, should be unified to improve our capacities to act collectively, effectively, and ethically in an informed way.[14]

Civic studies draws on strands of social science that emphasize collective capacity for action. For instance, the late Elinor Ostrom challenged the fatalistic idea that the "commons," symbolic and material foundations for a shared life, are doomed. She explored ingredients of effective collective action, beginning with a critique of Garrett Hardin's famous 1968 article, "The Tragedy of the Commons." "Ruin is the destination toward which all men rush, each pursuing his own best interest in a society that believes in the freedom of the commons," Hardin had written.[15]

Ostrom and her colleagues looked at actual cases of commons, including forest management, irrigation, inshore fisheries, and the Internet. They discovered that decentralized governance with high civic participation has advantages in terms of efficiency, sustainability, and equity. These advantages include incorporation of local knowledge, greater involvement of those who are trustworthy and respect principles of reciprocity, feedback on subtle changes in the resource, better adapted rules, lower enforcement costs, and redundancy, which decreases the likelihood of a system-wide failure. Decentralized systems working in isolation from larger systems also have disadvantages, such as uneven involvement by local users, possibilities for "local tyrannies" and discrimination, lack of innovation and access to scientific knowledge, and an inability to cope with large common pool resources. Ostrom argued for a mix of decentralized and general governance, "where citizens are able to organize not just one but multiple governing authorities at different scales." Such mixed systems may be messy, but in studies of local economies they "significantly outperformed metropolitan areas served by a limited number of large-scale, unified governments."[16] In 2009, shortly after she helped cofound civic studies, Ostrom won the Nobel Prize in Economics.

Work on governance highlights elements in *sustaining* the commons. Public work emphasizes another dimension, the effort involved in *making* it. "Such work," argues Levine, "builds social capital, strengthens communities, and gives people the skills they need for collective citizenship."[17] Public work shifts the emphasis from *users* to *producers*.[18]

Civic studies is also informed by strands of what is sometimes called "the new science," or dynamic systems theory. Esther Thelen pioneered such science in child development. She challenged views of infants as passing through predetermined "stages" of development, arguing instead that infants are experimental, self-realizing agents, profoundly relational and interactive with their environments. She also had a deep appreciation for nonscientific forms of knowledge and knowledge making. In her view, empowering knowledge grows not only from using the scientific method but also from experiencing a rich and interactive set of plural relationships, with "amateurs," parents, and families, as well as with other scientists. Her science suggested a conception of the person not simply as a problem solver but more broadly as a co-creator of the contexts in which problem-solving takes place. Drawing on many of her experiments, a group of former students and colleagues concluded that infants are constantly assembling holistic patterns, such as reaching or walking, out of many elements, including testing, perceiving, receiving feedback, and experimenting with ideas. "[An] integration of body and mind is a fundamental characteristic of all goal-directed activities. . . . Thought is always grounded in perception and action."[19]

After Esther's death in 2005, her husband, David Thelen, a leading American historian of democratic movements and an old friend of mine, convened a conversation among dynamic systems theorists of child development and people in our public work networks including Marie Ström, Scott Peters, Gerald Taylor, Bobby Milstein of the Centers for Disease Control, Bill Doherty, founder of the Citizen Professional Center at the University of Minnesota, and others. The concept of civic science that emerged from these conversations advances an understanding of science as a resource for human empowerment in which scientists see themselves as citizens. Civic science provided a way to name older democratic understandings of science. It is also a way to begin imagining how to rework contemporary scientific practices and science education, especially in fields related to human life and the environment. The Delta Center, founded by Esther's student John Spencer, himself a leading scientist of infant brain development and systems theory, was an anchoring partner. We organized a National Science Foundation workshop in 2014 on the concept and its implications.

Civic science addresses the knowledge war by stressing the need for multiple kinds of knowledge to deal with the biggest challenges facing our nation and the world, including climate change, energy security, health care, a sustainable and just food system, and many others, and the need for scientists to learn skills of public work. This process both generates and depends on new models of citizen or democratic professionalism.[20] The following presents three such examples that follow in the footsteps of educationally credentialed citizen experts and also arise from the tradition exemplified by beauticians who organized citizenship schools in the freedom movement and Oliver Harvey, the janitor at Duke who was a brilliant democracy educator. Those described below attended to the craft nature of their work, in the sense described by Mike Rose in his splendid book, *The Mind at Work*.[21] In this way, these examples are like the citizen teachers in special education described in Chapter 7 and the citizen staff, faculty, and administrators in higher education described in Chapter 8.

The first example is the group of faculty associated with the Citizen Professional Center at the University of Minnesota, which promotes the model of citizen professional in family therapy and health fields. The second is the doctoral program in nursing practice at Augsburg University, which prepares nurses to be citizen nurses. A third example, Clear Vision in Eau Claire, Wisconsin, was born when Mike Huggins, the city manager, used the idea of government as catalyst for citizens' public work. Huggins is an example of a city manager as citizen professional. Clear Vision is generating citizen professionals in other fields by creating a culture of active citizenship across a whole community.

A Citizen Therapist on a Bus Tour

"Are we headed for a national divorce?" asked Dan Balz, chief national correspondent of the *Washington Post* on NBC's *Meet the Press* on August 6, 2017. On the show, "Our Broken Politics," Chuck Todd showed how major campaigns no longer seek to engage "the middle" but rather try to mobilize their base. The numbers of congressional representatives who regularly try to work on legislation across the divisions between Republicans and Democrats, the "Red and Blue divide," dropped precipitously from 137 in 2002 to four in 2013. Such divisions in formal politics are rooted in different ways of knowing, which also are polarizing. For instance, the NBC reporter Andrea Mitchell reported that 58 percent of Republicans now believe colleges and universities "have a negative effect on the way things are going in the country." Heather McGee, president of Demos, a progressive policy group, agrees with David French, a conservative writer for *National Review*, that "the system is not working."[22]

While some in America's media and political establishment worry about the erosion of civic bonds, people at the grassroots are doing something about it. Bill Doherty, our colleague in developing the public work philosophy through citizen professionalism, is an example.

The idea of citizen professionalism emphasizes the civic dimensions of professions, through which professionals learn to work *with* other citizens in relational and empowering ways, rather than *on* them or *for* them.[23] Albert Dzur has detailed how professionals' work can be catalytic and energizing when they "step back" from the cult of the expert. He chronicles democratic trends in medicine, law, the movement against domestic violence, and elsewhere that enhance the authority and efficacy of lay citizens.[24]

Bill Doherty, Tai Mendenhall, Jerica Berge, and other colleagues and students associated with the Citizen Professional Center at the University of Minnesota have pioneered the practices and theory of such professionalism. Adapting public work concepts and practices to family and health sciences, their citizen professional model begins with the premise that solving complex problems requires many sources of knowledge. They often argue that the greatest untapped resource for improving health and social well-being is the knowledge, wisdom, and energy of individuals, families, and communities who face challenging issues in their everyday lives. The Citizen Professional Center has generated multiple partnerships embodying this civic philosophy. FEDS, a project on diabetes led by Indian elders in the Twin Cities, brings together community members and medical practitioners. It has shown strong positive health outcomes according to conventional assessments. Other partnerships include a movement of suburban families working to tame overscheduled, consumerist lives; a project in Burnsville, Minnesota, in which families are developing strategies to counter obesity among children; an African American "Citizen Fathers" project fostering positive fathering models and practices; a project with Hennepin County to change civil service practices into public work; and a pilot program with Health Partners Como Clinic called the Citizen Health Care Home, which stresses personal and family responsibility for one's own health and opportunities for leadership development of patients.[25]

In early 2017 Bill traced "Psychotherapy's Pilgrimage" in a major overview of developments and the public impact of the profession in the main working journal of the field, *Psychotherapy Networker.* He explored "the intimate relationship between what goes on within the seeming sanctuary of therapists' offices and the hurly-burly of the wider culture." Bill's work with the Citizen Professional Center shows that it is possible to translate core skills of therapy, such as group process and understanding the complexity of every person, into empowering public work. Trump's campaign—and similar signs of the rise of authoritarian and divisive trends around the world—was a "bugle call that therapists must begin to take seriously so as to move beyond focusing narrowly on individual mental health problems when the larger social glue is weakening." During 2016 he organized Citizen Therapists against Trumpism as "an association of therapists developing and spreading transformative ways to practice therapy with a public dimension, rebuilding democratic capacity in communities and resisting anti-democratic ideologies and practices." After the election, the group changed its name to Citizen Therapists for Democracy. "What is new is the democracy theme, which assumes that *everyone* has a stake in the public domain, can be affected by public stress (Trump supporters included) and can be part of the solution through personal action (such as talking about issues in their social networks) and collective action (by joining with others to work on change)."[26]

As the first major project of Citizen Therapists for Democracy, Bill teamed up with a new group called Better Angels, which sought to communicate and relate across partisan divides. They began by addressing the seeming chasm between Red and Blue voters in the rural community of Warren County, Ohio, between Cincinnati and Dayton.

The political geography of the United States has been described as "Blue" urban islands surrounded by "Red" rural seas. But people can live in segregated partisan bubbles in rural communities like Warren County. Andie Moon had doors slammed in her face while canvassing for Obama. She despaired about getting back to a time when people saw each other's humanity across differences. Angela Brown, an African American woman, said she didn't want anything to do with Trump voters, as she thought they must have bought into his racism. Gregory Smith, a Trump voter, said sometimes he wished he could speak with "someone who is not a conservative, someone of a different color," but it was hard to imagine how it might happen. "I feel afraid to open my mouth." Keith Johnson said he "loved Trump, but not because of his personality." He thought Trump was committed to the nation. "The challenge is how to get that message across." Kouhyar Mostashfi, a Muslim immigrant, expressed fear that if "this culture of animosity continues to grow it might give groups a blank check to touch upon violence."

Evidence of the desire many were feeling for a sense of shared citizenship across divides of party, race, and religion appeared in two weekend-long conversations after the election that brought together these and a few other voters, with roughly equal numbers of Trump and Clinton supporters.[27] At the end of the second conversation all agreed to a prepared statement that read, "A number of us on both sides began our meetings convinced that the other side could not be dealt with on the basis of rational thought. We say unanimously that our experiences of talking with rather than at or about each other caused us to abandon our belief." People described how their views had changed. "I did end up liking them as people," said Angela Brown. "If more people could have this experience I think our country could come back together and understand it's OK to be different," said Andie Moon. "I have permission to call him my Muslim friend," said Gregory Smith, talking about Mostashfi. "We're going to do what we just came from. He's going to attend a Christian church, and I'm going to visit a mosque with him." "I was very impressed with the dynamics," said another. "If you did twenty thousand of these across the nation you would change the world." The groups celebrated the weekend in a barn owned by a Tea Party leader, featuring a concert by the well-known progressive folk singer Peter Yarrow. Residents sang "We Shall Overcome" and "This Land Is Your Land, This Land Is My Land." Fifteen people, from both conversations, created a chapter of Better Angels to work together on issues such as parental leave and electoral gerrymandering.

In important ways the Ohio conversations succeeded because Bill had learned to put his professional training and experiences as a therapist to use in a public setting with a civic goal. He is a warm and curious family therapist and college professor. His easy manner can hide his pedagogical talents, which I have seen firsthand for more than twenty years. He is skilled at asking questions. He listens with great respect to people's stories, whatever their background. He sees hidden capacities and interests that highly partisan educators are likely to miss. He knows how to create spaces where people feel free to be themselves and to take the lead in their learning.

In the weekend conversations in Ohio, Bill used methods that allowed people to break out of stereotypes about each other and learn to see the "other side" in multidimensional ways. For instance, the conversations used a fishbowl process in which each side listened to concerns the other group had about their *own* candidate. They also heard their ideological opponents describe how they imagined others might see them. They learned that "the other side" had far more nuanced, complex, and insightful views than they ever imagined.

After the conversations in Ohio, Bill and a participant were featured on National Public Radio. Dozens of people emailed the station asking if he could come to their communities to organize similar encounters. Bill, his wife Leah, David Blankenhorn (cofounder of Better Angels), and two others set off on what they called a "One American Bus Tour." It began July 4 with a patriotic songfest, again featuring Peter Yarrow and the local Tea Party band in Warren. The bus tour, the first of a series, traveled to fifteen communities in eight states: Ohio, Tennessee, Vermont, New York, New Jersey, Pennsylvania, Maryland, and Virginia. New chapters of the cross-partisan group Better Angels are springing up in the wake of the local conversations. Meanwhile, in September 2017, at the Augsburg Nobel Peace Prize Forum in Minnesota, the theme of which was "Dialogue in Divided Societies," Bill teamed up with a group of college students in the Citizen Student Movement to host another Red-Blue conversation. For students in this movement, the concept of citizen professionalism provides a way to think about their future careers as change agents. Other students in the Twin Cities are also learning to think of themselves as citizens through their work, but there are significant challenges in the way.

Preparing Citizen Nurses

The nursing department at Augsburg has been a pioneer in challenging assumptions about the detachment of health professionals and incorporating public work skills and concepts. Augsburg in its early days encouraged students and faculty to organize a health society. Years later, the baccalaureate completion program in nursing was officially launched in 1974 with a particular emphasis on preparing students to take leadership roles and develop innovative practices.[28] In the fall of 1992, faculty and students, led by Bev Nilsson, chair of the nursing department, organized a freestanding health service for homeless people, the Augsburg Central Nursing Center (ACNC), at Central Lutheran Church in Minneapolis, where she was a member. It became much more than a service center, focused instead on mutual benefit and respect for human dignity. Most of the visitors in the ACNC experience homelessness, and many experience challenges of addiction and mental illness. For twenty-five years, the center has created a space for nursing students, who in most programs practice in acute care settings, to have meaningful interaction with "people living on the margins," building relationships, discovering strengths.

In 1999 a new program, the master of arts in transcultural nursing practice, was created to "prepare advanced practice nurses for population-focused practice in culturally diverse communities." The program grew out of a transcultural nursing course that Nilsson and Cherly Leuning had begun two years before. In the fall of 2010, the doctor of nursing practice (NDP) in transcultural nursing, the only such program in the country, was added. From the beginning, the program stressed epistemological pluralism, valuing indigenous and traditional healing practices. It included a strong commitment to social justice and health equity. In 2011, nursing faculty and students partnered with a nearby hospital and a local nonprofit health organization to find out concerns among the Somali immigrants in the area around Augsburg. "Nearby Somali immigrants had voiced concerns over the lack of culturally competent providers and access issues involved in seeking care. A group of Somali women expressed a need for a drop-in center they could access." The Augsburg nursing department responded by creating the Health Commons in the Cedar-Riverside neighborhood.[29]

Faculty members continued to struggle with the gap between vision and skills, a pattern common in nursing education. "Although social justice is a theme in many nursing programs' mission statements and core practice models the path of action remains unclear," write Kathleen Clark, Joyce Miller, Cheryl Leuning, and Katherine Baumgartner as they reflect on the evolution on their program in "The Citizen Nurse," an article published in the *Journal of Nursing Education*. They believe that "equipping nurse educators with foundational tools to address injustice in our communities is a critical first step toward igniting a desire to right the wrongs in society and create a healthier, better world."[30] The department embarked on an extensive curriculum innovation in 2014, working with the Sabo Center for Democracy and Citizenship to organize a series of seminars on the theory of public work and to incorporate civic agency skills into every level of the curriculum. The skills included the ability to act, a skill that emerged from learning a different kind of politics and developing a different view of power as the relational capacity to act. The department also included guest lecturers who were community organizers in a graduate course. "Students, faculty, and the community organizer discussed power in health care institutions, assumptions of the word [power] itself, and the importance of coping with tensions," write Clark and her coauthors. Students learn how to do one-on-one relational meetings and share their experiences, and to do power maps of their work settings or communities. Another skill, integrated across the curriculum, is learning how to create meaningful public relationships with community members. This also involves the nurse "immersing himself or herself in the local context to learn the resources, the influence of policies . . . while respecting the wisdom of cultural brokers." Finally, the curriculum teaches continuing reflection and collective evaluation.

One student studying abroad used power mapping with community health workers at a rural clinic in Guatemala to analyze power patterns in health. They "designed a power map of people who held decision making power in the clinic. The group then formulated a plan to conduct one-to-one relational interviews with people in leadership." The process allowed health workers to advocate for themselves, analyze and understand both formal and informal power relationships, and change the clinic model of care to incorporate indigenous wisdom.

Following the curricular changes, student feedback has been very positive. "Although I am in my second semester of the nursing doctorate program, I am already beginning to view problems in a new light," said one. Others said they were inspired by the idea of "citizen nurse" and had learned how to be much less judgmental.[31]

Like the program to develop citizen teachers in the Augsburg special education program, the effort to prepare citizen nurses at Augsburg is at an early stage and faces many obstacles in today's health system. But there is also considerable energy for this work. Clark and her coauthors conclude, "The goal of such curricular design [is] to produce citizens who can understand the importance of relationships, the urgency of taking action, and the means to lead change in the process of health and healing."[32]

Public work that brings relational organizing into health can sometimes lead to unexpected outcomes. Such is the case for the city government in Eau Claire, Wisconsin, which has become a demonstration site for government as catalyst for citizens' public work and for community-wide citizenship.

Government as Civic Catalyst

In recent years, most scholars and activists have seen government as an opponent or a target, not an ally. As the British political geographer Jane Wills has documented in detail, "in every field there has been a particularly strong collective antipathy to liberal democracy in favour of a form of radical politics that is understood to take place beyond the institutions of parliament, councils and official political organizations." Such perspectives prioritize "struggle and conflict," neglect "ordinary democratic politics," and pay scant attention to how governmental institutions might interact with citizens to promote "the common good."[33]

Yet against the grain, scholars such as Wills have argued that government institutions need to attend to the places and contexts in which they develop and have also described how they might be a resource for active citizenship. Their perspective revives a tradition once widespread in theory and practice. The Depression years of the 1930s and 1940s witnessed an impressive example.

From 1935 to 1941, a group of scientists and organizers in the Department of Agriculture (USDA) worked with land-grant colleges and their scientists, cooperative extension agents, and community leaders to develop a vast initiative on the future of rural America. "They strongly supported historical traditions, local knowledge, regional cultures, cohesive communities, and practices like family farming," writes Jess Gilbert in *Planning Democracy*. Discussions across rural America included farm organizations and unions, churches, youth clubs, professional and business groups, and government agencies. About sixty thousand discussion leaders received training, and more than three million people took part. Parallel "Philosophy Schools" on the challenges of modern society sought to broaden the perspectives of thirty-five thousand extension agents and other professionals beyond the disciplinary boundaries in which they had been socialized. "Their vision of democratic planning [envisioned] transforming rural American into a more egalitarian society [with] a wider distribution of power and resources for common people."[34]

We translated histories of government as partner and catalyst to contemporary public policy and practice in the Reinventing Citizenship effort I coordinated with William Galston and the White House Domestic Policy Council from 1993 to 1995. The aim was to develop strategies for overcoming the citizen-government divide. Before President Clinton's State of the Union, the administration held a meeting at Camp David to get advice. The late political theorist Benjamin Barber and I brought results of the project with current examples as well as historical precedents. Carmen Sirianni, our research director, had uncovered numerous practices of government as partner and catalyst for public work with citizens in health, the environment, education, and economic and urban development. We highlighted the erosion of civic life by the dominance of market and government-centered approaches. Several others at the Camp David meeting—Robert Putnam, Alan Wolfe, and Os Guinness—similarly stressed the need for civic work that government should not undertake on its own but that it could and should support.[35]

Clinton incorporated such ideas into his 1995 "New Covenant" State of the Union. "Our civil life is suffering in America today. Citizens are working together less and shouting at each other more," he said. "The common bonds which have been the great strength of our country from its very beginning are badly frayed." He urged Americans to revitalize "the work of citizenship" across partisan divides. We knew, from polling by Stan Greenberg, that the idea of government as partner and catalyst could find public support. But the day after Clinton's State of the Union, a friend with the *Washington Post* told me that while their polling showed the country was interested in the message, "everyone in Washington thinks he's lost his mind." He predicted Clinton could not sustain the message without citizen demand. It soon disappeared. I realized that the idea of government as catalyst needed strong examples in local communities before it could become a serious theme in national politics.

Eau Claire, Wisconsin, turned out to be a demonstration plot.

Eau Claire as a Demonstration Plot

In the educational traditions of cooperative extension, which was part of the rural conversations and public work in the 1930s, the concept of "demonstration plots" plays a large role. Demonstration plots involve places that people can visit and learn from.[36] This is a different model of dissemination than "replication" or "instruction." It is, in fact, much like the way Public Achievement spread in the 1990s with Saint Bernard's as the plot.

In the face of growing threats to democracy around the world, we need new demonstration plots for local democracy. Jane Wills's research on experiments to decentralize power around the world suggests "the need for new institutions" that "represent the diversity of local people . . . identify shared issues and concerns . . . articulate and mobilize around these, and . . . negotiate with other power-brokers in the locality."[37] She could be describing Clear Vision in Eau Claire, Wisconsin.

Public work approaches are best understood through the histories and cultures out of which they emerge and on which they build. Eau Claire, meaning "clear water," is named for the river that flows into the Chippewa River at the southern end of the Chippewa River Valley, a large watershed basin in northwestern Wisconsin that feeds into the Mississippi River. The community history has been marked by sometimes bitter conflicts, but also by patterns of collaboration.

In 1849, a delegation of Ojibwa Indians pressed their case against calls to remove them from the area. During a trip to Washington, DC, they used a pictograph to make their claim. It showed Ojibwa (Chippewa) clans with eyes and hearts connected to the chain of wild rice lakes in the Chippewa Valley. As early as the 1830s, lumbermen and land speculators had begun lobbying Congress for access to the area, part of the Northwest Territory, and for removal of the Indians. The United States government's acquisition of the Chippewa Valley in 1837 through a treaty greatly increased the dangers facing the Chippewa and other tribes. Over the next two decades they fought successfully for rights and against removal efforts. Nonetheless, conflict continued between Indians and European Americans.[38]

Ethnic segregation featured prominently in Eau Claire's history.[39] In 1900, six foreign-language newspapers were published in the valley, five in German. "Ethnic groups build churches, hospitals, schools, cooperatives, insurance companies, and community halls to sustain their heritage, build fellowship, bridge cultures, and provide financial security," describes the exhibit in the Chippewa Valley Museum.[40] In the 1910s and 1920s, Germans experienced persecution, and the Ku Klux Klan had several years of explosive growth after World War I, targeting Catholics as un-American.

If Eau Claire had conflicts, it also featured many kinds of civic organizing that built connections and skilled people in working through them. The community was at the center of cooperative, farming, and trade union organizing. Communal public work practices like barn-raising, quilting, volunteer fire departments, and civic groups bridging ethnic divides are featured prominently in the Chippewa Valley Museum.

Government structures also created norms and practices of collaboration, according to Kerry Kincaid, who has served as president of the city council for a decade. She believes that the city manager form of government, created in 1947, is inherently more collaborative than the mayoral form. She takes leadership in stressing the need for civility in city council meetings. But she also observes, "The city Council has a very flat organizational structure with weak power in the office of the council president. The office has no veto power, does not present an annual budget, and does not make appointments." In her view, "this structure helps us work together." Kerry points out that the city and county health departments are the first city-county health partnership in the state to share services, expenses, and a common director. "That is a practical model of saying we can be under the same roof."[41]

In the early twenty-first century, Eau Claire, with a population of sixty-six thousand, faced many challenges. The Uniroyal Goodrich plant, a mainstay of the local economy for decades, had closed its doors in 1992, putting twelve hundred people out of work. Cutbacks in state contributions to shared revenue funding beginning in 1995 resulted in a loss of $4 million annually. Sharp increases in fuel, energy, and health care costs resulted in larger classrooms in the schools and in less revenue for the museum, the senior center, low-income housing, and social services. In 2007, the city estimated that public infrastructure needs for schools, arts facilities, libraries, the courthouse and jail, sewage, and community centers totaled more than $400 million.[42] Mike Huggins, the city manager, saw an opportunity to build on and strengthen the collaborative practices of the community.

Mike Huggins had worked with the Center for Democracy and Citizenship in the mid-1990s as an assistant city manager in a community participating in a project on underage drinking. The Department of Epidemiology contracted with the center on a large grant from the National Institutes of Health to reduce underage drinking in eight small towns in Minnesota and Wisconsin. The epidemiologists promised a "community organizing" approach in their proposal. But it turned out that theirs was a mobilizing approach, not the civic organizing approach of our center. Epidemiologists believed that communities should adopt strict carding legislation, including punishment of bar owners who failed to query the age of drinkers. Research showed that this has some effect in lowering underage alcohol use. In other words, they had a predetermined solution. The scientists were well-intentioned, but their understanding of "civic engagement" was narrow: partnering as experts with communities.

For three years we argued that assuming "experts have the answers" robs communities of their agency and ignores moral, cultural, and local wisdom. We argued for a more open, jazz-like approach that developed people's skills to work across differences. About half the communities adopted mobilizing approaches, and the other half experimented with civic organizing. In one community, Tomah, the limits of the expert-knows-best approach were dramatized as the deliberation of a diverse group of community members led to the realization that carding wouldn't address the nub of the local epidemic of underage drinking. The roots of the problem lay in an annual "beer bash" that had created a norm of widespread casual drinking. The community organized to change the festival. The problem of teen alcohol use decreased significantly. Mike Huggins saw parallels between the epidemiologists and city managers. He became conscious of the hidden dynamic of technocracy, including narrow expert-knows-best training, overlooked in most civic engagement approaches. "If government is not the center of the universe for local problem solving, then what is the role of city managers as government leaders?" he asks. "It's a hard concept for many managers to get. The idea of citizen-centered problem-solving requires managers letting go of control, which is hard." City managers, in his view, are trained to be "master problem solvers" who "manage structures and processes to get the outcomes we think are important." Trusting problem-solving that puts citizens at the center, "expecting that the outcome is going to be good," is challenging.

It is difficult, in Mike's experience, to get city managers even to acknowledge power relationships. "As managers, we are uncomfortable talking publicly about power—what it is, who has it, how to build it, and how to use it." Yet for all the challenges, he also thinks local government needs a paradigm shift, "a twenty-first-century vision for local democracy centered on citizens." The question is how to do that. The public work approach impressed him as a potential framework. He became convinced it could be adapted to local democracy after coming to a conference of the Center for Democracy and Citizenship held at the Humphrey Institute, where he heard civic organizers such as Dorothy Cotton, former director of the Citizenship Education Program in the freedom movement, and Gerald Taylor and Tony Massengale, organizers with the Industrial Areas Foundation.[43]

In 2007 Mike Huggins organized an informal meeting of government and nonprofit leaders to discuss how to deal with the challenges of social services and infrastructure. The result was a highly unusual visioning and planning process that involved government but centered on the community. The group secured an initial $40,000 from a broad range of partners, including the city, county, Chamber of Commerce, United Way, Eau Claire Community Foundation, University of Wisconsin, and Chippewa Valley Technical College. They contacted the venerable National Civic League, a group dedicated to participatory civic life that had created a planning process involving both large group meetings and small working groups to set priorities, develop strategies, and generate measurable outcomes. A fifteen-member initiating committee included some of the initial leaders and eight others who reflected a cross-section of the community. The committee invited about five hundred citizens to participate in an extended yearlong process. When Mike reported to an international conference on participatory local governance, funded by the Ford Foundation and held at the University of Sussex in England in 2007, conference organizers recognized the highly unusual nature of Eau Claire's process and asked Mike for a more detailed case study.

Mike Huggins's report described how those invited reflected the diversity of the community by gender, age, geographic location, race, employment, and income. The initiating committee made special efforts to recruit from low-income and minority ethnic groups, including meeting with members of the Hmong community (a large new immigrant population in the city), African Americans, and local trade unions. "While the outcome was not a perfect representation of Eau Claire . . . it was an extremely diverse group of people," wrote Mike. Public meetings took place every several weeks, with participants sitting around tables to encourage everyone to speak. Two hundred came to the initial meetings, and about 120 stayed for the whole process, which concluded in June 2008. Clear Vision Eau Claire was born. The working groups identified priorities including community collaboration, education, health care, transportation, quality of life, and economic development.

The process was distinctive in several ways. It was highly diverse, citizen-driven, and respectful of the knowledge of lay citizens in ways that were virtually unique. In most public planning processes, "citizens provide input at designated times. In the Eau Claire process, citizens are actively involved in designing and conducting the process, determining the format and substance of recommendations, writing the final report, and determining the implementation strategies." Embodying Mike's awareness of the subtle but crucial dynamics of knowledge power, the process "blend[ed] citizen passion with technical knowledge and expertise."[44]

These elements became part of the identity of Clear Vision Eau Claire when the group integrated public work organizing skills, habits, and concepts. Elaine Eschenbacher and Dennis Donovan of the Center for Democracy and Citizenship worked closely with Mike and the Clear Vision board to provide training and develop a relational problem-solving model. Clear Vision developed a tool kit adapted from the Public Achievement coaches' guide. Like Public Achievement and other approaches based on public work such as the Citizen Leadership Programme of Idasa in Africa, continuing citizen training and development were crucial.

The mission of Clear Vision is "to engage our community for the common good." It was founded with three basic principles: preserving the quality of life, transforming the local economy, and empowering citizens. The overall purpose, according to the website, is "to convene, nurture and support diverse groups of community members for civic work that addresses the immediate and future needs of Eau Claire." Harvard University's Innovations in American Government Awards awarded Clear Vision $10,000 as a finalist for the Ash Award. The award points out the use of core concepts such as public work, power, public relationships, diversity, and self-interest in Clear Vision's highly innovative model and notes that Clear Vision teaches skills such as house dialogues, one-on-one relational meetings, power mapping, public evaluation, and action planning.[45] Mike Huggins, who teaches a course on local government at the University of Wisconsin–Eau Claire, develops these skills and concepts in his students, who are often coaches in Clear Vision.

In Clear Vision, teams tackle issues of community concern. Some have struggled; others have had considerable success, developing projects such as the Sojourner House homeless shelter created by a team project on preventing recidivism that included ex-convicts as leaders in the effort. Clear Vision has created community gardens, a project on public art throughout the city, and an initiative to make public services widely known to low-income communities (including vivid displays on buses). It has been the driving force behind the Confluence Project, a $45 million performing arts center connected to a $35 million commercial and residential development project. The most recent effort is a community-wide initiative to address poverty, emerging from a summit that sought people's views about new challenges. "Communities just don't know what to do about poverty," said Catherine Emmanuelle, a member of the Clear Vision initiating committee and member of the city council. "It's difficult, and people throw their hands up in the air. But Eau Claire is going to take it on and hopefully come up with some ways to address it."[46]

Community leaders observe many ripple effects. Kerry Kincaid, who was involved in the initial planning process, observes that the city is not immune from divisive trends in the larger society. She worries about the way social media empowers a radically individualist approach, encouraging people to "sound off" on issues, often anonymously, and about the bitter partisanship in America. "Eau Claire is not accustomed to heavy-handed partisan efforts in our local elections," she says. "In the past, candidates stood for election on their experience and points of view. But the spring election [2018] was non-partisan in name only." She fears that "partisanship in local elections threatens to fracture local governance." But she also hopes for continuing impact from Clear Vision. "Everyone knows what is a one-on-one and a power map," Kincaid says. She believes that Clear Vision has created a widely practiced "structure of deliberation."[47] Catherine Emmanuelle began her involvement in Clear Vision as a member of the first expanded initiating committee and continued as a board member. She was a young, single mother on public assistance, and the experience working with Clear Vision gave her tools and confidence that were transformative. "One of the biggest things that it taught me was building my civic muscles." She remembers, "I was on Food Share and other kinds of public assistance. I thought that people who influence the community are people with titles or money. I discovered I didn't need any of that to make a difference."

Emmanuelle used skills like one-on-ones and power mapping in many settings in Clear Vision and in her work as an extension educator. Catherine created a popular Latino leadership course in nearby Trempealeau County. "Public Achievement was at the heart of the leadership program," she describes. "I'd go door-to-door, speaking Spanish. I'd tell people my great grandmother came here from Mexico and we'd like to invest with you to have more power. We translated the Clear Vision Tool Kit, based on Public Achievement, into Spanish. We taught people to do one-on-ones, how to do power mapping." She also found the practices of public evaluation, incorporated into each meeting, highly valuable. "That helps me say my piece and also everyone else can have a say." Emmanuelle became regional director of three counties for the Wisconsin Extension service, with a staff of twenty-one. She teaches such skills and practices to all her colleagues, and they use them in many different projects. She identifies the approach as shifting from "town meetings," where government asks for input, to what she calls the Public Achievement model. "There is a function of having a public hearing, but there is also a value of sitting around a table and figuring things out. They're different." She gives the example of a controversy about public drinking in a neighborhood near the University of Wisconsin–Eau Claire campus. She introduced a process that would bring all the voices to the table, and the city council unanimously approved the change. "Now the city is hosting meetings with the bar owner and the police and the students and the neighbors at the same table, talking about what are the facts, what is motivating us, why we are here, what we are going to do." Whether the outcome is similar on paper to a public hearing process or not, the civic organizing process is crucial, creating ownership and civic agency.[48]

When she became vice president of the initial Clear Vision board, Vicki Hoehn was a highly respected business leader, vice president of marketing for the Royal Credit Union, with $2.3 billion in assets, branches in forty-two counties and two states, twenty-eight credit unions, and more than 180,000 members. In Hoehn's view, Clear Vision generated a framework shift in the community. "At the time we began, our community blamed government. People said nothing happened because the government was too slow." She believes that Clear Vision "opened a lot of eyes." Many came to see themselves as citizens. "It's not about relying on or blaming government. It's about taking responsibility and ownership ourselves as citizens." Hoehn has seen a shift in the outlook and behavior of the business community in the city. For instance, Bob McCoy, the director of the Chamber of Commerce, was involved in Clear Vision. She doesn't know whether it was the experience of being in Clear Vision itself or the collaborative tools and concepts he learned there, but she can see a difference. "The Chamber in the past often just turned to their members who are paying the dues. Now they work with others outside the business community as well." The collaborative approach has also impacted substantial decisions by Royal Credit Union. When Royal acquired land for a new large office building, their plan was to build it directly on the river. "We started talking to neighborhoods, and people said, 'If you build there we aren't going to be able to get to the river.' So we put a street and a park in front of the building. This never would have happened if we hadn't met with the neighborhoods, talked with the city, and found a solution." What she calls "the model" also affects her own work. Hoehn now has the newly created position of vice president for community engagement at Royal Credit Union. She gets to know the communities when Royal is opening a new branch. "Everything I do I say, 'How will this affect others?' I listen more. I ask questions, I probe on collaboration, I ask my staff, 'How do you work with other people?'"[49]

Ten years of work in Clear Vision have shown challenges and successes. Mike Huggins, aspiring to develop the civic and political capacities of thousands of citizens by teaching organizing skills and habits of mind of public work, also sees it as an experiment in local democracy. "A public life is not just a nice thing. It's an absolute necessity," he explains. "You can't lead a full life as a human without a public life, learning how to work with others to make your neighborhood and your community and your school a better place." He sees such work as vital to democracy's future. "Democracy is never a sure thing. It's a struggle, won or lost in local communities."[50]

A Nehemiah Moment

During the 2008 election, political candidates drew on a biblical repertoire to envision the kind of leaders we need as a country to address our problems. "It's a lot better to be with David than Goliath," Mike Huckabee told the Values Voter Forum on October 18, 2007, to show his identification with the little guy. Barack Obama, in a speech in Selma, Alabama, on March 4, 2007, commemorating the famous 1965 civil rights march, described himself as part of the "Joshua generation," picking up where the "Moses generation" left off.

Today, when the challenge is civic repair, we need the great story of public work in the biblical book of Nehemiah. Indeed, producing Nehemiah leaders who build open-ended, mutually empowering public relationships is one way to describe the mission of the new Obama Foundation. In *Common Wealth: A Return to Citizen Politics*, I had written about how the Nehemiah story inspired East Brooklyn Churches, affiliated with the Industrial Areas Foundation, to build thousands of single-family homes in the 1980s in previously desolate parts of the borough. Building what came to be called Nehemiah Homes helped the community to recover its confidence and identity. It became a model and inspiration for inner-city revitalization, even during the Reagan years of public policy that neglected cities. A diverse group of African Americans, Latinos, and white ethnics from Queens attended the opening ceremonies. At the Camp David meeting with the Clinton administration in 1995, I talked briefly about the *Common Wealth* book and made the case for "Nehemiah leaders." The story of Nehemiah has potential for wide appeal in our time.

Nehemiah was a skillful politician who gained permission from the king of Persia in 446 BC to return to Jerusalem in order to lead the Jews in rebuilding the city walls. "You see the trouble we are in; Jerusalem is in ruins, its gates have been burned down," he told the assembled crowd. But Nehemiah did not present himself as a Moses-like savior. Rather, he called people to hard work. "Come, let us rebuild the walls of Jerusalem and suffer this indignity no longer." The people responded: "Let us start! Let us build." The Bible recounts that "with willing hands they set about the good work." Nehemiah rolled up his sleeves and participated in the building of the walls himself.[51]

The walls, part of the commonwealth of Jerusalem, bear resemblance to America's vast infrastructure. The 2017 Infrastructure Report Card of the American Society of Civil Engineers, evaluating the condition of the nation's roads, bridges, drinking water systems, and other infrastructure, gave a grade of D+.[52] There is cross-partisan agreement that much rebuilding is urgent. Citizen involvement in issues such as road and bridge design and water usage is important, but usually overlooked. The broken walls of Jerusalem also suggest the deterioration of the larger commonwealth, from parklands to shorelines, clean air to schools and museums and art galleries. But the cultural aspects of the Nehemiah story hold the most important lessons.

During the Babylonian captivity of Israel, their enemies had multiplied, but the Hebrews persevered in the face of ridicule and posted guards at the gates. In the midst of persecution, however, a culture of greed and selfishness beset them. Morale and faith in the future had dramatically declined. More subtly and more profoundly, rebuilding the walls required civic restoration.

Nehemiah held together a motley crew—forty different groups are named, including merchants, priests, governors, nobles, members of the perfume and goldsmiths' guilds, and women. At one point he organized a great assembly to call to account nobles who were making excessive profit from the poor. As the Jewish people rebuilt their walls together they regained a sense of their purpose and identity as a people.

In today's America, as we have come to look to others—celebrities, experts, great leaders—to save us from our problems, we have similarly become afflicted by civic illnesses. Our bitter conflicts along lines of party, income, race, religion, and geography are fed by a devaluation of the talents and intelligence of people without credentials, degrees, and celebrity status. Our citizenship has declined as we have been entertained as spectators, pacified as clients, and pandered to as customers. Our leadership models are far too scripted and domineering.

We need Nehemiah leaders who call forth the democratic genius of America's self-reliant, productive, future-oriented citizenry who create, sustain, and care about our commonwealth. These are leaders who reject the rescuer role, summoning people to do the work of civic restoration rather than doing the work for the people. Such leaders develop and tap the talents of citizens to address public problems on which government action is necessary but not sufficient, from climate change to school reform. They challenge us to create healthy communities, not simply to provide access to health care. They recall that democracy is a jazz-like way of life, not merely a trip to the ballot box.

We are beginning to see such leaders. From Mike Huggins, Catherine Emmanuel, and Vicki Hoehn in Eau Claire to other organizers, educators, and citizen professionals who make their appearance in *Awakening Democracy through Public Work*—and many more not named here—a new generation of Nehemiah leaders is appearing, calling people to the work of citizenship.

In the process they are helping to build foundations for a democratic awakening.

NOTES

INTRODUCTION

1. Personal notes, October 26, 2017.
2. Quoted in Charles Payne, *I've Got the Light of Freedom: The Organizing Tradition and the Mississippi* Struggle (Berkeley: University of California Press: 1965), 68.
3. For a history of the phrase and song see Peter Levine's blog, March 9, 2011, *peterlevine.ws/? p=6105.*
4. Payne discusses traditional and grassroots leaders in Payne, *I've Got the Light*, 67, 68.
5. For the phrase, and a powerful account of such politics, see Luke Bretherton, *Resurrecting Democracy: Citizenship, Faith, and the Politics of a Common Life* (Cambridge: Cambridge University Press, 2015).
6. *CBS Morning News*, May 7, 1992, and May 13, 1992; *CBS Evening News*, May 24, 1992.
7. Alison Oosterhuis, "What Do You Stand For? The Citizen Student Movement Experience," December 19, 2017, directed study, Humphrey School, with Harry Boyte.
8. Steven Vogel, "The Citizen Student Movement," December 29, 2017, directed study, Humphrey School, with Harry Boyte.
9. Maria Avila, *Transformative Civic Engagement through Community Organizing* (Sterling, VA: Stylus, 2018), 43, 53.
10. Shankar Vedantam, "Social Isolation Growing in U.S., Study Says," *Washington Post*, June 23, 2006.
11. Dhruv Khullar, "How Social Isolation Is Killing Us," *New York Times* December 22, 2016.
12. Natalie Gil, "Loneliness: A Silent Plague That Is Hurting Young People the Most," *Guardian,* July 20, 2014. The Mental Health Foundation "found loneliness to be a greater concern among young people than the elderly. The 18 to 34-year-olds surveyed were more likely to feel lonely often, to worry about feeling alone and to feel depressed because of loneliness than the over-55s."
13. Personal notes, October 30, 2017.
14. "About the Foundation," Obama Foundation, *www.obama.org/about-the-foundation.*
15. On the Camp David meeting, see William Galston, "What He Should Say in the State of the Union," *Washington Monthly*, January/February 2011, 11; and Benjamin Barber, *The Truth of Power: Intellectual Affairs in the Clinton White House* (New York: Columbia University Press, 2008).
16. Danielle Allen, *Our Declaration: A Reading of the Declaration of Independence in Defense of Equality* (New York: W. W. Norton, 2014), 35, 34.
17. Allen's view of the declaration as advancing agency is akin to the argument by Josiah Ober, based on an etymological analysis of Greek, that challenges modern uses of "democracy" as "a voting rule for determining the will of the majority." Ober argues that the Greeks believed "*demokratia* . . . more capaciously, means 'the empowered *demos* . . . in which the *demos* gains a collective power to effect change in the public realm . . . the collective

strength and *ability* to act . . . and, indeed, to reconstitute the public realm through action." Josiah Ober, "The Original Meaning of 'Democracy': Capacity to Do Things, Not Majority Rule," *Constellations* 15, no. 1 (2009): 1, 7.

18. Alexis de Tocqueville, *Democracy in America,* ed. and trans. Henry Mansfield and Delba Winthrop (Chicago: University of Chicago Press, 2000), 491–92.

19. Sheldon Wolin, *Tocqueville between Two Worlds: The Making of a Political and Theoretical Life* (Princeton, NJ: Princeton University Press, 2001), 222, 224.

20. There are many renderings of "Let America Be America Again" in the public domain. One particularly powerful version, read by Hans Ostrom, is posted on YouTube: "'Let America Be America Again,' by Langston Hughes," April 19, 2011, *www.youtube.com/watch? v=78EKboznCTI.* It pairs pictures of injustice—like scenes from the segregated South—with images of freedom struggle and possibility.

CHAPTER 1

1. Matt Anderson, "Dr. Martin Luther King, Jr., and Public Achievement," *Creating the Commonwealth: Newsletter of the Center for Democracy and Citizenship,* Winter 2000, 2.

2. The story is told in Jan Shaw-Flamm, "Romping Room," *M: The University of Minnesota Alumni Magazine,* Fall 1999, 1.

3. James Walsh, "Young Movers and Shakers," *Minneapolis Star Tribune,* September 17, 1993.

4. Theresa Monsour, "Playing at Fame," *St. Paul Pioneer Press,* March 4, 1999.

5. Quoted in Shaw-Flamm, "Romping Room."

6. Alaina Lynch, interviewed by Dennis Donovan (email), April 17, 2017.

7. Carr, quoted in Walsh, "Young Movers and Shakers."

8. Jim Farr, quoted in Shaw-Flamm, "Romping Room."

9. Jim Farr, quoted in Walsh, "Young Movers and Shakers."

10. This story is taken from Harry C. Boyte, "Resurrecting Democracy: The Citizen Politics of Public Work," paper delivered to the Havens Center, Sociology Department, University of Wisconsin–Madison, April 11, 2001.

11. Quoted in Shaw-Flamm, "Romping Room."

12. Tamisha Anderson, interviewed by Dennis Donovan, June 6, 2016, Vadnais Heights, Minnesota.

13. Zach Baumann, interviewed by Dennis Donovan, June 15, 2016, Saint Paul, Minnesota.

14. Anderson interview; Baumann interview.

15. Baumann interview.

16. Lynch interview.

17. The ACORN story is adapted from Harry C. Boyte, "A Tale of Two Playgrounds: Young People and Politics" (paper presented to the Annual Meeting of the American Political Science Association, September 1, 2001, San Francisco, California), *eric.ed.gov/? id=ED458155.*

18. Quoted in Boyte, "Tale of Two Playgrounds."

19. Harry C. Boyte, Heather Booth, and Steve Max, *Citizen Action and the New American Populism* (Philadelphia: Temple University Press, 1986). The corporate mobilizations and citizen activist responses are described in Harry C. Boyte, *The Backyard Revolution: Understanding the New Citizen Movement* (Philadelphia: Temple University Press, 1980), ch. 1. See also Boyte, "Tale of Two Playgrounds."

20. Dana Fisher, *Activism, Inc.* (Palo Alto, CA: Stanford University Press, 2006).

21. Chuck Todd and Carrie Dann, "How Big Data Broke American Politics," *NBC News Report*, March 15, 2017.
22. Linda Honold, interviewed by Harry Boyte, April 3, 2018, St. Paul to Milwaukee.
23. Boyte, "Tale of Two Playgrounds"; also Harry C. Boyte, *Everyday Politics: Reconnecting Citizens and Public Life* (Philadelphia: University of Pennsylvania Press, 2004)
24. Charles Payne, *I've Got the Light of Freedom: The Organizing Tradition and the Mississippi Struggle* (Berkeley: University of California Press, 1965), 68.
25. Ibid.
26. Bernard Crick, *In Defense of Politics* (Chicago: University of Chicago Press, 1962).
27. Gene Sharp, *The Politics of Nonviolent Action: Part One, Power and Struggle* (Boston: Porter Sargent, 1973); for discussions see April Carter, "The Literature on Civil Resistance," in *Civil Resistance and Power Politics: The Experience of Non-violent Action from Gandhi to the Present*, ed. Adam Roberts and Timothy Garton Ash (New York: Oxford University Press, 2009), 25–42; and Mark Engler and Paul Engler, *This Is an Uprising: How Nonviolent Revolt Is Shaping the Twenty-first Century* (New York: Nation Books, 2016).
28. From Harry C. Boyte and Marie-Louise Ström, "Nonviolent Civic Life Worksheet," January 24, 2017.
29. For an account of my encounter with the Ku Klux Klan that led to this assignment, see "Populism in the USA: A First-Hand Account of Its Changing Nature from the 1960s, Interview with Professor Harry C. Boyte," *International Affairs Forum* 2, no. 1 (Spring 2017): 29–34.
30. Zeynep Tufekci, "Does a Protest's Size Matter? ," *New York Times*, January 27, 2017.
31. The roots of the march are detailed in Charles Euchner's *Nobody Turn Me Round: A People's History of the March on Washington* (Boston: Beacon, 2010), l; and also the CNN documentary, *We Were There: The March on Washington—An Oral History*, hosted by Don Lemon, 2013, *cnnpressroom.blogs.cnn.com/2013/08/01/we-were-there-the-march-on-washington-an-oral-history-debuts-friday-august-23-at-1000pm-et-pt*. Program notes in author's possession.
32. For a splendid description of Rustin's strategic vision for the march, see CNN, *We Were There*.
33. I wrote about COPS in detail in Harry C. Boyte, *Community Is Possible: Repairing America's Roots* (New York: Harper & Row, 1984); and about EBC and BUILD in Boyte, *CommonWealth: A Return to Citizen Politics* (New York: Free Press, 1989). Cleveland invited me to come to the institute after seeing the *New York Times* review of *Free Spaces: The Sources of Democratic Change in America* (New York: Harper & Row, 1986), which I coauthored with Sara Evans.
34. Harper quoted in Philip Foner, *The Voice of Black America* (New York: Simon and Schuster, 1972), 431.
35. Smith quoted in Boyte, *Everyday Politics*, 163.
36. David Mathews, *Reclaiming Public Education by Reclaiming Our Democracy* (Dayton, OH: Kettering, 2006), vii.
37. Oscar Handlin and Mary Flug Handlin, *Commonwealth: A Study of the Role of Government in the American Economy, Massachusetts, 1774–1861* (Cambridge, MA: Harvard University Press, 1969), 29–30.
38. Bertha Heilbom, "Second Generation Devoted to Pursuits of Culture," *St. Paul Pioneer Press,* December 31, 1933.
39. President Barack Obama and Marilynne Robinson, "A Conversation in Iowa," *New York*

Review of Books, November 5, 2015, *www.nybooks.com/articles/2015/11/05/president-obama-marilynne-robinson-conversation*.

40. Al Hammer, interviewed by Nan Kari, Minneapolis, May 27, 1995.

41. Blanchard and Leavitt quoted in Harry Boyte, "The Fight for America's Soul," BillMoyers.com, December 15, 2015.

42. Susan Faludi, *Stiffed: The Betrayal of the American Man* (New York: William Morrow, 1999), 39, 23, 599.

CHAPTER 2

1. Mike Rose, *Lives on the Boundaries* (New York: Penguin, 1989), 7, 8, 1, 2.

2. For a vivid account see Wayne Au, "Teaching under the New Taylorism: High-Stakes Testing and Standardization of the 21st Century Curriculum," *Curriculum Studies* 43, no. 1 (2011): 25–45.

3. Sue Halpern, "They Have, Right Now, Another You," *New York Review of Books*, December 22, 2016, *www.nybooks.com/articles/2016/12/22/they-have-right-now-another-you*.

4. Cathy O'Neil, *Weapons of Math Destruction: How Big Data Increases Inequality and Threatens Democracy* (New York: Crown, 2016), 3, 4, 5, 8.

5. Alyson Klein, "No Child Left Behind: An Overview," *Education Week*, April 10, 2015.

6. Ibid.

7. Diane Ravitch, "How, and How Not, to Improve the Schools," *New York Review of Books*, March 22, 2012.

8. Natasha Singer, "The Silicon Valley Billionaires Remaking America's Schools," *New York Times*, June 6, 2017, *www.nytimes.com/2017/06/06/technology/tech-billionaires-education-zuckerberg-facebook-hastings.html*.

9. Peg Tyre, "Can a Tech Start-Up Successfully Educate Children in the Developing World?," *New York Times Magazine*, June 27, 2017, *www.nytimes.com/2017/06/27/magazine/can-a-tech-start-up-successfully-educate-children-in-the-developing-world.html*.

10. Paul Barnwell, "Are Teachers Becoming Obsolete? ," *Atlantic*, February 15, 2017, *www.theatlantic.com/education/archive/2017/02/becoming-obsolete/516732*.

11. Duncan quoted in Allie Bidwell, "Duncan Relaxes Testing Push, but Teachers Want More," *US News and World Report*, August 21, 2014, *www.usnews.com/news/articles/2014/08/21/education-secretary-arne-duncan-loosens-reins-on-teacher-evaluations-testing*.

12. Ravitch, "How, and How Not, to Improve the Schools."

13. Ibid., 159–60.

14. Grant Wiggins, "A Veteran Teacher Turned Coach Shadows 2 Students for 2 Days—A Sobering Lesson Learned," *Granted, and . . . Thoughts on Education by Grant Wiggins*, October 10, 2014, *grantwiggins.wordpress.com/2014/10/10/a-veteran-teacher-turned-coach-shadows-2-students-for-2-days-a-sobering-lesson-learned*.

15. Juaquin Muñoz, "The Circle of Mind and Heart: Integrating Waldorf Education, Indigenous Epistemologies, and Critical Pedagogy" (PhD Dissertation, University of Arizona, Tucson, 2016), 56.

16. Quoted in Harry C. Boyte, "When Deliberation Becomes Democracy," Kettering Working Paper, July 4, 2016, 4.

17. Lawrence A. Cremin, *The Transformation of the School: Progressivism in American Education, 1876–1957* (New York: Alfred A. Knopf, 1962), 13, 12, 10.

18. Deborah Meier, "Who Is Making the Decisions," *Education Week*, February 28 2007.

19. On the disastrous effects of the efforts to engineer Newark's public schools from the outside, organized by then mayor Cory Booker, Governor Chris Christie, and Facebook

founder Mark Zuckerberg, see "Assessing the $100 Million Upheaval of Newark's Public Schools," an interview with journalist Dale Russakoff, National Public Radio, September 21, 2015.

20. Luke Bretherton, Review of *Public Engagement for Public Education: Joining Forces to Revitalize Democracy and Equalize Schools*, ed. Marion Orr and John Rogers, and *A Match on Dry Grass: Community Organizing as a Catalyst for School Reform*, by Mark R. Warren, Karen L. Mapp, and the Community Organizing and School Reform Project, *Perspective on Politics* 11, no. 3 (2013): 958. doi.org/10.1017/S1537592713001722.

21. Barack Obama, "Community Schools," July 15, 1007.

22. For views and experiences in these efforts, see Harry C. Boyte, ed., *Democracy's Education: Public Work, Citizenship, and the Future of Colleges and Universities* (Nashville: Vanderbilt University Press, 2015).

23. Description of coalition from Ira Harkavy, interviewed by Harry Boyte (telephone), April 14, 2017, and from Coalition for Community Schools materials, *www.communityschools.org*.

24. John Dewey, "Democracy in the Schools" (1937), in *Intelligence in the Modern World: John Dewey's Philosophy*, ed. Joseph Ratner (New York: Random House, 1939), 717.

25. John Dewey, "The School as Social Centre," *Elementary School Teacher* 3, no. 2 (1902): 73–86; also available at *www.jstor.org/stable/992485*.

26. Ibid.

27. Ibid.

28. Ibid.

29. On the Amendment 1 campaign, James Salzer, "It's Teachers' Union versus the Unknown in Georgia's School Amendment Fight," *Atlanta Journal Constitution*, October 4, 2016; Ty Tagami, "Opportunity School District Rejected," *Atlanta Journal Constitution*, November 8, 2016; Gerald Taylor, interviewed by with Harry Boyte (by telephone), April 23, 2017.

CHAPTER 3

1. Francis, "Speech to the Pontifical Catholic University of Ecuador," Quito, Ecuador, July 7, 2015, *saltandlighttv.org/blog/featured/pope-francis-in-ecuador-address-to-educators-pontifical-catholic-university-of-ecuador*.

2. Quoted in Herbert Gutman, *Work, Culture, and Society in Industrializing America* (New York: Vintage, 1977), 69.

3. As James Gee puts it in *An Introduction to Discourse Analysis*, "Politics is not just about contending political parties. At a much deeper level it is about how to distribute social goods in a society: who gets what in terms of money, status, power, and acceptance on a variety of deeper terms, all social goods. Since, when we use language, social goods and their distribution are always at stake, language is always 'political' in a deep sense." James Paul Gee, *An Introduction to Discourse Analysis: Theory and Method*, 3rd ed. (New York: Routledge, 2011), 7.

4. Meira Levinson, *No Citizen Left Behind* (Cambridge, MA: Harvard University Press, 2012), 12.

5. Ibid., 87–88.

6. I appreciate my Augsburg College colleague James Trelstad-Porter for introducing me to the field of intercultural development.

7. On the field of intercultural development, see Joseph J. Distefano and Martha L.

Maznevski, "Creating Value with Diverse Teams in Global Management," *Organizational Dynamics* 29, no. 1 (2000): 45–63.

8. Nan Skelton, interviewed by Harry Boyte, Saint Paul, Minnesota, March 30, 2017.

9. Quoted in Isak Tranvik, "The History of Public Achievement," working paper, Sabo Center for Democracy and Citizenship, November 16, 2015. See also "Youth Need Integration of Work, Education, and Community," *Minnesota Department of Education Newsletter* 23, no. 6 (March 1989).

10. People had diverse interests and institutional resources but shared a common commitment to youth development with a citizenship component that had explicit political but not partisan aspects. Dick Byrne, director of Minnesota 4-H, was involved, as was Billy Collins, a business leader in the Twin Cities; Josie Johnson, a longtime civil rights leader and a senior fellow at the Humphrey Institute; Carol Shields, who directed culture and arts programs for Minnesota 4-H; Nan Kari, who taught occupational theory at the College of Saint Catherine; John Kari with the Metropolitan Regional Council; Jim Farr from the University of Minnesota; Dennis Donovan from Saint Bernard's; and Juan Jackson, an activist in the HIV-AIDS movement. We also drew on other advisors, including Gerald Taylor and Tony Massengale, both of whom worked with the Industrial Areas Foundation; Deborah Meier, who is often seen as the midwife of the small school movement; and Dorothy Cotton, my boss in the civil rights movement. We also created a collaboration of groups and institutions experimenting with citizen politics in multiple sites and populations, not simply with young people. Called Project Public Life (PPL), it created a public stage for citizen politics that conveyed the sense that young people's action and school reform efforts were part of something large and important, addressing the general crisis of democracy. Coordinated for several years by Peg Michels and launched in cooperation with Frances Moore Lappé and her Food First Institute and with the Kettering Foundation as a learning partner, Project for Public Life included teams from Minnesota Cooperative Extension, the College (now University) of Saint Catherine; Augustana Nursing Home, and ARC (a group of African American parents with autistic children), in addition to Public Achievement.

11. Jim Scheibel, interviewed by Harry Boyte, St. Paul, March 20, 2017.

12. Contract in author's possession.

13. From program notes on conference, in Public Achievement archive. This material is taken from *Public Achievement Project Summary Year One*, Spring 1991. Here is how Public Achievement is described:

> Public Achievement is a pilot for a nationwide youth and politics initiative, a public life counterpart to Junior Achievement, the program that provides business experience with young people. We began in St. Paul in partnership with Mayor James Scheibel and a variety of community organizations in the spring of 1990. Teams actually came together and began working in the fall of 1990. Several questions framed our exploration the first year:
> - Can young people become involved in serious public problem solving?
> - Can they rename their work as politics?
> - What role might adults take in this youth political education process?

14. To date, Public Achievement has illustrated that teenagers are not so much apathetic about politics as they are usually placed in an outsider role. In Public Achievement poli-

tics stops being an unpleasant spectator sport and becomes something which is interesting, challenging, rewarding, and empowering.

15. Kay Miller and Richard Green, "The Minneapolis School Superintendent Believes 'When the Public Schools Have Failed and Ceased or Are Weakened This Nation Will Have Failed," *Minneapolis Star Tribune*, September 7, 1986.
16. Harry C. Boyte, "Catholic Teachings a Fit with Democracy's Future," *Catholic Spirit*, August 20, 1998.
17. Scott Peters, interviewed by Dennis Donovan, Saint Paul, Minnesota, August 25, 2016.
18. Andy Sturdevant, "Successive Waves of Immigrants Put Their Stamp on St. Paul's North End," *MinnPost*, March 11, 2015.
19. Jeff Mauer, interviewed by Dennis Donovan, Saint Paul, Minnesota, October 22, 2016.
20. Ibid.
21. Carmen Sirianni and Lew Friedland, *Civic Innovation in America* (Berkeley: University of California Press, 2001), 251–52.
22. Bill Salisbury, "Students Learn Lesson in Ways of Washington," *St. Paul Pioneer Press*, June 11, 1997.
23. Scott Peters interview.

CHAPTER 4

This chapter title is taken from the coaches' manual in Public Achievement. It was proposed by coaches themselves.

1. Miskat Az-Zubair, quoted in John Carras, "Developing a Civic Sense," *Kansan*, August 7, 1998.
2. Ken Burns, director, *Jazz*, PBS, 2000, quoted in Harry C Boyte, "A Tale of Two Cities" (paper presented to the American Political Science Association, September 1, 2001, San Francisco).
3. Shelly Robertson, interviewed by Harry Boyte (telephone), Johannesburg, South Africa, to California, July 19, 2017.
4. Ross Roholt, Robert Hildreth, and Michael Baizerman, *Year Four Evaluation of Public Achievement, 2002–2003: Examining Young People's Experience of Public Achievement* (Kansas City, MO: Kauffman Foundation, 2003), 3, 12, 5, 6.
5. Harry Boyte, "Public Achievement in Minneapolis: An Interview with Joe Groves," *Creating the Commonwealth Newsletter*, Winter 1999.
6. Frances Green, Katie Green, Pat Hennes, Cheryl Mandala, Matt Mohs, Jonathan Palmer, Darrell Washington, "Creating Public Work/Changing Private Lives: Public Achievement at Andersen Elementary," final paper, December 1997.
7. The account is taken from Boyte journal notes.
8. Jamie Minor, interviewed by Lena Jones, July 11, 2016, Minneapolis, Minnesota.
9. Adapted from Harry C. Boyte, "Reconstructing Democracy: Citizen Politics as Public Work" (lecture given at the Havens Center, University of Wisconsin–Madison, April 11, 2001), *havenscenter.org/vsp/carmen_sirianni_amp_harry_boyte*.
10. Joseph Kunkel, Clark Johnson, Heather Bakke, and Jason Miller, "Teaching Together: School/University Collaboration to Improve Social Studies Education," *Today's Social Studies Bulletin 98* (Silver Springs, MD: National Council for the Social Studies, 2001), 95.
11. Ibid., 99.
12. Ibid., 96.
13. Ibid., 101–2.

14. Ibid., 102.

15. Quotes from Scott Hanson, "We the (Young) People: Public Achievement and the Changing Face of Change," Center for Democracy and Citizenship at Augsburg University, posted by OAV, *vimeo.com/33221907*.

16. Brenda Kay Lewis, "St. Gregory Students Showcase their Public Achievement Participation," *Nodaway News Leader*, February 18, 1999.

17. Foundation mission and region from "Our Work: Healthy Communities," Heartland Foundation, *www.heartlandfoundation.org/what-we-do/healthy-communities*; Judy Sabbert quoted in Jan Greene, "Building a Healthier Community Starting with the Young and Alienated," *Hospitals and Health Networks* 84, no. 4 (April 10, 2010): 48.

18. Figures and subsequent stories from Shelly Robertson, email correspondence and notes, July 24, 2017.

19. Greene, "Building a Healthier Community," 48; and Shelly Robertson, interviewed by Harry Boyte (telephone), July 19, 2017.

20. Shelly Robertson, "Effect of Public Achievement on the Resilience of School-Aged Youth at Risk" (Master's thesis, Northwest Missouri State University, 2012), 13.

21. Robertson interview.

22. Cathy McKinley, interviewed by Harry Boyte, Saint Joseph, Missouri, August 21, 2017.

23. Bob Bush, interviewed by Harry Boyte, West Des Moines, Iowa, August 22, 2017.

24. Judith K. Sabbert with Christel A.K. Gollnick, *Come Together, Think Ahead!: Inspiring People, Organizations, and Communities to Thrive* (Kansas City, MO: Chandler Lake Books, 2015), 152.

25. Judy Slabbert, interviewed by Harry Boyte (telephone), September 20, 2017.

26. Marie Steichen, interviewed by Harry Boyte (telephone), November 20, 2017.

27. Heartland Foundation research report provided by Marie Steichen, December 6, 2017.

28. Heartland Foundation, "Our Work: Scholarships," *www.heartlandfoundation.org/what-we-do/scholarships*.

29. Thomas B. Coburn, "Peace Within, Peace Without," *Naropa! Magazine*, Spring 2006, 1; Eric Fretz, faculty profile, "Conversations in the Classroom," *Naropa! Magazine*, Spring 2006, 3.

30. Description of Centaurus from Susie Aquilina, "Student Introduction," in *We Are the Ones We've Been Waiting For: A Student Guide to Public Achievement*, prepared by Naropa student coaches (Boulder: Naropa, 2006), 6.

31. Ibid.

32. Leanne Bird, "A Letter to a New Public Achievement Coach," in *We Are the Ones*, 9–14.

33. Joseph Kahne and Joel Westheimer, "The Limits of Political Efficacy: Educating Citizens for a Democratic Society," *PS: Political Science and Politics* 39, no. 2 (2006): 289, 290, 293, 294.

34. Darwyn Fehrman and Aaron Schutz, "Beyond the Catch-22 of School-Based Social Action Programs: Toward a More Pragmatic Approach for Dealing with Power," *Democracy & Education* 19, no. 1 (2008): 4.

35. Warren and Randall quoted in "Making Citizens DC Launch," posted by National Association of Scholars, January 24, 2017, *YouTube* video, 2: 05: 07, *www.youtube.com/watch? v=6euzujOVVME*. Quotes on Public Achievement from David Randall, *Making Citizens: How American Universities Teach Civics* (Washington, DC: National Association of Scholars, 2017), 78, 83.

36. Notes from Center for Democracy and Citizenship, *Midterm Report to the Kauffman Foundation on National Expansion*, 2002.
37. RMC Research Corporation, *Public Achievement 2005–2006 Evaluation Brief* (Denver: RMC, 2006), 1–2.
38. Robertson, "Effect of Public Achievement," 38.
39. R. W. Hildreth, "Theorizing Citizenship and Evaluating Public Achievement," *PS: Political Science and Politics* 33, no. 3 (September 2000), 629.
40. Ibid., 630.
41. These figures and quotes from papers come from the Mankato Public Achievement website in 2002, accessed in 2004.

CHAPTER 5

1. On the launch of and the statement of Northern Irish educators see Harry Boyte and Dennis Donovan, "Public Achievement Goes to Northern Ireland," *Creating the Commonwealth* (newsletter), Spring 1999, 1–2. Angela Matthews is interviewed in the newsletter on 3–4.
2. "Salzburg Global Seminar: Anniversary Video," filmed 2017, posted by Salzburg Global Seminar, June 28, 2017, *YouTube* video, 3: 08, *www.youtube.com/watch? v=BW7dDr3ulKo.*
3. Dennis Donovan, interviewed by Tami Moore (telephone), August 11, 2017.
4. Ibid.
5. Brian Porter, "The 1989 Polish Round Table Revisited: Making History," *Journal of the International Institute* 6, no. 3 (1999), *hdl.handle.net/2027/spo.4750978.0006.301.*
6. Alicja Derkowska (from Nowy Sacz, Poland) and Julie Boudreaux (from Boston, Massachusetts), interviewed by Tami Moore (via video conference), September 16, 2017.
7. Ibid.
8. Alicja Derkowska and Julie Boudreaux, "Measuring Educational Initiatives: How and Why?" (paper presented at the Annual Meeting of the Comparative and International Education Society, Chicago, Illinois, March 1–5, 2010), 1.
9. Mission statement retrieved from the school website, *www.splot.info/s7-misja.html.*
10. School Plus Network Mission Statement, retrieved from *www.schoolplusnet.org/mission.html#History% 20* (now inactive).
11. Alicja Derkowska and Julie Boudreaux interview.
12. Donovan interview.
13. Alicja Derkowska and Julie Boudreaux interview.
14. Ibid.
15. Alicja Derkowska and Julie Boudreaux, interviewed by Tami Moore (via video conference), Nowy Sazc, Poland, September 15, 2016.
16. Initially, this discussion of the tasks of the PA coach appeared on the *www.paunite.org* website maintained by PA organizer Serdar Degirmencioglu in Turkey. The site is no longer available online; content formerly published on the site was provided to the authors by Ala Derkowska from the MTO archives, July 2016.
17. Ibid.
18. Derkowska and Boudreaux interview, October 15, 2016.
19. "PA Monitoring in Bakhchisaray UA Groups" (unpublished document from School Plus Network archives, provided by Alicja Derkowska, July 2016).
20. Ibid.
21. Ibid.

22. Ibid.

23. Derkowska and Boudreaux interview, September 16, 2017.

24. David Sobel, *Place-based Education: Connecting Classrooms and Communities* (Great Barrington, MA: Orion, 2004).

25. Elemer Hankiss coined this term to refer to the shadow culture that exists in private relationships that are not sponsored or influenced by the state, particularly those existing alongside Communist governments. See Elemer Hankiss, "The 'Second Society': Is There an Alternative Social Model Emerging in Contemporary Hungary? ," *Social Research* 55, nos. 1/2 (1988): 13–42; and Elemer Hankiss, *East European Alternatives* (Oxford: Clarendon, 1990).

26. Derkowska and Boudreaux interview, October 15, 2016.

27. Halima Fattulayevah, interview by Tami Moore (video conference), October 15, 2016.

28. Ibid.

29. Ibid. See also Harry Boyte, "A Democratic Educational Awakening Begins with Public Relationships," *Huffington Post*, February 27, 2017, *www.huffingtonpost.com/entry/a-democratic-educational-awakening-begins-with-public_us_58b41caoe4boesfdf61974a4*.

30. This draws from Marie Ström, "Citizens at the Centre" (unpublished manuscript, for a book on Idasa, October 14, 2014).

31. Quoted in Harry C. Boyte, *Constructive Politics: The Contributions of the Institute for Democracy in South Africa (Idasa)* (Pretoria: Idasa, 2004), 10–11.

32. Ibid., 62.

33. Strom, "Citizens at the Centre," 4.

34. This draws on Marie-Louise Ström, "Democracy on a Hillside: Developmental Politics, Democratic Pedagogy, and the Christian Missional Imagination" (final paper, CL8530, December 12, 2012, Luther Seminary).

35. Mamphela Ramphele, *Laying Ghosts to Rest: Dilemmas of the Transition in South Africa* (Cape Town: Tafelberg, 2008), 147.

36. President Harry Truman, "Four Point Program for Developing Countries" (1949), quoted in "Point Four Program," Wikipedia, *en.wikipedia.org/wiki/Point_Four_Program*.

37. Vijayendra Rao and Michael Walton, eds., *Culture and Public Action* (Palo Alto: Stanford University Press, 2006), 259.

38. This article in the Dutch magazine *The Broker* is a good summary. Harry Boyte was one of the original organizers. Willemijn Verkoren, "Civic Driven Change," *Broker*, July 22, 2009, www.thebrokeronline.eu/Articles/Civic-Driven-Change.

39. Citizenship DRC, *Blurring the Boundaries: Lessons from a Decade of Collaborative Research on Citizen Engagement*, 2011, 4–5, *archive.ids.ac.uk/drccitizen/pages/overarching-lessons.html*.

40. Ibid., 9–15.

41. Ramphele, *Laying Ghosts to Rest*, 147.

42. Harry C. Boyte, "Civic Driven Change and Developmental Democracy," in *Civic Driven Change*, ed. Alan Fowler and Kees Biekart (The Hague: ISS, 2008), 119–38.

43. On the "technocratic paradigm," see Harry C. Boyte, "*Laudato Si'*, Civic Studies, and the Future of Democracy," *The Good Society* 25, no. 1 (2016): 46–61.

44. This is treated at length in Harry C. Boyte, "John Dewey and Citizen Politics: How Democracy Can Survive Artificial Intelligence," *Education and Culture* 33, no. 2 (2017): 13–47.

CHAPTER 6

1. "Public Achievement in Fridley—Transforming Special Education," posted by publicwork-citizen, *YouTube* video, 38: 26, June 2, 2013, *www.youtube.com/watch? v=VaRimtavig8.*

2. Jane Addams, "A Function of the Social Settlement," *Annals of American Political and Social Science* 13 (January–June 1999): 8–9.

3. Peter L. Berger and Thomas Luckmann, *The Social Construction of Reality* (New York: Doubleday, 1966), 15; Isaiah Berlin, *Concepts and Categories: Philosophical Essays* (New York: Penguin, 1981), 4, 10.

4. Quoted in Harry C. Boyte, "The Struggle against Positivism," *Academe* 86, no. 4 (2000), *eric.ed.gov/? id=EJ613215.*

5. Addams's view of education taking place in whole communities is described in Nick Longo, *Recognizing the Role of Community in Civic Education: Lessons from Hull House, Highlander Folk School, and the Neighborhood Learning Community,* CIRCLE Working Paper, no. 30 (College Park, MD: Center for Information and Research on Civic Learning and Engagement, 2005), 3, 4, 5; Addams quoted on 5.

6. Jane Addams, "Educational Methods," in *Jane Addams on Education,* ed. Ellen Lagemann (New Brunswick, NJ: Transaction, 1994), 98–99.

7. Ellen Lagemann, introduction to Lagemann, *Jane Addams on Education,* 2–3.

8. Ibid, x.

9. Addams quoted in Boyte, "Struggle against Positivism."

10. Dewey, "School as Social Centre."

11. Myles Horton with Herb Kohl and Judith Kohl, *The Long Haul: An Autobiography* (New York: Teachers College Press, 1997); also Longo, "Recognizing the Role of Community"; and Nick Longo, *Why Community Matters: Connecting Education with Civic Life* (Albany: SUNY Press, 2007).

12. Katherine Mellen Charron, *Freedom's Teacher: The Life of Septima Clark* (Chapel Hill: University of North Carolina Press 2009), 224.

13. The story of finding a place for the school and choosing Robinson as the first teacher is told in ibid., 248–50; Robison quoted on 251.

14. The story of their conversation is told in Harry C. Boyte, *The Backyard Revolution: Understanding the New Citizen Movement* (Philadelphia: Temple University Press, 1980).

15. Ibid., 279–80.

16. Ibid., 259.

17. See for instance "Rosenwald School," Wikipedia, last modified March 18, 2018, *en.wikipedia.org/wiki/Rosenwald_School.*

18. Charron, *Freedom's Teacher,* 79.

19. Ibid., 294. On purpose, see Charles Payne, *I've Got the Light of Freedom: The Organizing Tradition and the Mississippi Struggle* (Berkeley: University of California Press: 1965), 68.

20. Charron, *Freedom's Teacher,* 302

21. Ibid., 284–85.

22. Ibid., 303–4.

23. Ibid., 338.

24. Ibid., 315.

25. Sarah Polus, "Full Transcript of President Obama's Toast at the Nordic State Dinner," *Washington Post,* May 13, 2016.

26. On Danish folk school influence on Horton and South Carolina adult education, see Charron, *Freedom's Teacher,* 219, 130.

27. N. F. S. Grundtvig and Niels Lyhne Jensen, *A Grundtvig Anthology: Selections from the Writings of N. F. S. Grundtvig (1783–1872)* (Greenwood, SC: Attic, 1984), 29.

28. Holger Bernt Hansen, "Grundtvig and the Third World: The Transfer of Grundtvig's Ideas to Other Peoples and Cultures," in *Heritage and Prophecy: Grundtvig and the English-Speaking World*, ed. A. M. Allchin et al. (Aarhus, Denmark: Aarhus University Press, 1993), 307.

29. "Living interaction" among learners and teachers, and among learners themselves, was one of Grundtvig's core educational principles. This was a radically different approach from the magisterial lecture.

30. N. F. S. Grundtvig, "The School for Life," in *Selected Writings*, ed. Johannes Knudsen (Philadelphia: Fortress, 1976), 156.

31. Ibid., 155. Although the very first folk high schools admitted only young men, it was not long before young women were also admitted.

32. Ibid., 157.

33. Grundtvig, "A Letter Concerning the Folk High School to Peter Larsen Skraeppenborg in Dons," in Knudsen, *Selected Writings*, 173.

34. Grundtvig, "School for Life," 154.

35. Ibid. 156.

36. Grundtvig, "The Danish High School," in Knudsen, *Selected Writings*, 162.

37. Ibid.

38. Anders Pontoppidan Thyssen, "Grundtvigianism as a Movement until around 1900," in *N. F. S. Grundtvig, Tradition and Renewal: Grundtvig's Vision of Man and People, Education and the Church, in Relation to World Issues Today*, ed. Christian Thodberg and Anders Pontoppidan Thyssen (Copenhagen: Det Danske Selskab, 1983), 383.

39. Paul Wellstone, *How the Rural Poor Got Power* (Amherst: University of Massachusetts Press, 1978), 211.

40. The founding statement of the BYNC is quoted in Robert A. Slayton, *Back of the Yards: The Making of a Local Democracy* (Chicago: University of Chicago Press, 1986), 203; Slayton describes the organizing work of BYNC in detail; see also Fisher, *People*, 54–56.

41. Payne, *Light of Freedom*, 68.

42. Sister Margaret Snipe, interviewed by Harry Boyte, Baltimore, November 6, 1987.

43. See Boyte, *Everyday Politics*.

44. Ernesto Cortes, interviewed by Harry Boyte, San Antonio, July 4, 1983.

45. Industrial Areas Foundation, *Organizing for Family and Congregation* (Huntington, NY: Industrial Areas Foundation, 1978), 13.

46. This process of change is described in detail in Harry C. Boyte, *CommonWealth: A Return to Citizen Politics* (New York: Free Press, 1989), especially chs. 6 and 7.

47. Max Thommes's paper from Dennis Donovan's PA 1401 class (Fall 2017), December 2017, quoted with permission.

CHAPTER 7

1. Rebecca Riffkin, "Climate Change Not a Top Worry," *Gallup*, March 12, 2014, *www.gallup.com/poll/167843/climate-change-not-top-worry.aspx*.

2. On the connections between race and poverty see Gary L. Cunningham, Marcia L. Avner, and Romilda Justilien, "The Urgency of Now: Foundations' Role in Ending Racial Inequity," *Foundation Review* 6, no. 1 (2014): 51–65.

3. Obama quoted in Michael D. Shear, "Obama Starts Initiative for Young Black Men Noting Statistics and His Own Experience," *New York Times*, February 28, 2014, A11.

4. For instance, anthropologist Annett Lareau has explored the split in K-12 education between community values and individualist, competitive school cultures in her study comparing what she calls "the cultural logic" of poor and working-class families with that of schools and educators. Educators, whether in suburbs or inner cities, are trained in what Lareau calls a "dominant set of cultural repertoires about how children should be raised," including individualist, competitive, and achievement-oriented norms. In contrast, for working-class and poor families, there is an emphasis on sustaining relationships with family and friends. Annette Lareau, *Unequal Childhoods: Class, Race and Family Life* (Berkeley: University of California Press, 2003), 4, 5. Research sponsored by the Kellogg School of Management at Northwestern University finds similar dynamics in much of higher education, showing how norms of individualist achievement generate inequality through their effects on undergraduates. Thus, the achievement norms such as "doing your own thing," "paving your own path," and "realizing your individual potential" make college "the ultimate symbol of independence" for middle- and upper-class students. But such norms are experienced far differently by students from working-class families. For the latter, "expectations for college center around interdependent motives such as working together, connecting to others, and giving back," Nicole Stephens reports. In four studies, Stephens and her fellow researchers found that as working class-students were exposed to the message of individual success and independence, a strong social-class performance gap emerged. Quoted in "Unseen Disadvantage," at *www.kellogg.northwestern.edu/news/unseen_disadvantage.htm*. For full article see Nicole M. Stephens, Stephanie A. Fryberg, Hazel Rose Markus, Camille Johnson, and Rebecca Covarrubias, "Unseen Disadvantage: How American Universities' Focus on Independence Undermines the Academic Performance of First-Generation College Students," *Journal of Personality and Social Psychology* 102, no. 6 (2012): 1178–97.

5. Atum Azzahir, interviewed by Harry Boyte, Minneapolis, Minnesota, May 23, 2006.

6. Diane Ravitch, "Schools We Can Envy," *New York Review of Books*, March 8, 2012, *www.nybooks.com/articles/archives/2012/mar/08/schools-we-can-envy*.

7. Alissa Blood-Knafla, "Experiences of Students with Special Needs in Public Achievement" (Master's thesis, Augsburg College, 2013), 1.

8. States may define disability categories differently; in Minnesota there are currently thirteen categories under which a student may qualify for special education services.

9. Renee Cameto, Phyllis Levine, and Mary Wagner, *Transition Planning for Students with Disabilities: A Special Topic Report of Findings from the National Longitudinal Transition Study-2 (NLTS2)* (Menlo Park, CA: SRI International, 2004), *www.nlts2.org/reports/2004_11/nlts2_report_2004_11_complete.pdf*.

10. Bonnie S. Billingsley, "Special Education Retention and Attribution," *Journal of Special Education* 38, no. 1 (2004): 39–55.

11. Jane Splean and Edward Caffarella, *Understanding Retention and Attrition of Special Education Teachers in Nevada through a Longitudinal Study: A Model for Other States* (Washington: US Office of Special Education Programs, 2010), *personnelcenter.org/documents/Understanding%20Retention%20and%20Attrition%00of%20Special%20Education%20Teachers%20in%20Nevada%20(abridged%20version).pdf*.

12. Linda Darling-Hammond, "Keeping Good Teachers: Why It Matters, What Leaders Can Do," *Educational Leadership* 60, no. 8 (2003): 7–13.

13. Jan W. Valle and David J. Connor, *Rethinking Disability: A Disability Studies Approach to Inclusive Practices* (New York: McGraw Hill, 2011), xii.

14. Ibid.

15. Christy Ashby, "The Trouble with Normal," *Disability and Society* 25, no. 3 (2012): 345–58.

16. Scot Dansforth, ed., *Becoming a Great Inclusive Educator* (Bern, Switzerland: Peter Lang, 2014).

17. Ellen Gelinsky, *Mind in the Making: The Seven Essential Life Skills Every Child Needs* (New York: HarperCollins, 2010).

18. Michael M. Gerber, "Emerging Issues in Teacher Education for Inclusion in the U.S.," in *Future Directions for Teacher Education for Inclusion*, ed. Chris Forlin (New York: Routledge, 2012), 71).

19. Children's names have been changed.

20. Blood-Knafla, "Experiences of Students with Special Needs," 16, 17, 18, 19, 21, 22.

21. Quotes from Blood and Ricci about their teaching in Harry Boyte and Jen Nelson, "A 21st Century Freedom Movement," *Huffington Post*, June 12, 2013, *www.huffingtonpost.com/harry-boyte/a-21st-century-freedom-mo_b_3421977.html*.

22. Cheryl McClellan, quoted in Wendi Wheeler, "From Problem Students to Problem Solvers," *Augsburg Now*, July 1, 2011.

23. In the fall of 2017, multiplying calls for revitalization of democratic purposes can be heard. See, for instance, Erika Christakis, "The War on Public Schools," *Atlantic*, October 2017.

24. Cheryl McClellan, quoted in "Problem Solvers."

25. Courtney Anderson, interviewed by Susan O'Connor, Fridley, Minnesota, May 25, 2016.

26. Krebs and McInnis quoted in Wheeler, "Problem Solvers."

27. Dana Lynn Wagner, Elizabeth Madson Ankeny, Susan O'Connor, Donna Patterson, and Diane Cole Vodicka, "Preservice Teacher Self-Efficacy and Public Achievement: An Exploration of Effects" (presentation to Minnesota Association of Colleges for Teacher Education, Bloomington, Minnesota, 2012).

28. Nora Ulseth, interviewed by Susan O'Connor, Minneapolis, Minnesota, May 13, 2016.

29. Jess Bowman, interviewed by Susan O'Connor, Minneapolis, Minnesota, May 18, 2016.

30. Noral Ulseth interview.

31. Elaine Eschenbacher, "The Oz behind the Curtain—Phil O'Neil: Public Achievement Coach," *Sabo Center News*, Augsburg University, April 22, 2016, *www.augsburg.edu/sabo/2016/04/22/the-oz-behind-the-curtain-phil-oneil-public-achievement-coach*.

32. Jess Bowman interview.

33. Personal communication from James Gnecco to Susan O'Connor, Minneapolis, October 27, 2016, used with permission.

34. Figures from Donna Patterson, "Special Education: Recruitment and Retention Survey," August 2016.

35. Becky Hamlin, interviewed by Susan O'Connor, May 16, 2017, Minneapolis, Minnesota.

36. Ehsan Alam, "Rondo Neighborhood, St. Paul," MNOPEDIA, June 14, 2017, *www.mnopedia.org/place/rondo-neighborhood-st-paul*.

37. Ibid.

38. Laura Yuen, "Central Corridor: In the Shadow of Rondo," *MPR News*, April 29, 2010.

39. Maxfield Elementary School, St. Paul, "Public Schools Start Class," August and October 2016, updated March, 2017, *public-schools.startclass.com/1/5007/Maxfield-Magnet-Elementary* (accessed September 10, 2017).

40. Elaine Eschenbacher, "Public Achievement in Maxfield, 2016–17," Augsburg University, October 21, 2016, Sabo Center for Democracy and Citizenship Blog, *www.augsburg.edu/sabo/blog*.

41. Elaine Eschenbacher, "R.E.S.P.E.C.T—Mukway Uses Public Achievement to Encourage Others to Respect Different Cultures," *Sabo Center News*, Augsburg University, March

4, 2016, *www.augsburg.edu/sabo/2016/03/04/e-s-p-e-c-t-mukwa-uses-public-achievement-to-encourage-others-to-respect-different-cultures.*

42. Brandi Pottle reflections on impact, Minnesota Civic Studies Civic Renewal Conference, October 24, 2017, Minneapolis.

43. Elaine Eschenbacher, "Brandi Pottle, Maxfield Elementary Teacher," Augsburg University Profile, September 2, 2016, *www.augsburg.edu/sabo/blog* (accessed September 10, 2017).

44. Atum Azzahir, "Maxfield Elementary School celebrates 125th anniversary," *Spokesman-Recorder*, May 5, 2016, *spokesman-recorder.com/2016/05/05/maxfield-elementary-school-celebrates-125th-year-anniversary.*

CHAPTER 8

1. Quoted in Rebecca Shamash, "Judging Higher Education on the Merits," *Good Society* 25, nos. 2/3 (2016): 341.

2. Quoted in John Allen Jr., "On New Year's Eve, Pope Francis Delivers His 'Silent Majority' Speech," *Cruz*, December 31, *cruxnow.com/vatican/2017/12/31/new-years-eve-pope-francis-delivers-silent-majority-speech.*

3. Francis, "Speech to the Pontifical Catholic University of Ecuador," Quito, Ecuador, July 7, 2015, *saltandlighttv.org/blog/featured/pope-francis-in-ecuador-address-to-educators-pontifical-catholic-university-of-ecuador.*

4. Lani Guinier, *The Tyranny of the Meritocracy: Democratizing Higher Education* (Boston: Beacon, 2015), 138.

5. The center and Harkavy have also played an important role internationally in raising the question and advancing practices of "education for democracy." See for instance the Council of Europe's videos of the twenty-fifth anniversary of the Netter Center: *www.nettercenter.upenn.edu/25th-Anniversary-Conference/Videos.*

6. President's Commission on Higher Education, *Higher Education for American Democracy* (New York: Harper, 1948), 102.

7. David Mathews, "Remembering the 1977 Arlie House Conference Report," Kettering Foundation, April 27, 2016, *www.kettering.org/blogs/airlie-report.*

8. Kenneth Wheeler, *Cultivating Regionalism: Higher Education and the Making of the American Midwest* (Dekalb: Northern Illinois University Press, 2011), 5, 45, 27.

9. This account of Michigan is from Lewis S. Feuer, "Dewey and Back-to-the-People Movement," *Journal of the History of Ideas* 20 (1959): 546; see also Brian A. Williams, *Thought and Action: John Dewey at the University of Michigan* (Ann Arbor: University of Michigan Bentley Library, 1935).

10. Liberty Hyde Bailey, *The Holy Earth* (New York: Charles Scribner's Sons, 1915), 41.

11. Andrew Jewett, *Science, Democracy, and the American University: From the Civil War to the Cold War* (Cambridge, MA: Harvard University Press, 2010); Bevier is quoted in Scott Peters, "Learning from Stories" (unpublished essay, 2017), in author's possession.

12. Kaylesh Ramu and David Hoffman, "On Campus, the Good Side of Politics," *Baltimore Sun*, September 4, 2012.

13. Charlie Carlson, Kat Gehl, and Zach Macon, "Beyond Polarization: Challenge Others and Yourself and You Will Learn a Lot," *MinnPost*, May 10, 2017. Other team members included Campbell Fisher, Katherine Xu, Spencer Williams, and Dupree MacBryer.

14. Taylor Morgan, final essay, PA 1401, for Dennis Donovan, "Organizing for the Public Good," University of Minnesota, December 12, 2017, quoted by permission.

15. Steven Vogel, "Prison Reflections," independent study with Harry Boyte, University of Minnesota, October 19, 2017, used with permission.

16. Quotes from Ali Oosterhuis transcription, "Social Media Deliberation," Purple Onion, Minneapolis, June 27, 2017.
17. Ibid.
18. Ali Oosterhuis, "Reflection on Blood Struggle," November 27, 2016, independent study with Harry Boyte, University of Minnesota, used with permission.
19. Ivy Distle, interviewed by Harry Boyte (telephone), September 15, 2017.
20. Erik Farley, interviewed by Harry Boyte (telephone), September 8, 2017.
21. Maria Avila, *Transformative Civic Engagement through Community Organizing* (Sterling, VA: Stylus, 2017). 34–35.
22. Ibid., 36.
23. Ibid., 45.
24. Ibid., 38–39.
25. Ibid., 48–49.
26. Ibid., 53–54.
27. Ibid., 55.
28. This profile of Weinberg is adapted from Harry C. Boyte, "Adam Weinberg—An Eye to Civic Agency," *Huffington Post*, September 30, 2016, www.huffingtonpost.com/entry/adam-weinberg-an-eye-to-civic-agency_us_57ee96a9e4b095bd896a0c85.
29. Jack Shuler, "Between Coasts" (unpublished concept paper, July 26, 2017), in author's possession.
30. Laurel Kennedy, interviewed by Harry Boyte (telephone), August 30, 2017.
31. Kennedy interview.
32. Matt Ferner, "Eleven Staggering Numbers That Help to Put the Harvey Catastrophe into Perspective," *Huffington Post*, September 3, 2017.
33. Manny Fernandez, "Plying the Urban Sea, Armed with a Boat and Raw Courage," *New York Times*, August 30, 2017.
34. Seth Howard, interviewed by Harry Boyte (telephone), June 29, 2017.
35. Richard M. Battistoni and Tania D. Mitchell, "Civic Identity and Agency after College," *Diversity & Democracy* (forthcoming, June 2018).

CHAPTER 9

1. Whitman quoted in Harry Boyte, *The Backyard Revolution* (Philadelphia: Temple University Press, 1980), x.
2. Battistoni and Mitchell, "Civic Identity and Agency After College."
3. The Center for Democracy and Citizenship merged with the preexisting Sabo Center after we moved from the University of Minnesota.
4. "Cardiopulmonary Resuscitation," *Wikipedia*, last edited April 6, 2018, en.wikipedia.org/wiki/Cardiopulmonary_resuscitation.
5. From Robert Gauger and Leo Christie, "Clergy Stress and Depression," course for Professional Development Resources, 2013.
6. American Medical News, "Warning Sounded on Demoralized Health Care Work Force," March 18, 2013. Also Laura Joszt, "Nearly Half of Physicians Are Discontent," *MD Magazine*, June 14, 2013.
7. Howard Fisher, "Why Is Public Employee Morale So Bad? ," *Governing*, August 23, 2016.
8. Brad Tuttle and Jacob Davidson, "5 High-Paying Jobs That Will Make You Miserable," *Money*, September 9, 2014.
9. Doris A. Santoro, "Good Teaching in Difficult Times: Demoralization in the Pursuit of Good Work," *American Journal of Education* 118, no. 1 (2011): 1–23, quoted in Tim Wallace,

"Teacher Burnout or Demoralization? What's the Difference and Why It Matters," *NEA Today*, January 18, 2018.

10. Naom Scheiber, "When Professionals Rise Up More than Money Is at Stake," *New York Times*, March 27, 2018.

11. Thomas Bender, *Intellect and Public Life: Essays on the Social History of Academic Intellectuals in the United States* (Baltimore: John Hopkins University Press, 1992).

12. Erin A Cech, "Culture of Disengagement in Engineering Education? ," *Science, Technology, and Human Values* 39, no. 1 (2014): 42–72.

13. Philip Nyden, "Public Sociology, Engaged Research, and Civic Education," in *Civic Studies*, ed. Peter Levine and Karol Soltan (Washington, DC: AAC&U, Bringing Theory to Practice, 2014), 109.

14. Peter Levine, "The Case for Civic Studies," in Levine and Soltan, *Civic Studies*, 7.

15. Garret Hardin, "Tragedy of the Commons," *Science* 162 (1968): 1243–48, at 1244.

16. Elinor Ostrom, "Polycentricity, Complexity, and the Commons," *Good Society* 9, No. 2 (1999): 37–41, at 39, 40.

17. Peter Levine, "Collective Action, Civic Engagement, and the Knowledge Commons," in Charlotte Hess and Elinor Ostrom, *Understanding Knowledge as a Commons: From Theory to Practice* (Boston: MIT Press, 2006), 247.

18. Public work partnerships have developed the concept of citizens as co-creators and producers, as well as civic agency developed through public work. On Boyte and colleagues' arguments, see for instance Harry C. Boyte and Nan Kari, *Building America: The Democratic Promise of Public Work* (Philadelphia: Temple University Press, 1996); Harry C. Boyte and James Farr, "The Work of Citizenship and the Problem of Service-Learning," in *Experiencing Citizenship*, ed. Richard Battistoni and William Hudson (Washington, DC: AAHE, 1997); Harry C. Boyte, "Public Work and Civil Society," in *Oxford Handbook of Civil Society*, ed. Michael Edwards (Oxford: Oxford University Press, 2011), 324–36; Harry C. Boyte, *We the People Politics: The Populist Promise of Deliberative Public Work*, with introduction by David Mathews (Dayton, OH: Kettering Foundation, 2011); Harry C. Boyte, "Constructive Politics as Public Work: Organizing the Literature," in *Democratizing Deliberation: A Political Theory Anthology*, ed. Derek W. M. Barker, Noëlle McAfee, and David W. McIvor (Dayton, OH: Kettering Foundation Press, 2012), 153–83 (originally published in *Political Theory* 39, no. 5 [2011]); and Harry C. Boyte, "Reinventing Citizenship as Public Work," in *Democracy's Education: Public Work, Citizenship, and the Future of Colleges and Universities*, ed. Harry C. Boyte (Nashville: Vanderbilt University Press, 2015) (a version was originally published by the Kettering Foundation in 2014, with an introduction by David Mathews).

19. John P. Spencer, Melissa Clearfield, Daniela Corbetta, Beverly Ulrich, Patrick Buchanan, and Gregor Schröner, "Moving toward a Grand Theory of Development: In Memory of Esther Thelen," 2005 Presidential Address, Society for Research in Child Development, Atlanta Conference; also see *Child Development* 77, no. 6 (2006).

20. See Albert W. Dzur, *Rebuilding Public Institutions Together: Professionals and Citizens in a Participatory Democracy* (Ithaca: Cornell University Press, 2018), a "Cornell Selects" publication of his lecture on receiving the Brown Democracy Medal for 2017.

21. For an excellent discussion of the remarkable craft in many manual occupations, see Mike Rose, *Mind at Work: Valuing the Intelligence of the American Worker* (New York: Random House, 2005).

22. "Our Broken Politics," *Meet the Press*, NBC, August 6, 2017.

23. Theoretical foundations of civic professionalism found early expression in the work of

John Dewey, who stressed the educative dimensions of "all callings [and] occupations." William Sullivan and Dzur further developed political theory of civic professionalism. See William Sullivan, *Work and Integrity: The Crisis and Promise of Professionalism in America* (San Francisco: Jossey-Bass, 1995), 28.

24. Albert W. Dzur, *Democratic Professionalism: Citizen Participation and the Reconstruction of Professional Ethics, Identity, and Practice* (University Park: Pennsylvania State University Press, 2008).

25. William J. Doherty, Tai J. Mendenhall, and Jerica M. Berge, "The Families and Democracy and Citizen Health Care Project," *Journal of Marital and Family Therapy* 36, no. 4 (October 2010): 389–402.

26. William Doherty, "Psychotherapy's Pilgrimage: Shaping the Consciousness of Our Time," *Psychotherapy Networker*, January/February 2017, *www.psychotherapynetworker.org/magazine/article/1070/psychotherapys-pilgrimage*.

27. Quotes from "Finding Common Ground in Ohio with Peter Yarrow," posted by Better Angels Media, *YouTube* video, 9: 27, June 5, 2017, *www.youtube.com/watch?v=9LSvR9Ahrhs*.

28. This history is taken from the draft chapter on Augsburg history, "Agency in an Avalanche," by Catherine Bishop, Harry Boyte, Kathleen Clark, Elaine Eschenbacher, Margaret Finders, Michael Lansing, and Joe Underhill, forthcoming in Tim Eatman and Scott Peters, *Democracy's Colleges,* a research project supported by the Kettering Foundation.

29. Ibid.

30. Kathleen M. Clark, Joyce P. Miller, Cheryl Leuning, and Katherine Baumgartner, "The Citizen Nurse: An Educational Innovation for Change," *Journal of Nursing Education* 56, no. 4 (2017): 247.

31. Ibid., 248–49.

32. Ibid., 249.

33. Jane Wills, "The Geo-Constitution: Understanding the Intersection of Geography and Political Institutions," *Progress in Human Geography*, prepublished April 15, 2018, 5, 10, doi.org/10.1177/0309132518768406.

34. Jess Gilbert, *Planning Democracy: Agrarian Intellectuals and the Intended New Deal* (New Haven: Yale University Press, 2015), 8–9. See also Harry Boyte, "Democratic Awakening," BillMoyers.Com, October 14, 2016.

35. On Reinventing Citizenship, see Barber, *The Truth of Power*; and Carmen Sirianni and Lew Friedland, *Civic Innovation in America* (Berkeley: University of California Press, 2001). The latter book includes detailed examples of citizen government partnership in health, environmental, urban development, and other areas.

36. See for instance, "Demonstration Farm," Wikipedia, last edited March 9, 2018, *en.wikipedia.org/wiki/Demonstration_farm*.

37. Wills, "Geo-Constitution," 15.

38. Account of Indian struggles against removal, "Anishinabe Akhi, 'Indian Country,'" historical marker erected by the City of Eau Claire Landmark Commission and the University of Wisconsin - Eau Claire, *www.hmdb.org/marker.asp?marker=75477*. The first settlers are described in Brian L. Blakeley, *A History of Eau Claire, Wisconsin, Volume 1: The Lumbering Era* (Eau Claire: Chippe Valley Museum Press, 2017), 24–25.

39. Ibid., 178.

40. From personal notes, April 7, 2018.

41. Kerry Kincaid, interviewed by Harry Boyte and Marie Ström, Eau Claire, April 21, 2018.
42. Mike Huggins, "Communities with Clear Vision," a case study for the Ford Foundation–funded Champions of Participation—Engaging Citizens in Local Governance project, University of Sussex, 2008, 1.
43. Mike Huggins, interviewed by Harry Boyte (telephone), August 9, 2017.
44. Huggins," Communities with Clear Vision," 2, 3, 4.
45. Clear Vision Eau Claire website, *ec.clearvisioneauclaire.org*; "Clear Vision Eau Claire," Government Innovators Network, Harvard Kennedy School, *www.innovations.harvard.edu/clear-vision-eau-claire*.
46. Julian Emerson, "Eau Claire Clear Vision Effort to Address Poverty," *Eau Claire Leader-Telegram*, July 26, 2016.
47. Kincaid interview.
48. Catherine Emmanuelle, interviewed by Harry Boyte and Marie Ström, April 21, 2018, Eau Claire.
49. Vici Hoehn, interviewed by Harry Boyte and Marie Ström, April 20, 2018, Eau Claire.
50. Mike Huggins, interviewed by Tami Moore (telephone), June 2, 2016.
51. Nehemiah 2: 17–18.
52. "2017 Infrastructure Report Card," American Society of Civil Engineers, *www.infrastructurereportcard.org*.

INDEX